Mary Elizabeth Fiske Sargent

Sketches and Reminiscences of the Radical Club of Chestnut Street,

Boston

Mary Elizabeth Fiske Sargent

Sketches and Reminiscences of the Radical Club of Chestnut Street, Boston

ISBN/EAN: 9783744652568

Printed in Europe, USA, Canada, Australia, Japan

Cover: Foto ©ninafisch / pixelio.de

More available books at **www.hansebooks.com**

SKETCHES AND REMINISCENCES

OF

THE RADICAL CLUB.

SKETCHES AND REMINISCENCES

OF

THE RADICAL CLUB

OF

CHESTNUT STREET, BOSTON.

EDITED BY

MRS. JOHN T. SARGENT.

BOSTON:
JAMES R. OSGOOD AND COMPANY.
1880.

UNIVERSITY PRESS:

JOHN WILSON AND SON, CAMBRIDGE.

TO

The Living and the Dead

OF

THE CHESTNUT-STREET CLUB

THIS BOOK IS DEDICATED,

By M. E. S.

PREFACE.

ANY details of meetings or discussions which have had a marked influence, or have indicated the growth and tendencies of public opinion, cannot but be interesting. This conviction has led to the collection of some of the essays given at the Chestnut Street Club, with a sketch of the discussions which followed their reading.

The volume has been made up from the recollections of friends, from notes and reports made of the meetings; and while I fear it will be found fragmentary and imperfect, still it is my hope that the words here preserved of many distinguished members of the Club, some of whom have now passed from among us, may prove not only of interest but of value to the reader.

M. E. S.

ORIGIN OF THE CLUB.

THE Radical Club may be said to have had its origin, in the spring of the year 1867, in the growing desire of certain ministers and laymen for larger liberty of faith, fellowship, and communion. In this respect it was akin to the Transcendentalist movement of earlier date. It was designed to meet a demand for the freest investigation of all forms of religious thought and inquiry. The Club existed with as little formal organization as was possible. It was composed of members of all religious denominations. Thirty persons were present at its first meeting; and at the closing sessions, in 1880, nearly two hundred were in attendance.

In its earlier years, the papers were chiefly confined to theological and religious questions; but during the last decade they were generally upon scientific and educational problems. The conversations were not less interesting than the essays. Rare thoughtfulness, deep human tenderness, and profound earnestness marked these reunions.

CONTENTS.

FOR M. E. S.

WHATEVER in love's name is truly done
    To free the slave, or lift the fallen one,
Is done to Christ.   Whoso in deed and word
    Is not against Him, labors for the Lord.
When He who, sad and weary, longing sore
    For love's sweet service, sought the sisters' door,
One saw the heavenly, one the human guest:
    But who shall say which loved the Master best?

JOHN G. WHITTIER.

SKETCHES AND REMINISCENCES

OF THE

CHESTNUT STREET CLUB.

I.

RELIGION.

By RALPH WALDO EMERSON, MAY, 1867.

WE know that the world was made at one cast; what we find in ourselves, we recognize all around us. Whatever man sees, that he has a key to in his own mind. All mythologies, the most barbarous and the most refined, he can translate into his own. The scholar can easily understand how the King of Crete came to be the Olympian Jove of Homer in old time, and how, in later ages, a saint of Nazareth became the adoration of nations; for the student is aware, in himself, that the religious impulse is the most revolutionary principle in human experience, uplifting and impelling the man beyond himself. Every nation of the globe is in our day, whether willingly or reluctantly, holding up its sacred books and traditions to our eyes, and we find in our mythology a key to theirs, and in our experience a key to their experience. There is in all these a general agreement to what we call good morals. In all these sacred books or systems, the anomalies can be accounted for in the peculiar conditions or geography of the people; and, as a rule, every one, of course with its share of nonsense, has some exceptional merit, some contribution of a wise and holy soul to ethics. In each appears the activity of the imagination in a barbarous mind, and the contemporary existence of a minority of comparatively wiser men holding fast to the simple rule of duty.

All the creeds claim miracles, but we do not therefore accept the creeds; we measure them by their civilizing power. Thus Christianity strives against the sensual instincts of man; we hold it therefore in honor. So does Buddhism, and every high enthusiasm. Just so far as they have this power, they prevail. You cannot resist a moral movement. "An arch never sleeps," say the architects. No more does a new truth, once clearly apprehended. You find a parallel truth in the very beginning of history for every noble inspiration of our religious history, as well as for every crime of ours committed under the sanction of religion or the claimed sanction of religion. That wise man that I spoke of as appearing always — the minority of thoughtful persons — is expressed in the mariner's prayer in the storm to Neptune: "O God, thou canst save me if thou wilt, and if thou wilt, thou canst destroy; but, however, I will steer my rudder true."

These cosmical statements occur in every nation, and in the sacred books of every nation. Every reader knows that almost every passage in our sacred books can be paralleled with a like sentiment from another book of a distant nation, and of such an age as to show that it was not derived from ours. And so many of the contributions in Eastern literature are so inestimable in themselves that one would think they could not be hidden in obscure translations, — translations which do not pass into currency. The immense energy of the sentiment of duty and the awe of the supernatural exert a powerful influence on minds that are often perverted, and a tradition is received with awe, but without corresponding action on the intellect. Then you find so many men infatuated on that one topic of religion. Wise on all other topics, they lose their reason the moment they talk of religious things. In a day not far off, these ridiculous attempts to patch the ecliptic of the universe with a piece of tin will come to an end.

We can never hold any false belief with impunity. It is claimed that the terrors of the old religious system were wholesome checks on the conduct of men, and that the gradual decline of the influence of the old religious system in this country, and in Germany as well, has been attended with a greater looseness of human action. But the lives of the believers were broken by it, their minds obscured, and their moral sense injured. One is struck with the manner in which clergymen of the old school, as we say, had their minds darkened by their gloomy opinions. When somebody said to the late Rev. Dr. Payson, of Portland, "How much you must enjoy religion, since you live always administering it," he replied that nobody enjoyed religion less than ministers, as nobody enjoyed food less than cooks. No doubt he enjoyed the remark, but still the remark was remembered because of its truth.

It is safe to say that no one holds the Christian traditions as they were uniformly held in the last generation. We rest on the moral nature, and the whole world shortly must. The church, you tell us, is an institution of God. But are not wit, and wise men, and good judgment whether a thing be so or no also institutions of God, and older than the other? The commanding fact which the true soul never does *not* see is the sufficiency of the moral sentiment. You can never come to any peace or power until you put your whole reliance on the moral constitution of man, and not at all in any history. George Fox had the courage to say that, though he read of Christ and God, he knew them only from a like spirit in his own soul.

There is at this time, as we all know, existing and in-

creasing, a disposition to complain of opinions that are
growing old.   In matters of religion, men merely fasten
their eyes on the difference between their creed and ours,
while the charm of the study is in finding the agreements
and identities in all the religions of men.   I think we
should not assail Christianity or Judaism or Buddhism,
but frankly thank each for every brave and just sentence
or history that is furnished us.   We should not contradict
or censure these well-meant approximations, but point out
the identity of their inspiration with every other inspiration.   The idea of this age, the idea of our Protestant
and Progressive Church, will not be truly reached or expressed until it attain the height which religion and philosophy reached in any former age.   One thing is certain,
— religions are obsolete when lives do not proceed from
them.   The worst adversary that the Calvinistic, the Episcopal, or the Methodist Church ever had was the discovery
that they, or some of them, would not be the friends but the
enemies of the emancipation of the blacks.

I look for the enlargement of that upper class in our
society, composed of those who enjoy the luxury of a
religion that does not degrade ; who think it the highest
worship to expect of Heaven the most and the best ; who
do not wonder that there was a Christ, but that there were
not a thousand ; who have conceived an infinite hope for
mankind ; and who believe that the history of Jesus is
the history of every man, written large.

Rev. JOHN T. SARGENT asked if Mr. Emerson had not
rightly measured and defined the absolute religion which
underlies all phases and forms of theology and church
religion.   He was impressed by what had been said of the
manifest changes which have gone on and are going on in
the doctrines of the church.

Mrs. JULIA WARD HOWE was conscious of that ; and this

was one reason why she thought they must not take too polemic and controversial ground with the churches. They complained, " You radicals do not give us a chance. You do not know what we preach or what we believe now. You take pleasure rather in representing us as intolerant as we ever were ; but we think we have learned as well as you."

Mr. T. W. HIGGINSON, when he read Mr. Emerson's Divinity Hall Address, felt that at last he had some glimpse of what was meant by religion ; the great thought of a universal religion dawned upon his mind, and he saw that, as Channing said, he had been trying to get religion through something else than religion itself. He did not know how it was with others, but all that was grand and noble that he had ever seen in life had been seen only in the light of that thought ; and it was with no feeling but one of shuddering that he looked back, not merely to the limitations of orthodoxy, but to any limitation which separated Christianity from religion. It seemed to him that such sentiments as had been expressed by Mr. Emerson had a vital bearing upon those great interests which Mrs. Howe thought they did not touch. So long as radicalism was negative, it was powerless ; it was impoverishing ; it took the life out of everybody : as soon as it became positive, it strengthened everybody. The members of the churches suppose what is positive is their little dogma, and if we reject that, we are nothing ; and, so we are if we think that dogma of sufficient importance to dwell upon much after we reject it. When we recognize the grandeur of all the religions in the world, when we get outside of our little temple and get upon a pinnacle and see the incense that ascends from all the temples in the world, and feel a sympathy for that, then we begin to be believers, and cease to be unbelievers. It had been affirmed that truth is something infinitely grander and larger than Christianity, and that was the true ground for a radical.

Rev. Mr. Tiffany related an anecdote of a Chinaman whose great grief was that an American friend was a Christian. This was such a complete turning of the tables that it made a powerful impression upon his mind. It seemed to him that the great outcry that was raised whenever anything was said about Christianity not being the root-religion came from the popular ignorance. The majority of men were too busy to read recondite books, but if they would read a popular book like Fortunies' book on China, they would see that all the benevolent institutions for the relief of human want and suffering which we have could be paralleled in that country. He thought the most important work was the spread of knowledge. People would accept the natural conclusions if they knew the facts, but so little had been brought before them that they believed all these beautiful things were only to be found in one quarter of the world.

Rev. John Weiss said that many years ago, when he was engaged in attending a course of lectures on Ecclesiastical History, he read a poem of Mr. Emerson's, —

> "Set not thy foot on graves,
> Care not to strip the dead
> Of his sad ornament,
> His myrrh, and wine, and rings,
> His sheet of lead,
> And trophies buried:
> Go, get them where he earned them when alive.
> As resolutely dig or dive!"

and that poem was a lesson in theology or religion to him, which considerably emancipated him from the routine of the school, and somewhat cast in the shade the wisdom which was being peddled out from day to day in the class. It set him upon a revision of his orthodox conception of Christ; and he found that if he would have personal religion, he must go and get it "where he earned it when

alive." He had clung to that discovery ever since, and
perhaps in consequence of that he had said more about
Jesus, and used the narrative and the parable and the
beatitude more than most radicals. When he read that
Jesus said to the people who stood around him, "Ye have
heard that other people have said so-and-so. I do not
care about that, — I say unto you so-and-so," it occurred
to him whether that was not meant for every man and
woman who was searching after religion. It was the first
act of personal religion to stand out alone and say, "I say
so-and-so;" and although a great many people might say
so who did not appear to have anything particularly well
worth saying, nevertheless he clung to it as the thing that
was to save mankind. How easy it was for them to state
what was the theism of Jesus! It was their theism, the
theism of Massachusetts, the theism of Mrs. Howe, of
Col. Higginson, of Mr. Garrison, of Wendell Phillips,
of the antislavery movement, — it was the theism of the
moral sense, that had interpenetrated the flesh of men and
women from the creation of the world; and it seemed to
him that Mr. Emerson, when he said, in his last sentence,
that "the history of Jesus is the history of every man,
written large," gave the reason why we all loved him.
And was not Shakspeare each man and woman sung loud
and clear and strong? Was not Beethoven each man and
woman played loud and strong, and sweetly too? All
stood upon the same platform, and shared in the theism of
God.

WENDELL PHILLIPS thought they ought not to fight
windmills; they did sometimes fight shadows. He had
never met a man of the old faith — one worthy to be taken
as a type of anything — who denied that the religious
sentiment had found meet and valuable and admirable
expression in the mythologies; and he thought that three
quarters of all the investigations which had been made into

Oriental religions, translations of their books, inquiries into their history, and analyses of their faiths, had been made by so-called orthodox men.   Yale College was as learned in all that matter as Harvard. He did not think, therefore, they could claim that the truth, as it appeared in those books and in those religions, had not been recognized by orthodox men.   The point where they separated was not there, by any means.   Of course, the old religions and mythologies grew out of an inspired religious consciousness, to a certain extent.   He never knew a man who denied it.   Every intelligent man that he ever met, of any sect, acknowledged the contributions to the literature of the West that had been made by many of the older faiths ; they had not neglected, they had not depreciated that development.   On all this we agree.   There is a great deal of astronomical speculation in the world, yet that does not interfere with the fact that there is a true astronomical method.   Because a great many scholars had speculated about the stars, did that show that Copernicus and Sir Isaac Newton are not upon the right track?   The question was, "Is there any indication anywhere that we have touched, even slightly, on absolute truth in any of the mythologies?"   When it was claimed that some parts of the New Testament could be found in Æschylus and Sophocles and Epictetus, he admitted it; but when any man said that the New Testament could be found in Confucius and Buddha, he stopped, and demanded the proof. He did not *know* that any Jew by the name of Jesus Christ had said, "Do unto others as ye would that others should do to you ; " but he knew that the best scholarship of Europe had scrutinized every line of the record in the most exhaustive manner, until we know, if we know anything, that three hundred years after his death, he was supposed to have said it.   So far they were on solid ground.   It was said that Confucius, five hundred years before Christ, said, " Do not do unto another as you would not have another do to you." There was a remarkable similarity in the sentences, and very little probability that a Jew, in that narrow valley, ever heard of a Chinese. How did they know Confucius said it? All they knew about the Chinese was not older than three hundred and fifty years. If they could prove to him that three hundred years after the death of Confucius, he was supposed to have uttered those words, he would believe it, but not now; and he did not give any more weight to the legends about Buddha. No story, forty years old, could be relied upon without scrutiny.

But suppose it was admitted that Confucius and Buddha did say just what Christ did? Steam and water were the same elements; but water would not move a locomotive, steam would. The Sermon on the Mount might be paralleled in Sophocles, they might find a great deal in Confucius: but one was water, the other steam; one had moved the world, the other had not. The proof that there was something unusual there was seen in the results. India had all the intellectual brilliancy that Greece had; she touched all the problems, exhausted all the intellectual debate thousands of years ago, and there she lies to-day. On the other hand, here was Europe. She had made marvellous progress; and, with the single exception of race, there was no element mixed in the European caldron to distinguish it from the Asiatic. Unless they were going to lay on this distinction of race the whole difference between European and Asiatic development, they had nothing but Christianity to account for it. It seemed to him that it was wiser to claim for Christianity the largest share in the merit of European civilization.

Everybody knew that the Chinese had hospitals before Christ, if we are to trust history; everybody knew all

about their progress in civilization; but they make no
progress to-day. The bee could make an eight-sided cell
better than Brunel could make it, but the bee can make
nothing else. The Chinese had not advanced for a thousand years. They had every spring-board and fulcrum
and motive power to go ahead, and had not. Europe had
constantly gone ahead. We had saved all we had got,
and gained more. We had taken the classic and the
Roman civilization, taken their law, their ethics, their
religious ideas, their idea of popular rights, and we had
carried them on. Europe was the hand and brain of the
world to-day; the pioneer, the constructor, the adminis-
trator of the world to-day; and there was nothing under-
lying her to make her so except race and Christianity.
Other portions of the world had had the same intellect.
Tocqueville had told us, in his report to the French Institute, that there was no theory or dream of social science
ever debated in Europe that could not be found in the
Hindoo discussions. The difference was not caused by
a lack of intellect. Here was a fact to be explained, and
it could not be brushed away by saying this man and the
other made a very near approach. No doubt that was so;
nobody ever denied it. God never left any race, nor any
man, nor any time, without Himself, and these twilights
and approaches to noon were seen everywhere in history.
But they had got at last the Copernican theory, and no
fact appeared that it did not explain. They had got at
last the true chemical analysis, and that went down and
weighed the atoms. That explained all new combinations
and all new discoveries. The reason why he believed in
Sir Isaac Newton was, that he gave the key to every fact,
discovered no matter where. Sir Thomas Browne could
tell a great many beautiful dreams about astronomy, but
they did not explain the facts. Christianity had faced the
facts and explained them. He claimed, therefore, that

there was something essentially different in it from the religious experience of other races.

Miss PEABODY asked if that " something " was a method of life.

Mr. PHILLIPS replied that what he meant was, that sugar and starch, considered chemically, were the same thing; steam and water were the same thing; but their action — how different! So if they showed him every line of the Sermon on the Mount paralleled in Confucius or Antoninus, it did not move him in the least. He still put the problem, How do you explain the fact that one arrangement of them has Europe as the result, and some other arrangement of them has no result, comparatively speaking?

Mr. HIGGINSON said that the history of the United States testified how well Mr. Phillips's theories fitted and sustained him; but he was sure there were others besides himself who felt that if they were compelled to look at the history of the world as he looked at it, it would stunt and paralyze them. As he listened to Mr. Phillips, it seemed to him that their eloquent friend did not say a single word in behalf of calling ourselves Christians in the sphere of morals that could not be adduced with precisely the same force in behalf of calling ourselves Shakspearians in the world of intellect. In each case, it was the difference between admitting the superiority of the individual, and separating him from the human race. When, at the end, he said the reason why he believed in Sir Isaac Newton was because he found all questions answered in him, it seemed to him. (Mr. Higginson) that he annihilated all his previous statements. If he believed in Christ as he believed in Sir Isaac Newton, as he believed in Shakspeare, it was all very well. Then the question remained, Could Christs be made by the study of Christ? He did not believe it, because Christ did not make himself in that manner. He would repeat, once for all, that he should feel weakened and paralyzed by taking what seemed to him the limited view of God's providence and of human history that Mr. Phillips took.

Mr. PHILLIPS explained that in speaking of the scrutiny to which the record of Christianity had been subjected, he only wanted to show that they ought to weigh equals against each other. He knew, so far as the most exact scholarship could tell him, that a certain act and a certain word were supposed, three hundred years after Christ, to have been done and said by him. They did not know anything with certainty about their Oriental Scriptures. Old Agesilaus said a very good thing when he said, as they were told, that "to work was infinitely better than to pray." It was a very brave, sound, and Christian thing; but did he say it? I do not know. Some fine thinker might have found one half of the story, and made the rest. I cannot tell. One half of Plutarch was poetry, the other fact. So, when considering the records of any religion, even Christianity itself, they must remember that principle. But he demanded that they should be put upon the same plane, that they should scrutinize the one as they did the other. The Eastern records were all story and legend until the same criticism was brought to bear upon them to which the records of Christianity had been subjected.

In regard to Sir Isaac Newton, he believed in him in astronomy. He had got the key to the material universe. When they came down to Laplace, they found they could reconstruct the universe on that principle. He would go to the stake on the correctness of the Copernican theory. When they came to religion, it was a different quality. He did not believe in Christ as he believed in Sir Isaac Newton, but he saw that the religious sentiment lay at the basis of civilization; it was the motive power and the check that could make human nature the highest product of the world. Europe had had a variety of religions which had never pro-

duced anything. We think we are now coming out into
the sunlight, and are on the right track to the right goal.
Take a single element in European history, — the sanctity of man as an individual, in his personal rights. No
other civilization of the world ever gave an inkling of it.
Greece knew nothing of it, nor Asia. Though each one
had the *idea*, neither *practised* it. Europe practises it.
With the variety of race there was in Europe, they could
not trace it wholly to race. He believed it was largely due
to the religious idea upon which Europe rested. It was
the natural outgrowth of Christianity, and was paralleled
in the civilization of no other race in the world. It was
just as much in antagonism to the race qualities of this race
as of any other race. The Saxon people from which we
sprung were as despotic and tyrannical as any other race ;
yet in spite of that, the quality of man was recognized.

In reply to a suggestion by Mr. Higginson, the speaker
said he was, of course, willing to allow the element of freedom in races ; but the question was, why it had not produced this regard for personal rights before. Europe existed before Christianity ; the Germanic race existed two
or three thousand years, perhaps, before Christianity.

Mr. POTTER wanted to know why, if they were to take
Europe as evidence that Christianity was different from
other religions, it was not fair to say that Christianity
failed in Asia for the same reason that other religions failed
there. Did not the facts tend to show that the difference
in result was really due to the differences of race and climate rather than to an essential difference in the religious
idea?

Mr. PHILLIPS replied that he thought Christianity took
possession of the Roman Empire, as it then existed. Civilization — what there was of it at that period — was a mere
belt around the Mediterranean. Up to the last five hundred
years, there was no civilization that penetrated a hundred

miles inward. Christianity took possession of the Roman Empire. He did not think they were necessarily thrown back upon race because it failed in a single province in Judea.

Mr. HIGGINSON reminded Mr. Phillips of South America, saying that even South America would compare favorably with the Chinese Empire, in her recognition of the great principles of the nineteenth century. He believed that the science of three thousand years ago was in many particulars as far advanced as ours. He thought they would find by-and-by that, with half-a-dozen exceptions, the older nations understood Nature about as well as we did.

Mr. WEISS sympathized very strongly with Mr. Phillips in regard to the emphasis which he put upon the humane and social developments of Christianity, but thought he overlooked certain points connected with the theory of the development of religious and intellectual ideas which were very important in the discussion of this question. Mr. Phillips doubted whether Agesilaus said, "It is better to work than to pray." Perhaps he did not, but *somebody* must have said it, else it would not have been attributed to Agesilaus. What particular consequence was it whether Confucius uttered the Golden Rule or not? *Somebody* must have uttered it, or it would not have come down to us. [Mr. PHILLIPS (*in an undertone*).—But *when* it was first uttered is of consequence.] The important point was, that everything of this kind was a stepping-stone in the stream of time, which led the nations from one position to another. He found an explanation of the whole problem in the relations of the great emigrations of the world to the development of the race. It was in the German nation that Christianity first found its aboriginal element,—Germanic regard for women; and it there gave the spiritual and theistic impulse to those humanitary and social ideas which have given it dominion over the hearts of men. The fact was

that, as mankind had been growing older, it seemed that
God had been growing older, for God expressed himself to
different phases and epochs of humanity. As men and
women were born into the world, and as the race became
more and more perfected in their organization or fibre by
the crossing of blood, by conquest, or by aboriginal purity,
its religious impulse took various forms; not merely the
theism of Christ, but the humanitarian idea of the Germanic
people. Christianity did not put woman where she belonged
until it touched the German races.

Mr. PHILLIPS. — They were not reached until the fifth or
sixth century. What was Christianity doing the first five
or six centuries?

Mr. WEISS. — It was mixing itself with the Greek and
Roman elements.

Mr. PHILLIPS. — Yes, but it recognized woman.

Mr. HIGGINSON. — It does not now.

Mrs. HOWE. — What does, if it does not?

Mr. WEISS continued, and said that he had reference to
a broad, general recognition. Of course, he understood
that when Christian women became food for wild beasts,
there was adoration paid to such women. There was always exceptional respect and adoration paid to those great
lights of the world's history. He thought they overlooked
that wonderful development of intelligence which sprang
from the Christian mind, which made Europe what it was.
He suggested this modification of Mr. Phillips's figure, that
the great principles of theism were always steam, for the
time being, wherever they were; but the trouble was, the
locomotive was not invented. The locomotive had been
built by the great and varied intelligence of modern Europe
and America, and thus we went ahead on the right track.

Mr. HALLOWELL wanted a definition of Christianity from
Mr. Phillips; whether it was his Christianity that overcame
the Roman Empire, or whether it was the Jewish, Messi-

2

anic idea which was held by all the churches. He wanted to ask Mr. Phillips whether he had faith in what is called "the atoning blood of Christ," and the other doctrines and theories of Christianity, or whether it was simply the moral law.

Mr. PHILLIPS replied that that was opening a very wide door; they could not discuss it to-day.

Mr. HALLOWELL said Mr. Phillips had admitted that Christianity found its parallels in other religions, but that the other religions had failed as civilizing forces. If the sentiment was there, he wanted to know why that sentiment did not operate? If the force lay in the idea, then the reason must be found in the difference of race, or climate, or something else that might be suggested; but if it was the man Jesus, the Messiah of the Jews, he wanted to know it.

Mr. SARGENT thought the question had been answered in Mr. Emerson's essay. It had been refreshing to him to listen to the teachings of Mr. Phillips. He felt that in his justification it should be said that, while others had been theorizing about Christianity, Mr. Phillips had been vigorously at work *doing* it.

In response to repeated and urgent calls from the company, who were anxious that Mr. Phillips should reply to the suggestions that had been made, that gentleman spoke again, very briefly. He said they did not come there to discuss the items of a technical creed: they were discussing Christianity as a great spiritual force, and he thought it distinct from all other religions. He believed that, in a certain sense, Buddha was inspired, but not in the sense in which Christ was. He thought the essence of Christianity was to be judged by its fruit. That was his Gibraltar. If a man tried to do a thing, he might be cut short, as Lincoln was, by death; he might be circumscribed by circumstances, — and therefore they could never judge of a man's character by his results; but if they gave an idea, a force, a thousand years to work in, they could judge of its essential character by the results. He thought the human race had never reached such a plane as Europe stood upon to-day, and therefore he claimed that no religion had ever done for the world what Christianity had done, or had ever given us that key to human nature which it had given us. Consequently no one of them could claim to stand anywhere near it.

Dr. BARTOL thought there could be no difference of opinion as to the fact that the name of Christ had taken up history, and that his teachings, as they had been organized, had socially succeeded. He should as soon think of abolishing the word "light" or "sweet" or "strong," as of abolishing the word "Christian." The only question was, whether the individual Christ, or any word or deed of Christ, was the essence and the beginning of the thing, or only a production of it, an illustration of it. Christ, as an individual man, was not the substance of Christianity, he only voiced it. He was the prophet of it, the saint of it, in the best sense, the orator of it; but Christianity altogether was but an illustration of something that lay behind and deeper. They might call it what they would. He did not like the word "theism" very much; but it was something that lay deeper than any particular person. Those stories of the good Samaritan, the Prodigal Son, and the rest, were only so many writings in invisible ink, which had been laid on the fire of the man's moral feeling until the characters were brought out; and what the fire in the man's own mind did not bring out, he could make no use of. They were all a part of this Christian story, and could not get out of it. He held all metaphysical notions on the subject of religion of no account that did not take right hold of human life, as Mr. Phillips had been doing.

People were getting very critical about reading the Bible. They found sentiments expressed which they regarded as untrue, irreligious, unscientific, and they could not abide them. He did not apprehend any evil from this resort to the interior feeling. He should as soon think of saying that the symphonies of Beethoven and the oratorios of Handel and Haydn were all of music, as of saying that the books of the Bible were all of religion.

II.

THE IMMANENCE OF GOD.

By JOHN WEISS.

WHEN Lord and Lady Amberley visited Boston, Mr. Ralph Waldo Emerson desired that they should meet persons who were interested in the reform in which they had been prominent in England. Lord Amberley had contributed valuable papers to the "Fortnightly Review," on the work of Conservatives and Liberals in relation to the English Church, pointing out the defects and limitations of that body, and making valuable suggestions in regard to its improvement. Lady Amberley was one of the signers of a petition, presented by Lady Anna Gore Langton, praying that married women and widows, duly qualified as rate-payers, etc., might be admitted to the privilege of voting for members of Parliament.

It seemed to Mr. Emerson that his object would best be accomplished by calling together the Chestnut Street Club; and at his request an extra meeting was held, the arrangements, as will appear from the following note, being left chiefly with him : —

CONCORD, Monday Eve.

DEAR MR. SARGENT, — My note to Mr. Norton, whom I requested to arrange with Lady Amberley about the day when our conversation could be secure of its guests, brought me no answer until to-night. Norton, it seems, put off his dinner, to which they had been invited, on account of the death of Governor Andrew.

To-night I have a note from Lady Amberley, saying that they will stay to attend the meeting at your house, on the 14th. So, if it is still agreeable to you and Mrs. Sargent to receive the company, we will consider it fixed for that day, at 10 o'clock, A.M. As it is not the true day for the club, I think Mr. Alcott rather wished to consult the best interests of the conversation; and instead of sending notifications to the whole society, to write to those members whom we could least spare, and also to a few ladies and gentlemen, not members, whose presence would essentially aid the meeting. . . . In your absence from town in the interim we cannot expect you to charge yourself with this care. . . .

With great regard, yours,

R. W. EMERSON.

At this meeting Rev. John Weiss read a very able essay, (since published in his works) on the immanence of God in presence and action everywhere and perpetually, in opposition to the popular theory of occasional miraculous intervention in past times, limited to those times.

I can do no justice to Mr. Weiss's boldness of thought and affluence of language. One of the guests said of him, "Then comes a voice from heaven. A man, one fifth flesh and four fifths flame, kindles under his inspiration into a miraculous light, and says words that can never be forgotten. I dare not try to repeat them. Who heard John Weiss can nevermore be quite as petty as his old poor self."

Mrs. LUCRETIA MOTT said she had been glad to hear an expression of the full faith of the Spiritualists in divine and eternal law; in view of this she heartily rejoiced in the obvious fact that their movement is doing more than any other movement to break up the ideas popularly called a "plan of salvation," a "scheme of redemption," etc. She believed this reform, like others, must be gradual in its operations, and that the various grades in religious society are still needed, and each must use its own method until it understands some other to be better.

DAVID A. WASSON did not doubt the continuity of Nature, but was not sure that that continuity was always traceable. "No doubt there is method," he said, "but many things in history cannot be apparently adjusted to it. The mythological stories of the Gospels, though quite unworthy of credit as facts, have yet a real value, because they express great and fruitful truths."

Rev. SAMUEL LONGFELLOW suggested that the word "supernatural" is used in such varied senses that discourse upon it cannot be well understood unless each person defines his idea of it.

Mrs. JULIA WARD HOWE commented on the essay, and ended by saying, "There is no antithesis between the real and the ideal. The ideal is to rule the future. The real is striving to overtake the ideal."

Lord AMBERLEY was glad to have heard an essay intended to show the unity and constancy of the operations of Nature, — an idea with which he thoroughly agreed. He had been favored with the opportunity of hearing the same paper read a few days before, and this second reading had given him a better understanding and a higher appreciation of it.

Mrs. MOTT was also with Lord and Lady Amberley at the first reading, and, far from finding the repetition wearisome, she wished she had a week for the careful study of the essay. "It is admirable in its methods of asserting Divine Providence and justifying the ways of God to man. Year by year more people are prepared to accept the plain statement of these ideas. Elias Hicks long ago taught this same doctrine, and when some timid members of the Society of Friends questioned him in regard to it, he asked impressively, ' Are we to go back to miracles?' Let us carry the high truths suggested in this essay into life, — into social and civil life, into business and politics. Our friends the Spiritualists are said not to be reformatory in practice. We need to show forth our faith by our activity in all good works. The natural and the spiritual ought never to be spoken of antagonistically. Both belong to man, and both should be recognized and cultivated in childhood, so as to give the benefit of both.

"Elias Hicks, at the close of a meeting where these ideas had been in controversy, once said, 'To the Christ who was *never* crucified, who never died or was buried, and who had no need to rise from the dead, I commend you.'

"The great fault in Spiritualism is its looking beyond the grave instead of attending to the present life and state. We need to apply all truths to life, to teach the gospel of truth and humanity for present as well as future uses. Most conversions are made to sects, comparatively few to truth and love. We dwell rather in Judaism than in Christianity, through the prevailing false reverence for the Bible, the Sabbath, and the sacraments. We have not yet learned to treat these things simply and naturally."

ROBERT DALE OWEN replied, referring to the criticism on nomenclature that had been made : " The French say 'spiritist' and 'spiritism ; ' but even if these terms are more accurate, they would mislead the mass of hearers here, and thus would be objectionable. When asked my own religious belief, I would prefer to call myself a Jesuit, if this term, instead of bearing its proper signification,— a follower of the ideas taught by Jesus, — had not been made by circumstances to convey a meaning far different. For the society with which I am identified I prefer the name 'Spiritualist,' as having a more extended meaning than the other.

"I like the essay because it teaches the universality of law. All that we perceive is natural. Between the two worlds, visible and invisible, there is but a thin veil. We should give as fair an examination to Spiritualism as to any phenomena of the natural world, and examine the ultra-mundane, so far as we can reach it, as carefully as the mundane. If the evidence for the Scripture miracles be unsatisfactory and insufficient, let that be plainly declared. Dr. Temple, the distinguished master of the Rugby School, and one of the authors of ' Essays and Reviews,' says that miracles have become a stumbling-block. The wonders of Spiritualism are not miracles. I believe them all to be in accordance with great natural laws ; and these are to be found only by patient and faithful searching."

III.

DEMOCRACY.

By DAVID A. WASSON.

MR. DAVID A. WASSON, the essayist of the day, and one of New England's cleverest thinkers, read an elaborate paper upon the elements of true liberty. Believing in the "Scriptures of Politics," Mr. Wasson handled his subject with the fastidiousness of a scholar and the sternness of a moralist. "In what sense is man free by nature?" he asked. "In reality, man is a victim to subjection, and it is only by the interposition of Art and Science that he breaks from his fetters. Co-operation is power; and as physical subjection diminishes, a moral sense steps in. The universe is one vast system and celebration of obedience. Civilization restrains, and man has not perfect property in the blood of his own veins. It is not surprising, therefore, if there be shown a preference for the freedom antecedent to civilization; and yet this same free life is a mirage. It fetters all man's human nature, and lets only the beast go free. Any freedom is fallacious, as it seems unconditional.

"Every man has an affection for his own will, and a desire to make it effective," continued Mr. Wasson. "This may be called subjective liberty, and is good as an element, but not as a principle. Yet this constrains; for, multiply one will by many, and man is surrounded by a network of such constraints as are productive of humanity's true emancipation. When two men come together there is a larger freedom, if they be rightly related; there is a convergence of powers to a focus of right reason. Man is not born free, but is born to become so, and attains freedom by prophecy and aspiration. Politically, it is man's effective application of right reason to himself and others that makes him free. The serviceableness of men depends upon their liberation in community; but liberation is not the liberty of thieves to elect thieves to office. Liberty is attained only through the medium of political community. Men shall be knitted together in unity, rational restraint being one of the factors of liberty. It is the shell of the egg, the husk of corn, without which disintegration and demoralization ensue. The ascent of life entails a progressive embodiment of restraint.

" All men crave a true liberation. Liberty in community demands discipline of the will. Had there ever been such discipline, History would have been different. Emancipators are victims, and the Cross is their symbol. Liberty that consists only in voting helps to oppress us. One of our greatest foes is fraudulent work, with its waste of labor and capital. Honesty would increase the value of labor one hundred per cent. We must get rid of reckless indiscrimination. There should be formation of guilds which should act as mutual-work insurance companies. It is democratic averages that keep human nature so low. We are forced to struggle against voracities rather than tyrannies that proclaim a law of chaos. The age of right reason will not be brought about by cheap sentimentality. Army hospitals did not conquer Richmond, nor will soup-houses conquer this century. Egotistic power, whether of one or two, must pass away as a dream, leaving to select men and women the divine reign of *recta ratio*."

Leading the discussion upon Mr. Wasson's paper, Mr.

RALPH WALDO EMERSON pronounced it an admirable comment on political society, and defective only in its attack upon suffrage. Its author's pointed pen would have undoubtedly destroyed monarchy more readily than democracy. Man has not skill enough to manage either. If offered reforms, Mr. Wasson would be unable to give up the public. The "rings" of New York simply prove the imbecility of any form of government in a bad population. With the exception of Connecticut, which is a suburb of New York, the New England States carry about with them their own cure for political distempers. Schools are the remedy for all populations; they qualify and remove all danger that threatens. History gives no preference over suffrage. We must stand for the freest form of government. In California it availed to make the best government among bruisers and gamblers. The best will is the average will. It is only upon extraordinary occasions that the world produces natural emperors, such as Abraham Lincoln and George Washington. In our democracy we show a better average than any succession of kings. The kingdom of God must come, and then all will be safe.

Mr. WEISS said Mr. Wasson's paper was most timely, and if the like were heard from rostrum and pulpit, the era of *recta ratio* would draw near. But it is too late to talk about limiting suffrage. The Plug Uglies have it, the negroes have it; and it would endanger the safety of the republic to take it away from one negro. He would establish a right balance of power by deploying women upon the field. In them is the emotional, intuitive, and moral element. There are women who have great power of synthesis, of ratiocination; there are men who are strongly emotional and intuitive; but both are exceptional, and the speaker did not believe there could be a democracy until man and woman stood side by side, — the one saying, "Here is my ratiocination," the other, "Here is my intuition." Then we shall have the whole power of the republic. When we have man, we have half a god. In Massachusetts, where there are 250,000 more women than men, we have more than our share of God. *Our safety lies in deploying all of God we have upon the field.*

"I appreciate," said Mrs. HOWE, "and value the justice and nicety of the criticism made by Mr. Wasson upon the faults and shortcomings of a democratic society. But while I heard him with pleasure and interest, I yet felt, in hearing him, like the disabled composer, whose cat, running over the keyboard of the piano, struck the third chord, legitimate and musical in its place, but asking the fourth as its solution. Incompetent as he was, he hobbled from his sofa, and struck the needed chord before he could again rest. The facts, indeed, are much as Mr. Wasson states them, and there are moments in our study and observation in which the evils of the popular rule confront us, and almost turn us back as insurmountable. But our great hope triumphs over these difficulties, and leads us on in the direction already indicated. This seems to be one of the *antinomies* of morals. It seems almost hopeless to reconcile the real evils of popular sovereignty with its ideal dignity and security. Yet the two, none the less, co-exist."

Mr. ALCOTT maintained that a democracy is impossible saving where the whole people are cultivated. Our theory is perfect, but in the absence of culture we are well-nigh swamped.

"No man," said Mr. OWEN, "is entitled to more liberty than he can use for his own and his neighbor's good."

IV.

LIMITATIONS.

By JULIA WARD HOWE.

OUR life begins with limitations. Very slowly are the liberties of the animal accorded to us ; yet more slowly those of the human being. Our human endowment comprises a little power of discrimination, a little memory, by which to-day is pieced out with yesterday ; and a little power of inference, by which to-morrow is prepared from to-day. . . . The human being soon finds that he has tasks before him. To the man in a wilderness all things belong, — sky, water, air, sunshine, trees ; but this liberty and fulness are savage, not civil. Man and the universe regard each other with no voice to interpret between them. Then the instinct of labor arouses the man to work. He clears his field, builds his house, and shuts himself in, that the elements may no longer visit him with unmitigated liberality. After awhile he invites another to share his house, and so divides all the goods he possesses, but, dividing also his labors, finds himself the gainer. . . . Provided after a while with material comforts, men begin to do their mental and spiritual work, and again discover in these directions their limitations. Thus the work of ascent from savagism to civilization shows a succession of limitations. Forbearance is an element of every perfect work. All arts tend to overproduction. When we thank a man for giving us one poem, we may thank him for not giving us ten. It is the same in friendship. One shall be better befriended by few intimates than by many, and more joy shall grow out of one great affection than out of a hundred easy likings. It is the same with religion, the character of whose demonstrations is more important than their frequency. The greater the power, the more imperious the necessity for its limitation. The perception of a high ethical good enables a good man to exercise the needful self-restraint and forbearance; and he who has a divine idea may be more hopeful in its neglect than in its celebrity.

Definiteness of object is essential to attainment, and good work presupposes subdivision and limitation. The limitations of the condition in life of Kepler, of Fulton, of Milton, of Jesus, were necessary for their marvellous achievements. Each life has its possible maximum. If it recognize its limitations, narrow its aim, concentrate its force, it will accomplish its highest possibility. Quantity and quality are factors of a constant product. The noblest genius becomes a hack when it sells all it can write for all it can get. The peculiar limitations of each person make the variety of human character which is essential to society. If any one were infinite in any direction, he would have no need of another. The original limitations of our structure are not accidental, but necessary. Every man needs a brain, but it would be of no advantage to have two. With four eyes we could not see more, nor with four hands do more, than we can with those we have. Rights do not change; they always exist. We discover them, and with each discovery a limit is set up beyond which we may not safely trespass.

In music, also, the seven rays of the prism of sound, limitation is essential both to melody and harmony. In a vocal concert the soprano is queen, and each subordinate voice maintains its own place. The soprano soars and trills, and scatters notes precious as diamond-dust; the tenor, who knows her intention, meets and supports her; the contralto, sweet and subject maid of honor, follows three notes behind her royal lady; and the basso, the basis and foundation of all things, says, "Here I set up my everlasting rest. I am the basso." Like the singers, each of us in the great harmony of life has his place and his limitation. In a given number of men there can be only one first man,—one Shakespeare, Dante, Garibaldi, —but each of us can strive to be his own best. Our birth makes one limitation, our breeding another. Our profession limits us to one function, our marriage to one partner.

Sects are the needful limitations of the religious idea. Religious intolerance is a failure to recognize the need of this diversity. There must be limitations in the education of children, whose early instruction is the title-deed to their estate. Honors and wealth also, to be valuable, must have their limits. In all things it is needful to know the metes and bounds of man's estate, and to conform one's self to them.

W. H. Channing said he must protest against the word and the idea of limitations. He thought the word "relations" would better express the thing intended; and relations, in his view, were not limitations. The problem of the Divine Being must be how to let the human creature be itself. All creatures must exist in Him; yet every human being is infinitely great in its essence. The ideal that comes to every human being is an image of the Infinite Mind. God does not limit us: he seeks relations with us by which we can increase.

A crowd of persons is blended in each single person. We cannot have merely a blending of the lives of two parents in each individual. There must be a germinal point where every person shall begin, and whence a new being may be formed, that shall find his genuine, harmonious relations to the persons and things around him. In short, he who seeks to realize God's ideal of him should look for it in harmonious co-operation with others, rather than by looking at limitations.

Mr. HIGGINSON objected to overmuch consideration of limitations or of prospective disappointments; he felt, with Thoreau, that he did not want to practise resignation in advance of the necessity for it. It was clearly undesirable that trees should grow so high as to lift their boughs into the sky, but not much trouble seemed taken by Nature to prevent it. To his thinking, limitations had their use in being something to struggle against; and these struggles against bounds are illustrated by all things. The very baby in arms struggles against its mother's bountiful breast and sacred knees. Nature is our mother, against whom we struggle. Some of us would be worsted, to be sure, and die failures; but let us struggle as long as we can. He believed in a vast power to enhance the gifts of Nature, even physically: spiritually, how much more! When Shakespeare comes into the world, his greatest work is to show what infinite things a man can do. And other men, not Shakespeares, have spoken single sentences which would emancipate whole planets, whole generations of life. See Bryant, after seventy, translating Homer, and Goethe writing "Faust" when still older. We do not yet know what we can do. He, himself, might yet invent a wonderful steam-engine after he was eighty, though now he could never attain to a clear understanding of the principles of one; and Heaven forbid that he should limit, even by a steam-engine, the future possibilities of Mrs. Howe. Let us stick to Pegasus as long as we can: be like Nick Bottom, who tries to play all the parts.

Mr. WEISS thought the Infinite Mind showed no objection to limitation. The first act of the Infinite Mind was to make nebulosity — then set to work to discriminate, to limit.   The further the Divine Mind travels from nebulosity, the more deeply it enters into limitation.   Mr. Weiss alluded to Mrs. Howe's musical illustration.   Pointing to a harp in one of the pictures of the room, he said that "every chord had its note because it was tied at both ends, and was limited to a portion of the infinite space which had been thus measured off to it as the bound of its activity."   So each individual had measured off to him his limited portion of infinity, within which his life might be made a sweet note, having its place in the grand harmony of the universe.

"Are you not confounding the limitations of matter with the limitations of soul?" asked Mr. Higginson.

Mr. Weiss replied that he thought both were subject to limitation.

"Would you say," rejoined Mr. Higginson, "that the progress of the soul is limited?"

"Certainly," said Mr. Weiss; "but the limitations of the soul may expand as it goes on.   You cannot say the soul has no limitations without saying that it is infinite; and thus you would people the universe with beings, each of whom is infinite."

Mr. McCauley alluded to Psyche, — her wanderings and perils before achieving immortality.   Being spirits, we were doubtless immortal, but might progress forever toward the infinite without attaining it.   Perhaps our limitations might be typified by those of the railway train, which may go on in one direction, but must keep to its track.   We may pursue the paths of our lives forever, but cannot deviate from them.

Mr. Wasson said our limitations served to compel us to singleness of aim and concentration of labor.   To attempt everything insures the accomplishment of nothing. Colonel Higginson may never achieve his steam-engine;

but if he does, it will be only by accepting his limitations and working on steadily within them.

Mr. CHANNING said it would have been easy for God to have made us infinite at once; and it was a sacrifice not to make us at the start as perfect as we shall ever become in eternity. That he has not done so indicates that now we are hedged about in certain directions, and, like every instrument in the orchestra, we must utter the tone that our condition makes possible for us as well as we may.

Mr. HIGGINSON did not like the orchestra illustration, notwithstanding it had been so beautifully used. The instruments were tied at both ends. He was sure that, on one side at least, he was not tied, and he did not intend to be. He preferred the railroad illustration, though probably, after a certain degree of progress, he should want to widen the gauge.

Mr. WEISS replied that if we were tied at both ends it was that each might vibrate, and sound his own note surely in the grand orchestra.

"I will compromise on one end," said Mr. HIGGINSON, "but must have the infinite part unfettered."

Mr. WASSON spoke of the races at fairs, where the combatants ran in sacks; and he thought Mr. Higginson considered limitation in the light of a hampering sack, while Mrs. Howe meant something quite other and different by it. He himself desired to be always so limited that he should stand in relations with others and be dependent upon them. In that consisted the happiness of being a family man. It was well that the heavens should be open, so that we were in no danger of striking our heads against them; but the grand sally toward the heavens comes early in all nations, and God is one of the first words. We must separate the human from the divine: one does one thing and the other another.

Mrs. HOWE said it was her own suffering under the

oppressing, hampering limitations of life, which seemed
sometimes not less than cruel, that set her thoughts in the
direction they had taken ; and she felt that in writing her
essay she was justifying the ways of God to herself.   She
asked Mr. Higginson if he did not think one who kept in
mind the limitations of time, the exact length of a day,
would accomplish more than one who worked on the theory
that the day had no end.

Mr. HIGGINSON was ready with a decided negative, and
he quoted a sentence from Goethe, " Time is infinitely
long, and each day will hold all you can put into it."

The last speaker was Mr. CHANNING, who said that our
planet will by and by be crowded, and that while there remains room to work comfortably, each person had better
do what he can do best.

At one point in the conversation Mr. Weiss was asked
why it was the Greeks did not understand music.   Mr.
WEISS replied the Greeks did not love music ; that the hour
for the development of that art had not struck.   The
work of the Greek genius was sculpture.   It was reserved
for the German genius to show the world the majesty and
the mystery of music.

V.

NATURE AND PERSON.

By HENRY JAMES.

MR. HENRY JAMES'S reputation as a profound metaphysician, and the brilliancy which he displayed in discussion at former club-meetings were sufficient reason for the large audience of listeners to his essay at Chestnut Street. The host, the Rev. John T. Sargent, called the club to order at eleven o'clock and introduced the essayist, who announced as his subject, "Nature and Person," saying that he had chosen it because he regarded Nature as the sole true theatre of creative power, and hence the sole true field of divine revelation, — the spiritual world being of no interest save as it shed light on the great problem of Nature, — our origin and destiny. The essay was devoted to showing the difference between nature and person, both as actualities and as forces, and to showing the evil results that have sprung from confounding the two terms and the two things.

Person affords ground for a moral or *quasi* individual development in man as good and evil, but it offers no hint of a future divine blending of these finite or contrasted men in a perfect, infinite, or unitary style of man. Thus Mr. James looked upon the element of person in human nature, which constitutes its finite identifying element, as designating the creature, and as being therefore the inferior element in the nature. And he looked upon law, which constitutes the infinite or individualizing principle of the nature, as indicating the divine or creative side of it, rigidly subjecting all persons to itself. In short, the

lecturer's fundamental idea clearly was that human nature
was originally a chaos or confusion of creator and creature :
thus of infinite spiritual good in the creator, with the utmost possible or conceivable natural evil in the creature.
But as "the utmost possible or conceivable natural evil"
is indefinite or *universal* evil, Mr. James considered the
creative end or purpose in the original constitution of
human nature to have been the vindication of its own
omnipotence or infinitude in begetting an offspring which
shall be in itself a most real or objective subjection of
evil to good.

After stating the general scope of his idea, Mr. James,
leaving abstract theory aside, soon proceeded to show the
mischievous practical results that flowed from an undue ex-
altation of the private or personal element in consciousness over the natural or social one.   He affirmed that the
rage for multiplying schools and colleges in our country
was a real insanity, as promoting an exclusively personal or isolated culture among us, and to that extent
retarding the development of a common or public consciousness.   In this connection he referred to the condition of England, which was spiritually rotting from
excessive personal culture, or the over-education of a
scholarly class, which could do nothing but criticise, from
its own idle, luxurious point of view, every scheme that
looked to distinctively general or race culture, and so
proved itself hostile to man's natural affranchisement.
But everywhere person is the born foe of nature; everywhere the vicious principle of personality — and nowhere
so much as in the religious sphere of life — erects itself
against the just principle of community in natural things ;
so that God, if we listen to our traditional pulpit-teaching,
would seem to have been the original inventor of the hell-
ish principle of emulation or competition in the human
bosom, instead of its mere assiduous utilizer.   Supposing

a stupid and limitary SELF-righteousness to be God's exclusive aim in man, and not a unitary RACE-righteousness, this is what alone we have gone on to crave at God's hands; and the only result of our ungodly prayers and pious strivings has been to impose upon the spiritual world the dread antagonism of hell and heaven, and perpetuate it there. The spiritual world consequently is fast becoming a complete nuisance to human thought, and men find themselves reverting to Nature with the ardor with which the child betakes himself to the sincere milk of its mother's breast. In fact, the believing world is becoming utterly atheistic to the deity proclaimed in the churches; and it would not be long before the entire honest or disinterested lay element in the churches themselves would demand a God for their worship capable of meeting the inexorable wants of human nature, rather than of ministering to the self-righteous cupidities of the individual heart.

Nature is the principle of community or identity in existence, and is the only just basis therefore of spiritual individuality; for an individuality in man which should acknowledge no common or identical basis in human life would be wholly inconceivable — like heaven without earth, or a house without a foundation. This natural or common principle in existence is called selfhood, and is in itself the source of all disorder and evil. For nothing can be easier to see than that common or natural selfhood (being the principle of unrelated or independent existence in the creature), however it may lend itself to the ends of the creative infinitude, is in itself the principle of hell in man. Every atom of creation on its natural or constitutional side bristles with selfhood, — *is* selfhood in fact, — else creature would be undistinguishable from creator. And the creator's spiritual omnipotence is displayed as a principle of free, spontaneous RELATIONSHIP among these discordant, warring atoms, binding them all in eventual harmony, and giving them the order of a unitary life. Thus, though self-hood (or unrelated, independent personality) be the stigma of created existence, giving us an insuperable felt remoteness to our Creator, yet without it creation would be, in a spiritual regard, mere sentimental rubbish. Personality is the dense mask behind which the Supreme Artist securely operates the enlargement of our nature in giving it gradual social form. Very slowly to our eyes, through marriage and the family unity constituted by it, and so on through all the successive expansions of that empirical unity in the tribe, the commune, the city, the nation, the republic, men's divine-natural consciousness struggles toward the light; for each of these successive stages of its development has been a stage of bondage to it. But the great final emancipation of the nature in social form and order has never been the least uncertain from the beginning. For it has always had the Divine omnipotence to guarantee it, and that omnipotence has found no surer tools to work with than the inveterate selfishness and imbecility of men.

At Mr. Sargent's invitation remarks were made by Dr. Clarke, Mr. Abbot, Professor Everett, and Dr. Holmes; the last speaker seemed to express the general feeling by saying that when he was invited to speak without preparation on a carefully written essay he always felt as he should if, at a chemical lecture, somebody should pass around a precipitate, and when the mixture had become turbid, should request him to give his opinion on it; besides, he added, the fallacies constantly arising in such a discussion, from the lack of a proper definition of terms, always made him feel as if quicksilver had been substituted for the ordinary silver of speech. He declared that he preferred to take the essay home, slowly assimilate it, and not talk about it until it had become a part of himself. This closed the discussion, but many of the members lingered to talk over the essay socially.

VI.

WOMAN.

By JOHN WEISS.

MR. WEISS began with a witty statement of the imperfections of our present political machinery, satirizing the attempts which men have made to give a monopoly of the regulations of public affairs to the rougher and coarser half of the human family. He gave a rose-colored view of the future, when women should combine with men in political not less than in domestic arrangements; claimed their right to such partnership, and seemed to expect a speedy if not an immediate change for the better in our state and national politics as soon as women should assist in directing them. To attempt to report the essay would be as futile as to attempt a description of Beethoven's heroic symphony.

Every one felt that the best had been said, and there was nothing left but silence. There was a spell upon us which none wished broken, and Mr. Emerson truly expressed the almost universal sentiment, when he said that he thought it would be far better to hold a silent meeting.

Mr. EMERSON seemed strongly impressed by the enthusiasm and confidence of the essayist. He believed it was for woman to decide what her political status should be. He had been accustomed to suppose that women of refinement and culture — those whose thought would be most available for political reform, if it were used in that direction — shrank from taking part in those labors, and were well content to keep the position public opinion had assigned to them. If it were otherwise, and thoughtful women *did* choose to apply themselves to efforts for improvement in legislation and government, he could not doubt the advantage of such action. When women of any State are accorded the rights of suffrage, it would be the graceful part of man to make all such arrangements as would be convenient for women; and he added that we are all the better for hearing of the riches in store for us, and can only await the eventful arrival.

Mr. WASSON thought there should be no more votes granted until preliminary steps were taken to base votes on quality. Mr. Emerson had remarked at a previous meeting that a government was no better than the people. It seemed to Mr. Wasson it were as wise to say that a ship is no better than the wood in a forest. "There is danger all round, and it is only the virtue of the structure that saves: the proper artisan must gather everything. The principle of selection comes in, — a principle that is absolutely necessary. There should be a qualification basis for suffrage, and certain departments of the government should be made over to women. I think that to bring the feminine element into political play would be a waste of good material."

Mrs. CHENEY replied: "Women would regard the ballot as a heavy responsibility. There will be no purification of politics until women do it. The finest men take no active part in politics so long as they can make excuses to their consciences. They shrink from this duty, until neglect becomes criminal. Women may be placed in the same category. They consider it as part of the solemn duty of life, and their very reluctance is an argument in favor of their fitness for the trust. It denotes responsibility. Character will be the only test. If the two classes, refined and intellectual men and women, would make the effort to work together for reform in politics, and no longer leave that department to the control of persons less competent and less worthy, an advance would be made such as the world has never seen."

Mr. ALCOTT argued: "Numbers need not embarrass . democracy. Magnetism must come from superior force. It is the rule of the best to magnetize the many. In the household there is real democracy. In men and women there is the polarity of magnetism. When did Saxon beauty bear its loveliest flowers? When Shakspeare wrote, and Elizabeth reigned as the ornament of history. Would Shakspeare and Raleigh have done their best, would that galaxy have shone so brightly in the heavens, had there been no Elizabeth on the throne? Give woman her place in history. She keeps the world in its orbit. If grace and culture mean anything, she should hold her rightful sceptre. The fine womanly element is culture, and begins with a sense of beauty. Can there be any culture or rule in government until it is made beautiful? Moore, in his 'Utopia,' spoke for women as well as for men, and educated his daughter as he would have educated his sons. In Plato's 'Republic,' women become rulers of the State after having given citizens to it. We practically theorize and fall behind antiquity. None of us can be sufficiently thankful for our essay to-day. It is feminine eloquence."

Judge WARREN placed the claim for woman suffrage in municipal matters upon justice, and supported the claim by the analogy of church and corporation voting, where women do vote. "Unmarried women can now make contracts, widows can administer the estates of their deceased husbands; these and other responsibilities and powers given women by our laws show their ability to discharge the functions of voters. Women would have especial influence in business relating to education, charity, administration, the issuing of licenses, and the like. Men and women are protected by government, but only men can vote. Suffrage is not a natural right, it is a question of expediency."

President WARREN gave as his only objection to women voting, their own indifference. He also regarded the question as one of expediency, and that the same principle should fix suffrage for one sex as for the other, extending it only to those who desire it, so as not to increase the number of disinterested voters.

Mr. WM. I. BOWDITCH spoke of the question as one of right, not expediency; but he believed that education should be made a qualification for all voters.

Prof. C. C. EVERETT favored a qualification as an incitement to the voter, and did not consider sex to be a ground of discrimination, if suffrage was not conferred on non-tax-payers.

Prof. W. W. GOODWIN considered that a property qualification would be better than the present ruinous system of voting.

Mr. TEDLOW recommended that women be given more power in educational matters, where they are of great practical benefit; but he doubted their success as public financiers.

Rev. Mr. ELDER began by enumerating the reasons which, if existing, might make it necessary to bestow the suffrage upon women. If it could be shown that it was needed to protect women in their rights, essential to insure the general welfare, it should be given to them. If it could be shown that the majority of women wanted the ballot, it would afford a presumption in favor of giving it to them. If it could be shown that men were generally indifferent to the privileges of women, then they should have the right to vote. He himself was opposed to granting women the right to vote, and contended that the laws were, if anything, rather more than just to woman.

Mr. D. A. Wasson dryly remarked that he should have been a believer in female suffrage if he had not heard the arguments in its favor.

This quotation from Theodore Parker was read as an appropriate ending for the discussion : —

" We want the excellence of man and woman both united ; intellectual power, knowledge, great ideas, — in literature, philosophy, theology, ethics, — and practical skill ; but we want something better, — the moral, affectional, religious intuition, to put justice into ethics, love into theology, piety into science and letters. Everywhere, in the family, the community, the Church and the State, we want the masculine and feminine element co-operating and conjoined. Woman is to correct man's taste, mend his morals, excite his affections, inspire his religious faculties. Man is to quicken her intellect, to help her will, translate her sentiments to ideas, and enact them into righteous laws. Man's moral action, at best, is only a sort of general human providence, aiming at the welfare of a part, and satisfied with achieving the ' greatest good of the greatest number.' Woman's moral action is more like a special human providence, acting without general rules, but caring for each particular case. We need both of these, the general and the special, to make a total human providence.

" If man and woman are counted equivalent, — equal in rights, though with diverse powers, — shall we not mend the literature of the world, its theology, its science, its laws, and its actions too ? I cannot believe that wealth and want are to stand ever side by side as desperate foes ; that culture must ride only on the back of ignorance ; and feminine virtue be guarded by the degradation of whole classes of ill-starred men, as in the East, or the degradation of whole classes of ill-starred women, as in the West ; but while we neglect the means of help God puts in our power, why, the present must be like the past, — ' property ' must be theft,

' law ' the strength of selfish will, and ' Christianity ' what
we see it is, the apology for every powerful wrong.

"To every woman let me say, Respect your nature as
a human being, your nature as a woman; then respect
your rights; then remember your duty to possess, to use,
to develop, and to enjoy every faculty which God has given
you, each in its normal way.

"And to men let me say, Respect — with the profound-
est reverence respect — the mother that bore you, the sisters
who bless you, the woman that you love, the woman that
you marry.   As you seek to possess your own manly rights,
seek also, by that great arm, by that powerful brain, seek
to vindicate her rights as woman, as your own as man.
Then we may see better things in the Church, better things
in the State, in the community, in the home.   Then the
green shall show what buds it hid, the buds shall blossom, the flowers bear fruit, and the blessing of God be on
us all."

VII.

THE RELATION OF JESUS TO THE PRESENT AGE.

By CHARLES CARROLL EVERETT.

ON this topic, Dr. C. C. EVERETT presented a beautiful, symmetrical, and logical essay. He regarded Christ as a problem and a power. In considering his relations to the present age, he considered each as a receiver, and each as a giver. Christ needs the present age, and the present age needs Christ. The opposition is only apparent. He spoke first of the external history of Christ, next of his teaching, and finally of his personality in relation to the present age. The external history of Christ contains elements which are opposed to the habits of thought most peculiar to the present century. He referred to miracles. The idea of miracle is so foreign to the spirit of the age that it has a fascination for it. There is a certain degree of right to both sides of the controversy. The very antagonism between the two shows that each has a contribution for the other which could be received from no other source. Law is infinite; the miracle itself can be only the manifestation of some grander law. For the first time miracle has its full logical meaning. No miracle, however stupendous, can prove the truth of a principle in morals. When the miracle testifies of the comprehensive law which it manifests, then first does it have a meaning. On the other hand, the miracle makes a no less important contribution to the spirit of the age. It demonstrates to the senses that physical laws are not absolute in their own realm ; that they are interposed and penetrated by spiritual force ; that matter is at the last subordinate to spirit.

————

Prof. CALVIN E. STOWE doubted that science was antagonistic to Christianity ; he did not think the essayist meant to convey that idea, but many do make that claim.   He did not see but that the moral worth and intellectuality and influence on the public mind was at least as great in the men who upheld Christianity as in the scientific men. He did not see why Christians should not be thought " the age," as well as scientific men.   " But I do think," he said, " that there is one thing that bids fair to be established, and that is, — a *fact* never can do any harm ; a well-developed *fact* should be received just as it is, regardless of consequences.   But if the thought of the age is opposed to Christianity, so much the worse for the thought of the age ; for Christianity is the only permanent thing there is. We know that the thought of the age has always been changing.   I think the human race have been a wonderfully foolish set from the beginning.   I think there is no history so melancholy as the history of man.   So far as I can see, it would have been a great deal more to the glory of God to have made fewer human beings, and had them of better quality.   But I have faith in God and faith in the New Testament.   I believe it is all going to come right.   I believe God knows more than I do, and more than the spirit of the age, and more than the Church, and that we shall all do better when we come to that."   He did not agree with the essayist in saying that Christ did not attach very great importance to his miracles.   He certainly did.   What he condemned was the constant longing of the Jewish mind for an external miracle.

DAVID A. WASSON acknowledged the system of miracles

as incomprehensible to him. He respected that open, broad something which took in the fact of the world, and did not push it aside with a thought. He did not want to put his personal feeling in place of the fact of the world, and could not sympathize with the idea that a man was good if he recognized no evil.

Dr. HEDGE said: "All we get out of fact, at last, is an idea, and that is what we get from fable. It makes no real difference whether the idea is suggested by fact or fable." For himself, he believed a large proportion of the New Testament narratives were fabulous, that what they related as facts were myths. But they were none the less important for that. Jesus is not the Christ. With reference to the miracles, we cannot put faith in those which affront our common-sense. The Positivist's denial of whatever is not reconciled with human facts is quite unsatisfactory. No individual really believes a miracle which affronts natural law. With many of the miracles of the New Testament he did not wish to raise a doubt. It was possible to account for them in other ways than by violation of the natural system of the universe. But the influence of miracles in this age is slight. They cannot be proved, and therefore nobody will believe them who is not originally disposed to. He disagreed with Professor Stowe about the Church and the thought of the age. They are not merely the representatives of men, but they influence men, and are the higher power which directs and determines individual thought. He also disagreed with Professor Stowe concerning there being too many people in the world. He thought a world of only good people would be a very useless world.

Prof. STOWE asked Dr. Hedge whether bad people could not be spared in the next world; to which Dr. Hedge replied, "No." Whereupon Prof. Stowe rejoined, "Then we must have the devil in heaven, after all!"

4

Dr. HEDGE continued. He once thought that Christianity would absorb all other religions, but he did not think so now. He found noble elements in all religions, calculated to inspire and content the human heart. There was one idea of Buddhism equal to anything in Christianity. It was the equality of all classes of the human race.

Prof. STOWE wanted to explain a little his idea of the human race. He had just been examining very closely the history of the Inquisition and witchcraft for three hundred years, and he thought that we could have got along without them, if the Lord had been so disposed. The only mystery I know of is the mystery of the human race, and the only solution of that is the eighth chapter of Romans. He could not agree with Dr. Bartol in his idea of Christ coming out of humanity, made up of Fiji Islanders and Iroquois Indians, etc. He did not want any such God as that.

Mr. SARGENT. — We might inquire whether that is humanity.

Prof. STOWE. — They are people on two legs.

Dr. BARTOL. — Had we not better take it all in — save it all?

Prof. STOWE. — I would not.

Dr. BARTOL. — Are they children of God?

Prof. STOWE. — In the sense of being derived from him, they are.

Dr. BARTOL. — Did he make them?

Prof. STOWE. — Just as he did the devil. He created him an archangel, and he made himself a devil. I suppose God was remotely responsible for it.

Col. T. W. HIGGINSON said emphatically that he believed this world was a very good world, both to live and work in. Men were ignorant; but they were not half so bad as they were represented. It would be too much to expect, in this age of the race, that it had made greater progress than it has. He had lived a long time among people who were said to be the most degraded on the continent, concerning whom he, and he supposed that others present, had written pamphlets to show how degraded they were. Perhaps the Digger Indians were lower in the scale, but they were not so much known then. He referred to the slaves, and the admitted lowest class of them who lived on the Sea Islands. He had learned to wonder, by his association with these people, at the great goodness of human nature. There was ignorance; but the degree of wilful wickedness was less than anybody would suppose. He had also known a great deal about criminals, in prison and out of prison, and the amount of goodness in their natures was surprising. He had seldom found a man anywhere in the world whose better nature could not be struck directly and effectively. "The more I know of my fellow-creatures," said Col. Higginson, "the more I am impressed with the general preponderance of good in them."

Prof. Stowe. — Here in Boston?

Col. Higginson. — Yes. But I was thinking of the Five Points, New York.

Prof. Stowe discharged a parting shot at the delicious optimism of Dr. Bartol. "I have the gout in my foot — *awfully*," he said. "I suppose Dr. Bartol would try to persuade me that it is a pleasant sensation." "And if I did," said Dr. Bartol, "you'd say I was a figure of speech."

VIII.

SYMBOLIC CONCEPTIONS OF THE DEITY.

By C. P. CRANCH.

MR. CRANCH considers that the importance of imagination, the symbolizing faculty, has been generally
underrated, inasmuch as processes of thought, especially on
theological topics, are almost impossible without symbols;
and he considers that one proof that imagination foreruns
theology can be found in language, as evidences of the
action of the air, heat, and light can be found in the geological strata.   There is a wide range of difference in the
symbolic representations of the Deity; a wide distance between the fetichism of the South Seas, the reverential attitude of those inquirers who own that they do not entirely understand God, and those who seem, from their own account,
to have held privileged interviews with him, and to be
perfectly familiar and confidential with him.   To the scientific man he is light and force; to the poet, an all-pervading soul; to the artist, eternal beauty; to the theologian, a
being of differing phases, — as, for instance, to the Hebrew
a Warrior and a King; to the Orthodox Christian a Father
and a Saviour; the Roman Catholic requires that the soft-
ening influence of the Virgin Mother be added to his ideal
Divinity; to the Calvinist he is a being to whom the natural man is perverted and corrupt; to the Swedenborgian,
he is the " *maximus homo*."   The Rationalist and the Radical refuse to accept any conception that savors of anthro-

pomorphism, and consider him merely as an " oversoul,"
to use an expression of Emerson's.

The essayist then dwelt at some length on the impossibility of the creation by any one race at any period of time
of a symbolic representation of the Deity which should be
adequate for any other race or any other era.   Such conceptions, in his estimation, cramp and maim rather than
strengthen.   To endeavor to adopt as correct the conceptions of Palestine is as if an astronomer should endeavor
to mingle the mystic formulas of ancient Arabian science
with the pure mathematics of to-day.   The monarchical
form of the Hebrew government tinged the whole conception of the divine economy, whereas the modern idea is
more republican, — man, instead of a subject, being considered as a co-worker of God, and as such entitled to some
credit.   How is theology justified in accepting the popular
conceptions of one age as formulated for all time to come?
Why should not the modern conception be framed to accord with the most advanced knowledge?   Precisely as the
Copernican system has displaced the Ptolemaic, as chemistry has thrust aside alchemy, so the changes of science
have pushed aside local religions, leaving only the vital
elements incorporated in them.   The great element in reform is an adequate conception of the Deity, and observations and calculations in all climes and lands the most
remote must be made for the settling of this parallax.   To
put one's thought of God into words is almost as difficult
as to translate a symphony of Beethoven into phrases.
Still, as we must use symbols, there is a choice.   How prosaic was the old conception of God as an artificer who
created the world, set it going, and has been watching it
ever since, ready, if a screw becomes loose, to step down
from his high stool and work a miracle !   The world begins
to see that character is salvation rather than anything else,
and to discredit the idea that any one religion furnishes its

votaries with a pass-ticket to the front seats of Paradise,
while infidels are relegated to seats in the pit less comfort-
able than those in any earthly theatre, and not calculated to
allow any enjoyment of the grand drama of redemption.
Mr. Cranch likened the popular mistakes in symbolic conception to the optical deception that causes a wharf from
which a steamboat is receding to seem, to a passenger, to
be in motion, and said that to him the substitution of the
Copernican for the Ptolemaic system seemed to strike the
keynote by which the great symphonies of all the religions
might be harmonized. In relation to the much-vexed
prayer question, he asked whether it would do any real
harm to believe that God did not come to the soul, but
that the soul moved towards him: it was simply substi-
tuting one philosophy for another, the real for the apparent
motion, explaining miracles by reference to subjective
and not objective causes. The old Hebrew pictured God as
rending the heavens to come down: the modern hymn is
"Nearer, my God, to thee." For himself, the essayist
preferred to conceive God as the oversoul in which we
live and move, the most real of all realities, whose perpetual presence we see by faith, and from whose worship
nothing can separate us.

The Rev. W. J. Potter said it seemed to him that
the imaginative element in theology was not sufficiently
recognized by those persons who used symbolic terms without reference to the poetic element in them, and by those
who refuse to acknowledge church and religion because
the former had not yet succeeded in finding accurate symbols for the latter. He said he thought the democratic
influence of which Mr. Cranch had spoken might bring
about a new phraseology, and thus, possibly, the religion
of the future. In regard to the question of prayer, why

should not God come to man as well as man go to God? Why, if immanent, should it not be in accordance for him to come if the avenues of approach are thrown open by prayer?

The Rev. JAMES FREEMAN CLARKE was the next speaker, and he began by declaring that he did not like to hear slighting allusions to theology, which is the queen of the sciences, and of a date long anterior to that of Judaism. For his part, there was nothing arbitrary or abnormal to him in a conception of the Deity that makes him as free as a human being. If man is able to rise to God, why should God not be able to come to us? He did not, he said, believe in the impossibility of knowing God; we could not comprehend him, for we could not comprehend even a human soul, but we could know nothing which is not a revelation of him.

Mrs. CHENEY agreed with Mr. Clarke, illustrating her belief by saying that the next step to learning that the earth moves was that the sun also moves. She believed that there were really sincere atheists.

Mr. W. C. GANNETT found the best symbols in modern science, and could best conceive of God as the universal ether. He spoke in deprecation of the spirit which could take a humorous view of another person's conception of the Deity, and he asked whether it was not almost impossible to talk of God.

In reference to this, Mrs. CHENEY asked whether any modern artist would be likely to attempt to paint God as the old masters had done.

Mr. HENRY JAMES begged to ask Mr. Gannett whether his symbol was capable of verification; and preferred society, as an element which surrounds and vivifies the individual, so that even his flesh responds. At present there is only typical society: physical necessities must be considered, and thus this form of society is justified. It can be verified; it is not, like the ether, a mere working hypothesis. We value society; we would give life to verify it; we all look to future harmony, else we were ready to abandon life.

Mr. CRANCH and Mr. JAMES discussed the word "over-soul" at some length, the latter gentleman protesting against it as inadequate; he did not know his own soul, nor that of any other person: he never should and did not want to. What was wanted was a humanitarian conception of God. He never heard any attempt to typify God as a soul, without thinking of Thoreau's remark to Alcott at a conversation when the Concord philosopher began by saying, "All souls are plural." "I'm sorry for that," said Thoreau; "one is more than I can take care of."

Mr. TIFFANY spoke of the universal interdependence of things, saying that, for instance, as the mind of Newton had the idea of gravity, the whole solar system was necessary to its production. He did not think religion and science to be hostile. The enmity between different medical schools was as bitter as that between theologians. As fine an inquisition might be organized in Paris among the Communists as ever there was in Spain. Neither did he think that theologians are slower to accept ideas than other persons. The human mind was always reluctant to adopt new theories.

IX.

BORROMEO.

By OCTAVIUS B. FROTHINGHAM.

ON taking up his manuscript, Mr. Frothingham observed that he was delighted to see so goodly a company, but rather appalled at the thought that he must entertain them. He should ask them to stand before an old picture which he had taken down from his gallery and retouched somewhat. Perhaps he had been bold in thinking it presentable, but if they should think so they were at liberty to say it — after he had finished. The portrait was that of "Borromeo, the Saint." The outline, with now and then a bit of coloring, is here reproduced.

Travellers going by the Simplon into Italy commonly stop at the tower of Bareno on the shore of the Lago Maggiore. There in a row-boat they visit the Borromean Islands, the most southerly of which, the Isola Bella, lies about a mile from the borders of the lake, like an emerald set in crystal. The island was once a barren rock, but wealth has converted it into beautiful gardens. Two terraces, rising one above another, one hundred feet above the water, contain most luxuriant products of the southern climes. By trellises of orange and lemon trees, beneath tall cedars and shadowy cypresses, breathing an air fragrant with aromatic shrubs, pleased by the gleaming of marble statues, detained by curious mosaic work, wonder-struck by grottoes of shells, fascinated by the colors of water and sky, the

wooded slopes and graceful outlines of mountains, the rav-
ishing green of valleys that shelter their tiny villages from
the world, and fairly tormented by the variety that every
turn in the path discloses, the visitor spends his hour in
an earthly paradise. A princely château opens to him
marble halls and galleries, rooms of state and collections
of paintings. The beauty of line and color of material and
workmanship is bewildering. But an observant eye fails
not to be struck at every pause by an inscription consisting of a single Latin word. It is emblazoned on tapestry,
carved in wood, let in letters of marble into mosaic floors,
fashioned in gay shells on the pavements and walls of grottoes, stamped on ornamental vases and even on earthen
flower-pots ; it is spelled in flowery characters on the green
turf. The word is *Humilitas*. It was the motto of the
man who has made illustrious the family of Borromeo.
Farther down the lake on the west stands the ancient town
of Arona. On the slope of a hill, at some little distance
from the town, on a height overlooking the whole district,
stands upon a pedestal of forty-two feet a colossal statue
seventy feet high. The head, hands, and feet are of bronze,
the robe is of wrought copper. The image has stood nearly
two hundred years in memory of the man whose motto we
have been reading on the terraced rock. From the city of
Arona the traveller pursues his way to the city of Milan.
There a miracle of architecture breaks on his view, — the
great white cathedral, next to St. Peter's at Rome and the
cathedral at Seville the largest church in Europe. It stands
in a vast square, — a mass of exquisitely carved marble,
gleaming in the soft sunlight, and making brighter the
bright moonlight of Italy, from plinth to the gilded ma-
donna that surmounts the spire, a masterpiece of skill.
Two hundred architects of renown, among whom were
Brunelleschi, Leonardo da Vinci, and Julio Romano, spent
their genius on the building. Sculptors of fame contributed

to the font and to the five thousand statues of saints and heroes that cluster among its pinnacles, fringe its cornices, or hide within its niches. The skill of Procaccini is displayed in more than one figure of silver; Celleni's delicate hand is seen in at least one graceful form; and Michael Angelo's bold thought is expressed in the majestic monument. The roof of the temple is adorned with ninety-eight Gothic turrets. Nigh two hundred statues have place in the superb façade, whose fringe of spires bears up twelve colossal images. Inside and outside the building one may count more than seven thousand marble statues, not a few of them worthy to be placed in a gallery of sculpture. The fifty-two columns that support the arches rise like the trunks of venerable trees, carrying the eye into a wilderness of tracery, and through the gorgeous windows the light wanders into the sombre spaces as through a distant opening in a forest. The bright sunbeam glides between the leaves to give a parting glory to the grass. As we wander over the structure, we are perpetually reminded of the single name. The high altar suggests it; the choir, the subterranean chapel, the spacious gallery and colonnade, the porphyry font with its beautiful canopy, the carved pulpit and screen, and many a precious bit of workmanship in metal, jewels, and stone. The power of this name breaks upon us, as, descending a broad flight of steps, traversing a spacious gallery lined with finest marbles, and passing under a portal with perfect columns, that flash out glory as the guide's lamp goes by, we enter a small octagonal chapel. Eight massive bas-reliefs in silver record, in fairest modelling, scenes in the life of a saint. Eight busts, also of massive silver, represent in allegory his virtues. Costly tapestry of gold woven upon crimson silk after artistic designs covers the spaces not occupied by the silver. The chapel contains an altar; and above the altar stands a bronze casket with silver mountings. The guide

lets down the front of the casket, and displays within a
sarcophagus of rock crystal bound with silver bands, the
gift of a king of Spain. Numerous small images of silver,
tokens of respect from princely donors, impart an air of
quaint sumptuousness to the whole. In the midst of all
this splendor, robed in pontifical dress, the golden staff
beside it, the golden crown and cross of emeralds above,
lies a shrunken brown body. It is the body of the man
whose motto, *Humilitas*, was inscribed all over the Isola
Bella, and whose crystal statue looked down from the
hill above Arona, where he was born, towards the Lom-
bardy that he blessed. Who and what sort of man was
this, whose crystal coffin royal people have adorned with
gems that would have glorified the state of any earthly
majesty?

The ruins of a castle at the southern extremity of the
Lago Maggiore mark the place where he saw the light,
October 2, 1538. Like the rest of us, he was predestined
from the cradle. His father was a noble, a knight, and a
devotee ; his mother a court lady, the sister of a cardinal,
and, best of all, a womanly woman. The child was a
priest in petticoats. He made a convent of his nursery.
This boy will never outgrow his altar forms. He is a
priest by nature, a saint in the bud. At the University of
Paris he is a fair scholar, a gentle companion, courteous
and amiable, but still a priest and saint. Borromeo was
no sentimental, morbid milksop : he was a youth who bore
under his silk gown an iron will. His father, dying, en-
trusted to him the management of his household. When
Borromeo was twenty-one, Pope Paul IV. died, and John
Angelo Medici, own uncle to the young man, was elected in
his stead. The new pope was all cordiality and condescen-
sion. He felt himself fortunate in having a nephew gifted
with genius for labor and goodness. The jovial old man
piled toilsome honors on the youth of twenty-two. In the

course of a single month he was made cardinal; nine days
afterward he was created archbishop of Milan. The main
conduct of the pontifical government was committed to
his care. Borromeo is now in the bloom of youth, rich,
handsome, the pride of a luxurious court, the kinsman of
a genial pope. The delighted old pope gathers up his
crosses, keys, and ribbons, heaps them on the young man,
and mounts his horse for a ride on the Campagna. The
youth accepted the burdens, but, instead of mounting a
throne, dropped on his knees. Frequent and absorbing
were his acts of devotion; fasting and the scourge reduced
his flesh; lonely vigils took the bloom from his cheek.
The citizens wondered to see a prince in the open day
bestowing alms on the beggars, himself in appearance
more squalid than they. Borromeo was in earnest: he
went to the root of things. He purged the libraries of
immoral books; he instituted a rigid control of the press,
that works of irreligious tendency might be suppressed;
he bade his agents search travellers for heretical tracts;
he forbade intercourse with the Jews. In his zeal he
became a persecutor. But to the ugly habit of persecution he added the lovelier habit of compassion for the
persecuted. He pleaded, warned, and wept before he
punished. In the heat of summers and the rigor of
winters his frail form was seen among the lonely passes,
with Alpine staff in hand, going from village to village,
consecrating churches, dedicating altars, hearing confes-
sion, and granting absolution for sin. No sigh of fatigue
ever escaped his lips; no complaint ever strayed from his
patient heart.

In Milan, Borromeo was not popular. Was ever a reformer popular in a great city? He is praised who beauti-
fies a temple. He is cursed who would beautify men's
lives. The common people complained that he put an
end to their harmless amusements of brawling and getting

drunk; the magistrates complained that he encroached on their jurisdiction. A new pope summons the faithful to celebrate in Rome the jubilee of the holy year. Borromeo obeyed the summons. It is winter, but the pilgrim lingers at every wayside shrine and worships at every holy grave. Arrived in the great city, he retires at once to a convent, and passes several days in meditation. Issuing thence, he marches forth murmuring prayers. He walks with down-cast eyes; he returns no greeting; nobles dismount to salute him, but he takes no heed of them. A story gains currency that he has been miraculously saved from the bullet of an assassin who fired at him as he knelt at prayer. The bullet struck him fair, men said, and dropped harm-less from the folds of his garment. From that moment his fame as a saint is established.

And now Milan is to hold jubilee. Devotees flock into the city. Day and night the streets are thronged with processions. The archbishop sets example of unwhole-some austerity. The feet are naked again; the money is flowing in streams to the beggars; the sacraments are administered in chapels stifling from close and fetid air. The example is contagious. Nobles, men and women, go about with bare feet and coarse, dirty raiment. The city is full of strangers, beggars, pickpockets, diseased persons, carrying pestilence in their clothes. The odors of sanctity and the stenches of depravity infect the air. And in the midst of the jubilee a gaunt figure, unexpected though not uninvited, stalked into the city. The plague is in Milan. Borromeo's theory of the plague was simple. Of secondary causes he knew nothing; of natural laws he had never heard. In his view the pestilence was a special dispensa-tion, sent by the immediate will of Heaven in judgment for some terrible sin. That it came in consequence of his own imprudence; that it was the result of the crowding, the suffocating heat, the promiscuous assemblies; that riotry and dissipation had anything to do with it, could not occur to him. It was a doom to be averted by suffering. His only thought was of offering himself instead of his people, in hope that by his stripes they might be healed. How he watched and prayed, and slept his hour or two on the floor; how marched up and down the street in penitential attire, and devoted himself to daily death, — is related by his biographers with touching simplicity. The poor wretches crowded to the windows of the pest-house as Borromeo passed by, thrust their hands through the bars, and with poisonous breath called for the consolation of religion. But the great soul does not despair. Scattering his wealth like sand, toiling night and day, aiding the living, shriving the dead, he bears the iniquities of his people. From sixty to seventy thousand persons are living on daily alms. Yet the brave soul does not faint. He adopts orphaned children. Two horses laden with provisions go with him on his marches. A purse hangs at his girdle. People fling themselves at his feet, call him father, worship him as an angel of light. The privations he undergoes are incredible. At length the pestilence abates. It has burned up its fuel. The archbishop spends himself in praises as he has done in prayers.

Borromeo is now forty-six years old. The flame of sanctity has burned his material part away. In Rome, in Venice, in all high places, Church and State vie with one another in rendering honor to the man who made the Infinite wrath relent, and turned aside the heavy hand of the Lord. Seven years after the plague, Carlo Borromeo fell an early prey to a fever which struck him in the solitudes of Mount Varallo.

Borromeo was a typical man, — an ideal saint and hero. His personal virtues were matchless. He was saintly, though a prince. His faith, trust, devotion, have been justly celebrated outside of his own church. His charity knew no bounds; he could forgive his enemies. In the great virtue of self-abnegation he has no superior.

The saint all over the world is one who resigns his will to the Supreme. The narrow doctrine makes the narrow saint. There was about Borromeo's saintliness an air of limitation. His rule in regard to temptation was to keep out of its way, to run from it. He avoided society, never looked in a woman's face, ate his meals alone, and never looked out of a window. He published a letter against beards as a weak concession to nature, but was as scrupulous as a dandy about the cut and color of his priestly vestments. He was jealous of his office because it was the gift of the Church, and the symbol of the Church outranked in his eyes even the rights and duties of kings. Let me beg you to remember that the Supreme Power may be apprehended otherwise than as Borromeo apprehended it.

The modern saint will not be behind in the singleness of his devotion to Divine Power. To it he will give himself; to it he will belong; to it he will bring the rich but unworthy offering of his substance, his capacity, his talents, and his time. In meek service to it he will find his absorbing occupation, his high privilege, his sufficient joy. But the Divine Power will stand revealed to him in the awful yet gracious laws that guard his well-being. By obedience to the organic conditions of health, by loyalty to the rules that secure happiness in personal and social relations, by allegiance to the larger human principles of kindness and equity that watch over the prosperities of communities and the steadfastness of States, — by doing his best that the best may prevail, the modern citizen will be the modern saint. It will be his distinction to make saintliness and manliness one, to marry liberty and law, to reconcile renunciation with gladness, satisfaction with sacrifice, self-development with self-denial, desire with duty. He at length will prove the proverb true, "He that loseth his life shall find it."

————

Rev. W. J. Potter thought it was so beautiful a story and so beautifully told that no one could feel like adding a word. None denied the beauty of Borromeo's character, but a little difference of opinion existed in relation to his usefulness, — whether, according to the light of his age, his life was wisely directed. Mr. Potter recognized the power of soul over matter, the superiority of goodness. The belief in miracles rests in the power of goodness.

Dr. Bartol said it was not a restored picture, but a new one. He thought there was a species of selfishness in this self-sacrifice. Not *self-sacrifice*, but self-forgetfulness, is, he thought, the true state.

Mrs. Howe admired the great onward sweep of Borromeo's life. Most of us have to stop for business. She believed in this great power of religion. The great defect in Borromeo's life was that it was not a human life. Christ's life was human and simple. The piety of those days we might call imitative Christianity; not the spirit. The last antithesis is self-denial, development.

Mr. Higginson thought the great force of this life grew from its limitations. Roman Catholics can bring all their power to bear. In weak moments we choose limited ways. He sympathized with Mr. Frothingham's view of the character, and compared it to a beautiful river turned from its true course. He was concerned lest the glamour of distance should cast a fascination over a character whose example modern Christians ought not to seek to imitate, but rather to avoid.

Dr. C. C. Everett thought Borromeo's was a high life; he did his best with his light. If we would all do that, we should do well.

Mr. Higginson objected to the word "saint." He

thought we were passing into a broader state, in which there is something better. Some one remarked that there are saints to-day of equal value.

Mr. GANNETT asked if any one of our helpers combine so much as Borromeo.

After a little further conversation of this nature the meeting broke up.

X.

THE UNSEEN.

By W. C. GANNETT.

W. C. GANNETT'S essay attempted to evolve the real harmony from the seeming discord between science and religion, and he entitled it "Looking at the Unseen."

When Paul says, "We look not at the things which are seen, but at the things which are unseen," he speaks for all of us. It is not specially the scientific, not specially the religious, but the human attitude. The outside never satisfies. What lies behind? What is it made of? What is it for? How came it to be? Such are the questionings with which men have always stood before Nature. We are all philosophers in our search for causes and destinies. The child in his nursery is an irrepressible asker of conundrums. And how his science runs into his religion! "What makes my gun go bang?" he begins with; but soon it is, "Who made me?" and, when that is answered, "Who made God?" "Who was the first mother, the very first?" asked one small questioner; and "Where did God stand to make the world before there was any place to stand on?" asked another. "How could Satan have been so wicked, before there was any devil to put him up to it?" wondered a third. The savage is also a philosopher, seeking with his childlike reason into causes; and with him, also, science and religion are not two but one. The thunder rolls above him. "Hush!" said the old-time German, "Hush! The god Thor is hurling his mighty hammer." The moon passed between the earth and the sun, eclipsing it: "It is the great Dog-monster swallowing the sun," and the Indian would shout and shoot his burning arrows into the air to drive him off. That was the savage's science, his theory of the cause, to account for the seen effect; but his theory took him at once to the gods and the demons. In this respect the child is only father to the man; and the savage — why, every professor in Harvard College is the son of a savage. We of to-day peer more eagerly than ever into the unseen, and the more we see convinces us the more how little we see. Every anxious guess at our origin or our destiny, every sacred aspiration, testifies how truly we look at things not seen.

And this we are in the habit of calling the looking of religion. Is the looking of science altogether different? When the chemist seeks to find the treasures of the snow, and the astronomer the place where light dwells, and Owen studies his fossil bones till he calls back the day that passed a million years ago, they also are looking at the things not seen; and this we call the looking of science. We are wont to separate religion from science, but their attitudes before Nature are just the same; and that suggests that child and savage may be essentially right, after all, in making them not two but one. Science looks at the things not seen in three ways, — of educated eyes, of improving instruments, and of careful reasoning, — each method adding new realms to her gaze. The very beginning of a scientific education is to learn to see — really to observe, with minute and accurate attention, what is going on around us. For many a long century eyes were all there was to see with. Now the eyes are armed with instruments which give far, new worlds to our vision. As one looks into telescope or microscope, great realms of the

Unseen burst into the Seen; Infinitude seems to open in both directions, toward the all of space and toward the nought of space. But Science does not stop with the vision of her instruments. She feels her way to the laws of events, and dares to predict what instruments and eyes shall see. These foreseeings are the feats of science. On what was thought to be the verge of our system, a planet showed strange haltings and quickenings in its pace around the sun. At last astronomers began to guess that some unknown body might exist outside, which held our neighbor in its spell. Adams and Leverrier set themselves to calculate from these irregularities whereabout in the wide circle of the heavens the strong outsider might be found. The figuring was finished, and the telescopes were turned to the designated place. And then, punctual to the appointment, a new planet swam into their ken, — the one we now call Neptune. And farther on, into infinity, Science is still making magnificent guesses, suggesting and theorizing things which cannot yet be seen. But, all through her growing vision, she has not yet passed beyond the material. The matter, at its finest, is matter still, — unseen, indeed, but strictly conceived of as seeable. The motion is quick beyond all possibility of our catching, but not beyond the possibility of catching if eyes were better. The universe to her, from farthest space to the brain-cell, is nothing but matter and motion. This is all that Science sees when she looks at the things unseen, and so we call her Physical Science; and some say, and more half fear, that there is nothing in the universe but matter and motion.

What is Religion when it begins its witness? Is it not this same Physical Science? Does not this, itself, betray something in the universe beyond its mere matter and motion, — something that is not only unseen but unseeable? Look again at the three steps of Science. What is that

reason with which she trod the last one so confidently, into
limits where no instrument could follow her?   In the
second step, what is the cunning that calculates the curves
of the lens-surfaces for her instruments?   Nay, in the first
step what is the mere sensation of sight when our eyes
open and we see?   Traced along from the Without toward
our Within, the process is first that rapid flashing of the
ether waves; that is, of course, physical.   They strike
through the eye-layers to the retina, and there give up
their motion to certain nerve-filaments behind; still we
are in the physical.   The thrill passes inward to a certain
spot of gray nerve-matter in the brain, and thence, perhaps, further to the upper brain.   And all this, too, is
purely physical; matter and motion account for all.   But
now what happens?   A mystery that no one has yet
fathomed.   This physical becomes psychical.   The nerve-
thrill becomes consciousness.   Through the organ of sense
something has passed into a sensation.   Religion says that
this consciousness which we find in ourselves, overlying
all the matter and motion of our brain-cells and our body,
overlies the whole universe of matter and motion; and
that what we can fairly trace as the facts and laws of this
Self-Consciousness of ours belongs, in a dim way at least,
to some Great Consciousness that overlies the Whole; that
our Will betokens Will there; our Reasoning betokens
Thought there; our Sense of Right, Sense of Right there;
and so we make God in our own image.   Some people cry
out at this as fetichism, but there is reason in it.   Nature
must be in some degree conscious in order to evolve consciousness, for that is a part of Nature; but her consciousness must be a conscious unity.   In every atom, then, of
this vast material world, in every faintest thrill of its physical motion, the other side — the spirit side — must be
somehow represented.   This makes Nature alive and God
immanent.   But self will always make God in its own

image; and as the self becomes more conscious, wise, and noble, so will Nature fill and fill to us with a wiser, nobler God-life. The man who is thoroughly imbued with a sense that Nature is the life of God is everywhere a worshipper. What others call accident, he feels sure is invisible law; what seems confusion, he doubts not is hidden order. What seems horror, he cannot help trusting as unknown goodness. To him the universe is a temple.

The discussion which followed was more brief than usual. Dr. BARTOL said it seemed strange that there should be any alarm about the tendency of Materialism when it was continually taking the direction toward spirit. Before science, as before the Great White Throne in Revelation, the heavens and the earth flee away, and nothing is left but pure force. Some scientists carry their theory beyond the atom. One Frenchman in particular goes behind the atom to atomicities. When it gets so far as that, Materialism has committed suicide. Putting on immortality is not the first step: the first step is for spirit to put on matter. Matter clothes us, and introduces us to each other. Spirit is the first term.

Mr. POTTER saw no reason for going back to a beginning, when soul existed without world. It seemed to him less rational than the notion which puts matter and spirit together in the beginning, and never separates them.

Dr. BARTOL explained, in reply, that he did not believe in a beginning of the universe, any more than a beginning of God. It was not chronologically that matter comes after mind, but logically, psychologically; matter is the servant of mind.

Rev. R. COLLYER. — I do not feel afraid of the revelations that come from the other side. I think the more we know the better it will be for all around, — for ourselves, for those to whom we minister, and to the whole world. I do not want to have the two things separate for a moment, but made more intimately one.   So that, if possible, I want to believe that God is present in every rush of the waves or the billows of the fiercest sea-storm, as well as in the quiet of the New England meeting-house on Sunday morning. Mr. Collyer related a prairie experience which he had had years ago, in a tremendous storm, when everything seemed so bleak and woful on his journey that the idea of God was almost obliterated ; but when he got to the house of a friend, who had a happy, cheerful home, he was instantly cured.   He found God there.   He thought if we could find God anywhere, we could find him in a cheerful, happy home, nestling and shining in human hearts.   And while he would try to realize God in the forms of Nature, and trace him deeper and deeper into the infinite depths of the universe, he would at the same time cling to the realization of God as he comes into and out of the human hearts fitted to receive him ; he would find him in this temple of the Holy Ghost which we call man.   He did not want God set up aloof in a picture painted on a roof.   "If I have to go through anything that pulls upon the last inch of manhood, I want him to go through it too.   He came here before I did, and knows all about it, and I do not want him to come here and be alone and have a good time all the while.   If I have something that wrings my heart, he has got to have his heart wrung too.   I do not want science to take away the sympathy of God from me.   If it does, then I fight science. But I think it will bring us into sweeter and deeper rela- tions to him to know the universality of his presence. Some great French thinker says it is not hard to believe in God if you do not try too much to define him.   Thackeray says, 'It is not the right thing to open a rose with a penknife : if you let the sun shine on it, it will open time enough.'"

XI.

THE CHRISTIAN NAME.

By WILLIAM H. CHANNING.

MR. CHANNING'S subject was suggested by an essay with the same title read by another member at a former meeting of the Club. After speaking of the need of careful discriminations upon this subject, and saying that, in the strict acceptation of the word, no nation, no community in the world, was now or had ever been Christian, and that the customary attitude of civilized nations toward savage nations was by itself sufficient to prove the former unworthy of this name, — Mr. Channing went on to say that the word " Christian " (whatever our theological theories might be) stood for the idea of a heavenly life. The beginning of the Christian religion is faith in a divine humanity, in a ministry of heavenly reconciliation to make all human life new and pure. Mr. Channing then enlarged upon the idea of divine humanity, God making himself man, set forth by such writers as Schleiermacher, Schelling, and Hegel. God identifying himself with man, man becoming godlike, total devotedness and disinterestedness, — man knows not himself until he discovers the germ of these divine ideas within him. Mediation, however, is universal, not after one type only. We can learn its meaning only as we put away our own antagonisms.

Do we enter into the meaning of a ministry of reconciliation, — of an atonement, — of God taking on himself the sins of the world? "I," said Mr. Channing, "accept this idea. The well-beloved Son gave his life for man. Yet the Church has put upon this fact an interpretation far too narrow, too exclusive.

"The Church! — have we exhausted its idea? Do we understand all its numerous branches? The true Church is a body of the children of God, giving themselves for the welfare of their brethren of mankind. The organized bodies which call themselves Christian churches have never yet come up to this standard, and hence the Christian religion has had a far deeper influence than theirs on the world. It has implanted the germ of that reverence for humanity which is spreading through society, — the conviction that every human being is a child of God. This idea will not only put away the distinctions between classes, but will prevent us from attempting to divide men into good and bad.

"The influence of this idea on the community has already been most powerful. It has broken the chains of slavery, it has raised our estimate of useful labor, it is going on to dignify all ministries of human service. It has put away the view of woman as merely an appendage to man. It will go on to introduce the spirit of peace and love between nations, in opposition to the law of force."

This expression led Mr. Channing to say that he had formerly accepted the doctrine of non-resistance, but that this persuasion had given way when he saw the Boston court-house girdled with chains for the maintenance of Slavery, and again when he saw a gigantic rebellion arise for the same purpose. Then he had taken down the peace flag. Yet he must still declare his conviction that the influence of peace is a divine influence, and that it must ultimately prevail.

As to the present time, the Christian religion seems

passing out of its local and partial forms to appear as
the universal religion. Every one of us is welcomed by
God and the well-beloved Son. A divine germ is within
each of us. God is centred there, and will fill us in proportion as we welcome and cherish him. Each of us may
say, By the grace of God I am what I am. We are to
be transformed into his image. Our constant effort should
be to be perfect, as the Father in heaven is perfect. God
means that we should be his well-beloved children, and
we should keep ourselves in attitude to receive all the
high influences which he pours upon us. If we really
believe that the work which God assigns to us is to trans-
form earth to heaven, our daily lives will give token of
this conviction.

Every human being should be a reconciler of all differences. Dare not to draw back from this mission. Strive
for the perfect life. To gain this needs the mutual help of
all. We must be redeemers together of the human race,
as the Christ has never yet been. We must embody in society the true idea of the Christian Church, and look into
the sources of human degradation that we may know how to
combat them. "The difference between me and the people
classed as criminals is that I have been helped more than
they. It is thus my duty to help them. I renew, with ten-
fold emphasis, the assertion of the possibility and duty of
a union of interests and efforts in human society."

He had learned from the venerated relative who was
his teacher how glorious the Christian ministry might be.
Yet while in the domain of speculation, and before entering on the *work* of the ministry, his position might perhaps
have been classed as Deism. His first attempts at preaching did not extricate him from this position. His doubts
were not relieved until he went to Europe, and studied
society and theology there. In the midst of this examination, his feelings rallied around " the well-beloved Son "

in his ministry to the poor. He returned to New York, and entered on a system of ministry to the poor, understanding himself to be a Christian. Livingly, as a matter of fact, he found himself ready and glad to devote all his powers to that work. He wished to be a brother of that well-beloved Son.

.   .   .   .   .   .

Can we cut ourselves off from all the noble souls who have illustrated the excellences of the Christian system? To hold by that system is not to recognize Jesus as the Jewish Messiah. Who does so recognize him? The true Christianity is girdling the earth, and Providence is using this great central power to bind the nations together, and fuse them into one. Neither the nations nor the churches now represent Christian society. Our work is to make them do it.

————

At the close of Mr. Channing's address, Mr. SARGENT, the host, referred with deep feeling to his own experience, in former years, of the hostility of the clergy and the churches to reform, and the exercise of their influence *against* that fraternization with the suffering and oppressed which his friend, Mr. Channing, had declared to be the essence of Christianity. He (Mr. Sargent) was not particularly zealous for the retention of the name Christian. What he valued was a life manifestly devoted to human welfare, such as the lives of Wendell Phillips and John G. Whittier, both of whom, he was happy to inform the Club, were then present.

Many persons expressing the desire to hear Mr. Phillips, he came forward from the side-room where he had been sitting.

Mr. PHILLIPS was glad to be strengthened by the experience and testimony of the friend who had addressed them. "Christianity," said he, "is a great moral power, the determining force of our present civilization, as of past steps in the same direction. Jesus is the great religious genius who has given its peculiar type to the modern world. Speculations as to the why and the how may differ, but we see the fact. We cannot rub out history. Europe shows a type of human character not paralleled anywhere else. The intellect of Greece centred around power and beauty; that of Rome around legal justice. The civilization of modern Europe was inspired by a great moral purpose. Imperfect as it was, and limited in many ways, the religious element there had steadily carried those nations forward. The battle for human rights was finally fought on a Christian plane. Unbelief has written books, but it never lifted a million men into a united struggle. The power that urged the world forward came from Christianity. Mr. Channing has explained to us its origin. I look at its results, and they lead to the same conclusion. He claims to be Christian. So do I. The best part of the life of Europe may be traced to Christianity.

" The religious literature of Asia has been compared with the Christian Scriptures. The comparison is not just. That literature has many merits, and contains scattered sayings and precepts of great excellence; but there are heaps of chaff in that and in the writings of the early Christian fathers; none in the Gospels and Epistles. Of the mediæval writings one half was useless. Of the boasted works of Confucius seven tenths must be winnowed out to find what the average reason of mankind would respect."

T. W. HIGGINSON said that nothing would have more amazed him, twenty years ago, than to be told that he would come to differ, entirely and absolutely, with the two friends who had just spoken. Yet he did so differ. The address of Mr. Channing was like the song of a seraph to people in prison, bidding them to be content with their lot. For his part, Mr. Higginson said, he preferred to be out-

side the walls, and even to fight, if necessary, for a larger
liberty. He could not agree that all spiritual life was an
effluence from Jesus. The system he accepted must be
such as would leave him still a man.

The defect of the doctrine taught by his esteemed friends
who had just spoken was that it was not true. The New
Testament was not so free from chaff as had been represented. What was true in the Gospels was written in the
world's life before Jesus was born, though it had never,
perhaps, been so sublimely carried out.

Jesus was a *man*. He took in not only the sublimity,
but the delusions of Hebrew Scripture. He taught his
disciples that he was the literal as well as the spiritual
Messiah, and that he was to come again in that generation
to judge the world. He was so far in error. How can
I found a hope for the redemption of the world on the
basis of an error? We can afford to put Jesus into the
category of men ; and examination will show that *all* our
best lessons did not come from him.

From whom did we learn resistance to Slavery? Not
from Jesus, but from Garrison. From whom did we learn
the rights of women? From Frances Wright and from
Lucy Stone, who found the call of duty in the promptings
of their own hearts.

Mr. Phillips should have claimed for enthusiasm that
motive power which he ascribed to Christianity. The same
mistake had often before been made. Instead of clinging
blindly to the past, we should recognize the great teachers
of our own time. Mr. Abbot's fifty affirmative propositions, published in " The Index," are not surpassed, either
in boldness or in truth, by the famous theses of Luther.

Multitudes have for years been longing to step out of the
limitations of Christianity into the glorious liberty of the
sons of God. As to myself (said Mr. Higginson), I am
never clouded in this faith, the belief that God inspires

every man that comes into the world. Inspiration is common to all. We all have intellect, and we must seek our supplies where the ablest men of all ages have sought theirs.

Mr. PHILLIPS replied to Mr. Higginson very briefly, controverting his doctrine respecting the origin of the Anti-slavery struggle and the Woman's Rights cause. Both these movements, in his opinion, grew out of Christianity. The sweep of centuries of this influence had removed slavery and would elevate woman.

Mr. WEISS believed with Mr. Higginson. It seemed to him, however, that Mr. Channing held the same idea. What the latter praised as Christianity was not the system now commonly called by that name. The presence of God everywhere, at all times, and now here in this room, which Mr. Channing has described, is the thing to be believed in. His inspiration was in Jesus, no doubt, and so it was in Burns, when he wrote of the field-mouse and the daisy.

"Our phraseology," added Mr. Weiss, "is one of our obstacles. I enjoyed Mr. Channing's words, because I interpreted them with a running commentary. We must recognize the fact that we, as well as Jesus, are inspired of God."

Mrs. JULIA WARD HOWE said: "While we were hearing Mr. Channing, we were one. He is a reconciling medium. Those are the choicest speakers who show us wherein we agree." She was surprised that any one could think that Mr. Channing's view of Christ excluded any other human being from God's inspiration.

Dr. BARTOL. — We have grown out of the past. We do not bear the root, but the root us. I cannot believe that God has set us to copy only one of his lines of beauty, the Judæan line. He is himself drawing a line in the heart of each of us.

JAMES FREEMAN CLARKE said that the differences expressed here seemed to him to be mainly questions of words. He agreed with Channing, and he agreed with Weiss. There were excellent things in the Asiatic Scriptures ; but the doctrines of Confucius would never have raised the Chinese to effect the emancipation of slaves. When men are questioning whether Jesus called himself the Jewish Messiah, he would inquire what was meant by that phrase. For there were two Jewish views of the Messiah ; and we know that Jesus did *not* identify himself with that one of them which contemplated taking arms against the Romans and holding temporal rule over the Jews.

One of the parables of Jesus represented him as praising the deeds of some who were quite ignorant that they had done the things in question. They did not know that they had ever fed or clothed, or otherwise relieved him. Perhaps some of the speakers here would hereafter find their position cleared up in a similar manner.

Rev. John Chadwick, from Brooklyn, expressed his gratification at having heard the discussion. The true meaning of any old myth, he thought, was the best and highest meaning that would fit it. So of the word " Christian ; " the best meaning of it is that which stands for our highest ideal of manhood and womanhood. In this view, how can we wish to call ourselves anything but Christians, though others make a point of denying us that name?

As to the relative rank of Jesus, it is certain that God does give to one man five talents, to another two, and to another one. We are the creatures not only of organization, but of circumstances. We must always recognize that God is as near the world now as he ever was, and that his laws of inspiration remain the same ; and yet we may hold Jesus to be the greatest, as having been born in the fulness of time. We accept his words, not by constraint, but when the God in us responds to the God in him.

Mr. Potter, of New Bedford, had great satisfaction in

hearing Mr. Channing. He thought the chief difference between them was where he had pictured the universal church as that which Christianity was to open. Rabbi Ellinger has lately pictured the ultimate messianic era from the Jewish standpoint, and his view of it greatly resembles what we have just heard from Mr. Channing. Our wisdom will be to seek in all religions the universal element, emancipated from the specific form.

Mr. WASSON felt very little interest in claiming, or making any reference to, the name Christian. He thought facts more important than names. In regard to Jesus, he had no sense of any personal relation to him. Still, he would not fail to acknowledge the function of Jesus in history. Christianity has had immense influence on the Western world, but not through the person of Jesus. He would long since have been forgotten had he not been called God. Christianity never has by itself transformed the world. Where it entered into the inheritance of Greek and Roman civilization it succeeded; elsewhere it failed. Christianity in Asia has been unprogressive, both in former and latter times. Only where helped by European civilization did it prosper. There was no reason, Mr. Wasson thought, to choose Christianity for *our* system, either at present or in the future.

WENDELL PHILLIPS reaffirmed his idea, — the moral earnestness of the world lives in Christianity. To a question by Mrs. Cheney, " What abolished slavery in Tunis?" he answered that this was an outgrowth from the moral earnestness of Europe.

Mr. WASSON replied with some details of the early civilization of India and China, before the mention of Christianity there, and then the lateness of the hour dissolved the meeting.

6

XII.

THE PEOPLE.

By W. J. LINTON.

A REAL democracy is the beginning of the republic, an assembling of the free in order to turn their freedom to its full account for the good of the whole. This organization of the powers of all, this government of all, by all, for all, is the republic. Democracy is either the basis of this or it is anarchy. Among kings and aristocrats had been wise rulers and lovers of order; and there might be some justification for the rule of the One or the Few in old days, when the great truth of human brotherhood was unknown. The essayist spoke of aristocracy as only monarchy held in commission; the two opposing principles are monarchy and democracy, or authority and conscience. Yet democracy alone is insufficient. It has but one word upon its banner, — "THE PEOPLE;" but one definition, — "the People as the sole source of power." There is no aim in this, no religion. It is the mere egotistical assertion of power, of universal rights, not to be universally used. "Your fathers," said Mr. Linton, "did their best for the time they lived in; but the Christian assertion of rights has done its work: we need advance our programme to the higher realms of duty." The republican banner bears upon it a religious creed, giving also the aim of the republican life. The European republican formula — "GOD AND THE PEOPLE"

— implies the organization of the whole people in order to do the will of God; the association of the whole people, men and women, not merely to make such laws as may suit the tastes of some party conspiracy, a majority for the nonce, but to enact the laws of God in human statutes to rule the current life of all, to realize in human life the prayer of all life to the Father which is in heaven, — "Thy will be done on earth!"

Is there such organization now? Mr. Linton did not find it in Europe, where they are yet struggling against that old dynastic division and disintegration of the world, of which the Austrian empire is the type, — struggling even for national existence. Without political organization social organization is impossible. He referred to English and Irish poverty and emigration, to the demoralization of France under the ruffianism of a Napoleon, and, turning to the young republic of America, asked, What organization is there here? What in Georgia and Tennessee and Texas? — nay, what in New York and Massachusetts? In your magnificent Empire City there is not organization enough to sweep the streets after a snowstorm. In the city of the Puritans you may have the cleanliness which is next to godliness; but of the godliness how much? What chance of virtue with the present ordering of labor and of trade? Is your labor ordered for the benefit of all? And your buying and selling, — is it not the greedy game of middle-men, robbing both sides, in vindication of the Jewish proverb, "As mortar sticketh between stones"? Organization of society! Ask your criminal population; ask the unfortunate women of all Christian streets; ask the unhappy strangers you take into your families as servants. Are you decently organized even in your homes? Organization! You dare not, as a nation, even whisper an encouragement to the struggling republicans of other lands. And the best-natured, the most gifted among you, keep out of politics from a very proper disgust at what is called " politics," — stand by without attempt at organization.

Then Mr. Linton proceeded to define his ideal republic, imagining a ship-load of emigrants, men and women, landing in a new country and founding their government; conferring as to this or that law, and adopting or rejecting each according to the will of the majority, excluding none from their council and excusing none, avoiding the tyranny of a permanent majority by confining the majority to each law, and so changing the majority with every law. This is the direct sovereignty of the people, which he claimed as a religious duty. What service more acceptable to the Eternal than the devout considering what law, or alteration of an old law, shall make our lives more honest, more holy, and more God-like? Why should not the town-hall and the church be one? And why should the increase of the community render this more difficult? Is this republican organization a mere Utopian dream?

On one day you cast the votes of the whole land for President. Would it be more difficult to cast them for a certain law?

Two things would be gained by having the people thus directly vote their own laws. Their will and conscience would be represented, and the habitual voting as a patriotic duty would be of educational value. In war you excuse none. Why excuse any in peace? In great crises the need of a convention of the whole people is admitted. The direct sovereignty of the people is only a permanent convention. And when is not consentaneous action necessary for the common weal?

And three questions not able to be answered now might then obtain solution, — the religious question, the woman question, and the educational question. The labor ques-

tion and that of money must also wait for a real republic.
Men will no longer be ashamed to be thought religious
when all the business of life is organized on a religious
basis, when religion is recognized as the science of life,
and politics as only the practical application of religion.
Woman, not wanted now in the political arena, will then
take her right place as the helpmate of man, the Priestess
standing beside the Priest; and the whole current of life
will be educational, educational and religious, bearing us
on and onward to the Eternal Peace of God.

When an essay is so true that little else can be truer,
and when the force of its truth strikes home to an audience,
there is room for a great deal of eulogy, but for little of
argument. Mr. Linton's paper was severely critical,
unsparingly caustic; but, however certain details might
be objected to, it defied contradiction as a whole. No
one attempted the task.

Mr. SARGENT said that, though the pill was a bitter one,
the most graceful act we could perform would be to swallow
it without a murmur. He for one accepted the criticism,
particularly in its reference to Boston.

Mr. ALCOTT thought the essayist merited the thanks of
all assembled. Americans are braggarts in words, braggarts in deeds, and refuse to recognize themselves when
the mirror of truth is placed before them. The highest
friendship admits of the bravest truth-telling, and is
attained when a man or a nation is told of faults even by
an enemy. Much more should we be grateful to the critic
who is a friend. It was delightful to see any one who
believed anything. Mr. Linton is his own republic; and
if there be one of the opposite sex who subscribes to his
tenets, then does it exist on earth. But Mr. Linton has

taken us into the middle of the next century, where many
now living belong. We may walk the streets of modern
Athens, and yet feel very solitary. Such papers, however,
make contemporaries, and he subscribed to this one with
his whole heart. Thirty years ago an attempt had been
made to carry out a similar idea, and for a time success
attended the efforts. When indeed its moving spirit again
took his place in the world, he left Brook Farm, feeling
that one day it would be a reality. Mr. Alcott was happy
to hear of its counterpart.

Mr. Weiss, who always carried in his heart the lighted
torch of eloquence, recognized the ideal republic, that
which mild and respectable republican journals are wont
to call the serenely Utopian. Our skilful engraver but
pours a little acid over the plate to eat away extraneous
substance and leave a work of art. The little child of the
republic is born, or if not born we are bearing it in our
bosoms. He liked the criticism, sharp as it might seem.
It was from berries pressed harsh and crude. The critic
was not drunk with new wine. Mazzini and his disciples
had tasted of the vintage gathered when God put the
world up. It was the aboriginal wine, all ready to be
opened and quaffed by mankind; and America, in spite of
the shoddy element, was not unprepared to put its lips to
the sacramental cup. We hold our opportunity, born of
the bloody throe of the last four years. Mr. Weiss
thought that there could be nothing so ineffably mean as
our treatment of struggling nationalities. It is ours to
say, " God bless you, old Greece! God bless every man
who believes that every other man has a right to share in
the divine presence! We are going to stand by that young
people." It was a part of our mission to stretch out a
hand to all peoples that cry aloud, " I want to be a part
of the United States of the world," though they be Greek
or French, Italian or Spanish.

Mr. Powell felt greatly indebted to Mr. Linton. The doctrine was good, but it would take the people a long time to see and understand it. Mr. Linton's doctrine was, after all, but the kernel or substance of Quakerism. Quakers, more than any associated people, have upheld this ideal government of God in the human soul, and their decline is because of an ideal beyond popular conception.

Mr. Robert Dale Owen thought the first part of the essay masterly, but was not prepared to agree to its later details. In the earlier portion of his congressional experience there was not such corruption as now exists. Looking back a quarter of a century, he remembered well that there was not a member of Congress who was even accused of a willingness to accept a bribe. He did not say that there was not a certain amount of lobbying, but positive corruption there certainly was not. This could not be said of recent years. It is almost an impossibility to pass a bill through Congress without money; and if the States go on twenty-five years longer under the present regime, there will not be honesty enough to keep the body politic together. Mr. Owen could recall the time when intemperance in the West was so terribly prevalent as to cause four fifths of all the crime. At last it became so bad that a remedy was found in total abstinence.

He was himself not a devoted adherent of total abstinence, but as the lives of the best are spent in choosing between the less of two evils, he hailed the new dogma with gratitude. Now there is not one drunkard where there were ten. Mr. Owen thought that in like manner public opinion would rise up against political corruption. There ought to be protest, but we should lose hope did we look at the reverse of the shield. He had never expected to live to see Slavery abolished, yet his eyes had beheld the impossible. What may not be foretold of the

" Woman's Rights" movement? He could go back to the time when married women in Indiana had no right to their own property. Since then there has been the greatest progress.

XIII.

NEWSPAPERS.

By F. B. SANBORN.

WHEN Horace Walpole was furnishing his fine house, his friend and former tutor, the poet Gray, wrote him that his chairs ought to be new, unless he would cramp or torture his guests. "Every chair that is easy is modern," said Gray; and with quite as much truth we may claim that all newspapers that are good are recent. Sydney Smith was fond of dating events before or after "the invention of common-sense;" and certainly the common-sense that controls the modern newspaper does not go back many centuries.

The newspaper of to-day is a very different thing from the newspaper which Dickens satirized in "Martin Chuzzlewit." Not only have the means of communication been infinitely enlarged, so that our news flashes to us with the speed of lightning from every quarter of the world, but the newspaper has ceased to be the vehicle of mere news. Moral and scientific questions are ably discussed, reforms are advocated, discoveries are chronicled, — in short, the newspaper holds its mirror up to every aspect of the times. Thoreau was in the habit of condemning newspapers. He read them once a week, but considered himself the worse for even so much dissipation. "Read not the Times," he said, "read the Eternities." But there came a season when Thoreau read every newspaper he could find. It was when

John Brown lay wounded at Harper's Ferry, and his enemies, thronging about and questioning him, drew from him
those answers which rang through the country for years,
and still thrill the heart as we recall them. It was the reporter of the New York newspaper who then and there
noted down the undying words, which might else have been
lost; and thus was it made manifest for what reason the
New York newspaper had been allowed to exist all these
years, since no other paper could have had a reporter there.
In those days the Times and the Eternities got printed
on the same sheet, as they always do when a hero appears. .
Of late years there has been a marked increase in the courage as well as in the resources of newspapers. Contented
formerly with following in the wake of public opinion, they
have sprung to the front, and aspire to lead where they
used to follow. In the last ten years the tone of our own
journals has greatly changed. If they are not yet models
of courage, they are by no means deficient in boldness, and
no longer deem it their duty to " feel round for the average judgment of their readers and express that," as Wendell Phillips used to accuse them of doing. One reason for
this change is the rapidity with which, as a nation, we have
passed from a provincial to an imperial position among the
nations; for, waiting on our prosperity, have come fabulous wealth, increased culture, a prodigious diversity of
tastes and interests, and a wide expansion of the horizon
of individual ambition. Under the spur of these excite-
ments a new class of newspaper editors has appeared. An
English traveller, in 1833, spoke of the American editors
as "shrewd but uneducated men;" the description no
longer applies. Nearly all the rising or lately risen journalists in the country are educated men, many of them
highly accomplished in scholarship or literature. They are
travelled men, too, — familiar with foreign countries and
with their own. Either as editors or correspondents, jour-

nalism is drawing into its service the highest culture and
the best brain in the country, whether of men or women.
When Mrs. Child, that genial grandmother of feminine
journalism in America, wrote her "Letters from New
York," when Margaret Fuller went to the same city to help
Mr. Greeley edit "The Tribune," how daring and strange
their ventures seemed to their countrywomen! Now their
successors in the same field are legion. But, with so many
recruits to the ranks of journalism, it must be confessed
that the number of really able editors is still small. Brilliant, forcible, and sensible as American journalists are,
they seldom develop into marked superiority; each has his
drawback, and does not rise beyond a certain standard.
Had Franklin lived in our day, and devoted himself to a
newspaper, he might perhaps have come nearer than any
one else to being the ideal editor; but even of Franklin
Timothy Pickering observed that "he was never found in
a minority," and the ideal journalist, like the greatest general, must sometimes lead a forlorn hope. Courage, high
moral courage, is still the quality most lacking in journalism, though we meet it not infrequently, and believe that
it is constantly increasing, as the temptations to cowardice
are decreasing. It becomes every year more difficult to
hire or buy a successful newspaper; for the successful
newspaper is rich enough to live without bribery. Moreover, papers thrive now by their advertisements rather than
by their subscribers. One of the besetting sins of the journalist, especially of the war and Washington correspondent, is self-conceit. "I wish I knew anything," said Lord
Melbourne, "as positively as Macaulay knows everything;"
and it were surely a high enough ambition for the most aspiring scholar to be certain of everything as is an American editor. But our daily or weekly instructors have, after
all, the right to a little comforting self-glorification. It
is no mean talent which they use, and they do not use

it ill.   It is sometimes objected to journalism that it is
anonymous ; a newspaper is always responsible for what it
prints.   The shield of anonymous publication is necessary
to the man who is to criticise fearlessly; without it he
would be exposed to the reproaches, the hatred, the bribes,
and the blandishments that would certainly interfere with
his proper duty.   There are enthusiasts who hope for the
model newspaper which they have never yet seen : whenever it is established it will require in its editor the deepest
purpose, the broadest thought, the highest culture, the
most tolerant heart, the noblest manhood, of which humanity is capable.

Mr. WEISS followed, and spoke of his own enjoyment of
newspapers.   He never took one up without wanting to
cut a scrap from it.   The relative importance of the press
and the pulpit would bear discussing : for his part, he
thought the press had filched a good deal of power from
the pulpit, and preached its sermons quite as effectively.

Dr. BARTOL wondered whether the press, as well as the
church, might not need its Luther.   He was struck by the
blind, irrational belief of the great journalist that he is
not a responsible man, but a gigantic behemoth who shall
bear down all prejudices.   He was once entertaining
Thackeray at breakfast, and they fell into talk about
Goethe.   Dr. Bartol made some strictures on the morals
of the great German ; but Thackeray shook his head.
"We can't judge such a man," he said, "by ordinary
standards.   He is too great for our measurements."   Simi-
larly the editorial mind seems to think itself beyond common
judgment ; and we are afraid of the press, all of us, as we
are of the Irish vote.   The facility with which newspapers
change their minds is something amusing to watch.   A
savage one day was talking to some missionary about
virtue, and betrayed his opinion that people are good be-

cause they are afraid. "When he grow strong he grow bad," said the savage, commenting upon human nature as he saw it: might not the same be said of newspapers?

Mr. WASSON did not think newspapers became bad in proportion as they grew strong, but the reverse. The richest paper could afford to be the bravest; and the worst paper in New York was one struggling to establish the fact of its existence. But there was one danger about newspapers, and the better the paper the greater this became, — the danger that we should be *satisfied* to get our information from them. Mr. Weiss always wanted to cut " scraps " from them, and their tendency was to make one's *mind* run to scraps. The diminution of the faculty for concentrated study may be largely traced to newspapers; and this is not at all the fault of the newspapers, but of those who are contented with mere mention. We are, indeed, no longer provincial, and that is a great gain; but it is bought dearly by the loss of the power of long and close thinking. Thought itself is worth quite as much as the results of thought. Will not some editor begin by and by to define the province of journalism, and tell people that they are not to depend on newspapers for their opinions?

Gen. ARMSTRONG had just been spending an hour in a convention of orthodox ministers. They had been discussing the bondage of the pulpit, and they concluded that the escape from it must be through the force of strong conviction: so about the press; if journalists have strong convictions, to which they dare not be disloyal, the force of truth will make them free.

Mrs. HOWE thought neither pulpit nor press could supplant the other. The newspaper is indispensable, — God forbid we should be deprived of it! but the church also is indispensable, — God forbid that we should be deprived of that! It is the old fable of the hare and the tortoise. Let the hare do the swift running: we need the slow, safe

tortoise as well.   The people must not forget that the business of the Church is to set forth high ethical culture.

Mr. ROBINSON said that he did not believe newspaper
influence was really increasing ; he thought the newspapers
of to-day followed the people rather than led them.   He
entirely agreed with Mr. Wasson about the danger of believing in newspapers. ⁻ He detested newspapers, but he
read them constantly.   After he had flung a paper upon
the floor, he would pick it up and look at it again, and all
the time he knew that newspapers were the worst possible
reading ; and if he was not ruined by this reading, it was
because he did not remember what he read.   He then spoke
of some papers having a definite personality, as, indeed, is
characteristic of all newspapers more or less.   There is a
paper called " Our Society " ("I even read that," he par-
enthesized), which he considered as the most offensive
result of this rage for newspaper gossip.

There was a general laugh, a general enjoyment of this
sharp fusilade from the prince of newspaper correspondents, and after a few words more the meeting broke up,
never more reluctantly ; and then one began to see the
various faces come out of the corners, and to find that
Samuel Bowles, of the " Springfield Republican," had been
a listener to this newspaper talk, to which he could so well
have contributed.

XIV.

THOU SHALT.

BY DAVID A. WASSON.

SCIENCE does not satirize history more than it does
physical nature. In either case it assumes in the
observed facts, however remote in time or grotesque in
appearance, a significance to be found in harmony with
all existing truth. In respect to organic truth, Goethe
divined the truth now generally acknowledged, — that one
and the same type governs growth through all its stages
and transformations. We await the Goethe or the Lyell
who shall apply this law of uniformity to history, sustain-
ing the identity of principles in all the ages of civilization.
An apprehension of this fact is fast spreading, — Nature
instructing us how to study civilization, with all the ideas,
institutions, customs, and formative processes which belong
either to its history or to its present state; and historical
criticism, at once animated and disciplined by the scientific spirit, is steadily becoming graver, more appreciative,
more disposed to assume as its guiding clew the identity of
type and uniformity of ideal force in all that upbuilding
of humanity, all that organic vivification, structure, and
growth which modern speech is accustomed to designate by
the term " civilization."

It is incontestable that man recognizes somewhat as
sovereign over his will so soon as he has any sentiment of
the kind which distinguishes human nature. By the first

civilizers, law and rule were thought to come only from above. It is precisely this notion of their origin that gives them authority and engages obedience. Primitive senti-ment knows nothing of law-makers, but only of law-givers. It is obvious that Moses, in saying, "Thou shalt not kill," sought not to impose his individual will upon others, while he as little professed, or was understood to be, the mere reporter of their wills. He was accepted as an interpreter. Homer's Themistes signify the same. May it not be that in their instinctive reference of all authority to a ground above any will or inclination whatsoever we also find an old friend, though one who awaits our recognition? Prin-ciples are sovereign; men are so but as the media or exponents of principles. The laws of social welfare date from the foundation of the world, and are as unchangeable as its constitution. Men may discover, acknowledge, apply them, but are as incapable of making them as the eye of making what it sees. These laws every man is, by the fact of his existence as a human being, bound to obey; while any obedience enforced upon him otherwise than in furtherance of their claims is injurious and odious. Po-litical thought which does not begin here, and thence pro-ceed to all political functions, is *ipse facto* discredited.

But beginning here, we are led to an unqualified rejec-tion of all *mere* personal authority, whether of one or of many, of king or of people. To this intent government is organized, — not to render some dominant over others, be it the few over the many, or the many over the few, but to make reason dominant over all. The State exists, it has been a thousand times said of late, to express the will of the people as supreme. The State exists in truth, to express the loyal submission of all wills whatsoever to the laws of social welfare, as by the best lights of reason de-termined, — to express an allegiance we all naturally owe. A sovereign human will — let us have done with that.

Authority is vicious; it lacks the genius of authority in the degree that its ground is any mere will, however compounded. A compound, indiscriminate personal domination, on the mildest scale, is democracy; the sovereignty of the laws of welfare, represented by qualified agents whose sole title to that function is found in their translucency to authoritative principles, is Republicanism. The latter is the ideal aim of the modern world; but, unhappily, in passing over the crust of a period of transition it has slumped into the former. Our chief question, therefore, should be, not *who* it is, but *what* it is in which authority resides. This may seem an abstract way of contemplating the matter, but it is not more abstract than science and common-sense must be.

The speaker proceeded to define political obligation as having two factors independent of any man's will. The first is found in necessary conditions, — necessary either absolute or relative, — including necessary laws of consequence and the like. These make a certain conduct matter of moral necessity. For this necessity human authority is to stand, representing the imperative requisition of the facts. An enforced mandate is a crime against nature if it be not a mandatory form of the truth, having a deeper ground than mere volition. Public duty can as little be willed into existence as the force of a syllogism. The facts are thus and so; therefore duty is thus and so. A rational inference, a considerate judgment, mediates between the facts and the duty. Government, then, is a means of getting the considerate judgment where it is wanted, that the facts may speak through it and afterward be rendered obligatory in force as in right.

Now it is obvious that just force can be represented only by the considerate and judicious mind, as only a polished surface can serve the purpose of a mirror. Only such mind, therefore, is capable of a political act in the proper sense

7

of the term. There is much in every demand, and an obvious preponderance in some, of force that is good while it is kept under, and infernal when it is not kept under. We are brute beasts, every one of us, and none the worse for that so long as our brute part does not attempt the *rôle* of law-giver; but when the beast in the individual or society proceeds to legislate, Satan's statute-book receives the record. I hear much of each man's superior knowledge of his own interest, and of this supposed or pretended fact as the one from which the theory of government should be derived. Well, the prisoner at the bar is above all interested in the event of his trial. Does his interest call him to the place of judgment? It excludes him. Do we say the will of the people is sovereign, and has a right to acquit or condemn at pleasure? That were barbarous or below barbarism. What is to decide? The special facts of the case placed in proper relation to those general facts and truths which all men ought to regard submissively. What can reflect these accurately? Considerate and judicial mind.

Political obligation also presupposes a purpose which is of such à nature that all men are under obligation to recognize it. The ideal ends of life, of which those of government form a part, have a claim to regard which is simply indefeasible. Good alone is regal; all the lines of just authority derive from it and lead to it. We are under a natural obligation to seek welfare, to accept the condition of it, to adjust the conduct to the laws of it.

Are not these discriminations important to others besides theorists? A critical hour has struck in the world. That time must be critical when general principles reflectively distinguished gain practical importance and give the initiative to action. So long as men act instinctively Nature charges herself, so to speak, with their guidance. Like bees, they build better than they know.

In politics, as in other provinces, the epoch I have hinted at has arrived. But, because this epoch has come, we must distinguish, as men never had need to do before, the principles which justify authority. In this time, when class is taking up arms against class, and avocation against avocation; when capital is imperilled by lawless wealth, and labor compromised by the spirit in which even its just demands are made; when fraud and rapacity occupy the very citadels, and we know not whether to fear most those who make the laws or those who stand ready to break them, — I discern one point, and after long reflection see it even more clearly, where reformation, to be at all radical, must begin. We must put authority in a condition to engage respect. At present the very principle of authority is in disgrace. The actual authority is always a makeshift, an expedient for the hour. Indeed, it is esteemed endurable only because it is ephemeral. Rule is submitted to because we are so soon to be rid of it. It is a tooth which we do not have out because it aches but a little while at a time; the twinge would be in another place before we could reach the dentist's. The national attitude toward its governing power is much like the mutual attitude of a husband and wife, who should each, the day after the wedding, purchase and keep always in view the other's coffin, by way of strengthening the marriage tie! "There is a divinity doth hedge a king," said the Old World. That generous delusion dignified obedience, if it did no more; and to do this was much. To obey what you honor is wholesome and elevating; to obey what you do not and cannot honor is debasing, and in the end morally destructive. There's a divinity doth hedge a caucus, — the poetry of our politics has come to that. Power now is simply power; we submit to it, but we do so much in the spirit of the ancient Pistol, dining upon leeks: "I eat, and eke I swear." The degradation of our civil service and the absence of any public sentiment to be shocked by its degradation; the great American principle, "Rotation in office;" and the great American maxim, "To the victors belong the spoils," — these things and a great many similar ones might suggest a set of political urchins, who, while capable, like other urchins, of fine sallies of bravery and generosity, know not the value of what they handle, and would burn an insurance policy to fire a toy cannon.

Mr. Wasson closed with the following summary: —

1. To the laws of welfare, which are the ratio between necessary conditions and obligatory ends, every man's allegiance is due. But welfare is a qualitative term, signifying an elevated manner of life. Only to this are we ideally bound; any other bond imposed is enslaving.

2. Human government arises to represent the just force of that system of laws, and human law is legitimate when it stands transparently for their authority.

3. A quality in man adequate to the representation of these laws is Nature's basis for all governing function; rule which does not signify a respect to quality in man, and through that an allegiance to right ends of life, is a barbarism Nature may tolerate for a day, but surely will not tolerate forever.

———

Rev. WILLIAM H. CHANNING said that "extemporaneous remark on a theme so grand, and so ably treated by the essayist, must needs be insufficient. Also, before commenting on the essay, there was need to know more precisely what the author meant by 'will,' what by 'welfare,' and what by 'law.'"

"We can find no ultimate source of authority," Mr. Channing said, "except being, personal being, God himself. Essential goodness is the will which presides over us. We have heard that there is no sanctity in a caucus, and there is a sense in which it is so; nevertheless we see that God sometimes speaks in the hearts of a whole people. It is on account of this unquestionable fact that I trust in universal suffrage. Also, I expect great benefit from the next step towards getting the voice of humanity as a whole, — namely, the voting of women. Let us listen religiously to the voice of God which will speak through the heart of woman. If she apprehends this responsibility aright, and uses it aright, she will be to us a prophet, a savior."

Mrs. Howe said : " Though I know how solid and logical Mr. Wasson's work has been, and I followed with intense interest as one must follow when he reads, I have wanted several times to say, 'Stop, you are not leading me right.' I do not see where morals can be found, if when we tell a man 'Thou shalt,' he is unable to say 'I will.' The foundation of morals, the very first thing which religion appeals to, is to raise and exert the will; it is energizing and inspiring, — that is the real and palpable element of command and authority. And I feel there is something very divine about a caucus. I have a great and very tender reverence for it, no matter how badly it may do. Then I don't like the words 'beast' and 'brute' applied to anything human. However debased a man may be, I do not think of him in that way one instant. I should say to such a man, 'What you do is brutal; what you are is divine.' That, I think, would be the way to touch the right string; the other is demoralizing."

Mr. Weiss. — We must accept the situation. The criticism of the paper was particularly suggestive. It instantly awoke and sent flashing through every vein of my thought a belief in the old ideal of the republic, toward which all criticism, the most hostile, the most searching, is tending; and as in all the cases where our friend Mr. Wasson has treated this subject, this one thought has always occurred to me : " How are you going to get your best men, how are you going to get your best minds to assume that authority which all the other minds and consciences will recognize as being the best?" And so I ask in the case of Mr. Wasson, though I love to hear the criticism and agree to every word of it, and I do not think there is a man living who can paint the gold ring, or the caucus ring, or the whiskey ring, or the railroad ring, in colors too black for the truth. How are you going to get the conscientious men, the true and just men?

It seems to me we have to recognize one plain fact, — as we have to do in everything which relates to this universe, — that here we are; we are not different from what we are, and we are not in any other place. Here are the tools; we have nothing else. We cannot go to work and forge tools for the future out of the impalpable. You must take men and women just as they are born into the world. All the men and women of this republic are the people who compose the future welfare of the republic. Mr. Wasson spoke of the beginning of superficial equality; and it is only in the beginning of superficial equality that the cereal product of earth becomes fit for the food of man. When the forests which covered the earth and usurped the nourishment of the soil were cut away, were the victims of a cataclysm or a catastrophe, the buried grass first began to appear; and it was superficial equality. Each blade was very hirsute, and not fit to eat; yet it contained the life of the human race. The ancient people understood it perfectly well, in the tradition that the grass which grew on the mountain-side was transformed into men. I only mean to say that in America it is superficial equality which is going to furnish you with the staff of life. It is by having all the men and all the women turned into it that this mill of government is slowly going to refine itself in the future: I do not see what else. I would like to ask Mr. Wasson to reflect upon that point. Has he any other way of eliminating the best mind, and best justice, and best authority, to secure the universal welfare? Is not that the practical point, — that here we are, such as we are; and we have got to work with the good that is within us?

. Mrs. LIVERMORE said: " While Mr. Wasson was reading his paper, I could not but assent to all that he was saying concerning the evil tendencies of the times, concerning the terrible upheaval of the late war which has brought all sorts of uncleanness to the surface. And then I said, ' Does it follow that the republic is a failure; that, after all, this experiment that we have tried of a government carried on by the people is bearing us to anarchy?' and I thought, Why, we have not a republic: we have tried a form of government in which we have allowed the masculine mind to rule, but we have never yet invoked the feminine nature. I have great faith that whenever the men of our country — our misgoverned country — call to their aid the female half of nature, — which may not be better, but is different, and was intended by God to supplement and complement the other half — that we shall find we have taken a new departure from that hour."

ABBY KELLEY FOSTER observed, " I would remark that the old adage, ' There is a power behind the throne that is stronger than the throne,' and which moves the power, is the whole sum and substance of the great general conception uttered here. As Mr. Gerrit Smith once said, ' The power behind the throne is made up of the masses; and because the masses have not felt their responsibility, the rulers have not felt it. Shall it be said that because the masses have not been educated up to the point to which they need to be, that then the government is a failure? The very business of government is to raise the moral and intellectual standard of the people.' "

Hon. GEORGE B. LORING said, " I am happy to say that I have heard more of just such talk as this among the

common people in their caucuses and assemblies than some
of the more refined might suppose.   There is an immense
amount of common-sense, conscience, and humanity in the
masses of the common people, — more than we think there is,
sometimes ; and I assure you it is the hardest thing in the
world to lead the masses of men astray.   Their sense of justice is keen. 'I am not surprised that so much is said of
corruption in means.   Wherever the carcase is, there will
the eagles be.   But they are not all eagles.   I don't believe
anything is pure.   I think there is a spot somewhere in the
heart that we all have to get rid of the best way we can ;
and the individual heart is a type of the public heart.   In
spite of all the discouraging facts of the situation, I have
great hope.   I have seen through all our history one great
fact, and that is, that that which is dominant, that which
has ruled all men, has been obedience to nationality."
The speaker commented on the purity of Washington,
and said : "There never has been a time in this country
when the great ruling thought of the country has not been
saved by universal suffrage.   It is not a question of education, a man is not required to know the alphabet to teach
him right and wrong: and so, I think, one of the great
marvels of our time has been the way in which the masses
of the people have reasoned up to the great ruling thought,
and supported it."

The discussion was thus terminated, and the company
dispersed.

XV.

MUSIC.

By JOHN WEISS.

THOSE who have been accustomed to hear Mr. Weiss need not be assured that his essay on "Music" was full of melody and harmony, and that it wrought the effect of rich and deep music on the hearers. I can only give the scattered fragments which follow.

Mr. WEISS began by saying that every age has its own style of art, which, after serving the purpose of its time, gives place to another. The voices of Nature are variously interpreted by men, and each period finds its own appropriate form of expression. The ancient Greeks wrought wonders in stone. Instead of expending our strength in the attempt to imitate or surpass them, should we not rather assume that the Phidian exigency has passed, and turn to labors more suitable to our own time?

He cited the somewhat remarkable fact that there were certain great writers, like Ben Jonson, Pope, and Burke, who had no music in their souls, cared nothing for it. This he explained satisfactorily to himself. His theory was that the microscopic disks in the *cochlea* of the ear — discovered by Helmboldt — were in the above instances disarranged naturally, and could not recognize and telegraph to the brain the pleasure in harmony that is the delight of other ears. But most great writers and noted men — like Shakspeare, Milton, Tennyson, and of all others the last to be thought of, Nero — were fond of music and capable to a large degree of appreciating its appeals to the soul.

Mr. Weiss then went on to show what music is, by pointing out where it fails us, or, in other words, what it is not. For instance, music cannot imitate anything. The imitations of the voices of animals, which the performer on the violin executes with good effect generally, are only perfect so far as we anticipate and make an effort to recognize them as such. To be brief, music is in no way descriptive; it cannot describe anything. As illustrative of this point, the essayist referred frequently to well-known symphonies by Beethoven, Mendelssohn, and others, in which the word attributed by some writers on music might be replaced by its opposite, and the description still hold good. In the latter part of his essay Mr. Weiss sought to define to some extent the place that music occupies among the arts, or rather to sum up in a few words what it has to do with us. It speaks to us in language to which words cannot possibly be adapted: and, in fact, if a symphony could be completely expressed in words, the need of conveying it to us through music would be eliminated.

Mr. Higginson had highly enjoyed Mr. Weiss's testimony to the superiority of words over music as a means of description: words have this advantage, — that *exact* description or criticism can be given only in them. He doubted whether there was any soundness in the claim of superior expressiveness in music. Odors are as suggestive as sounds, and the power of association belongs to all our senses. External life is secondary, human life is primary, as even Thoreau, the champion of external nature, had felt himself obliged to confess.

Dr. Bartol quoted the opinion of Mendelssohn that language was less definite than music, but declared his own opinion to be otherwise. Words contain most and suggest most. Genuine, sincere words surpass musical notes in the expression of spiritual as well as material things. He referred to the experience of Dr. Channing, who found new tones developed in his voice through his experience as preacher and pastor.

Mrs. Howe thought that by the alternation of words and music a ladder of ascent might be formed, reaching heights greater than either by itself could bring us to.

Mr. Weiss, referring to an apparent misunderstanding of his meaning by some of the speakers, said that he had not intended to declare music superior to speech, but to say that it produced some effects, recalled some impressions, which words did not produce or recall. Something is done to the appreciative hearer of the best music which is not done to him by Shakspeare or Dante.

Mr. Higginson referred to the fact that no woman had ever excelled in the composition of music, though many had admirably illustrated it by performance.

Robert Dale Owen said that even if women have not composed highest music, the lady who wrote "Charles Auchester" taught us better than most composers have done the power of music.

A lady expressed her conviction that music is the highest kind of language. An orchestra, she thought, has greater power over the audience than any speaker. Music represents God to the soul better than words can do. It gives a clearer expression to spiritual things. If women have not yet distinguished themselves in musical composition, it is because their time has not yet arrived; and she declared her conviction of the superiority of Robert Schumann to all other musical composers, and found in his pieces a clearer expression of the thought and feeling

intended than in those of any other composer.   This merit
she ascribed to the remarkable combination, in him, of
masculine and feminine characteristics.

Mr. SARGENT closed the conversation by remarking that
the best music is that which quickens human emotion to
move towards the promotion of the welfare of humanity.

XVI.

SAPPHO.

By THOMAS WENTWORTH HIGGINSON.

THE lovely city of Mitylene, on the island of Lesbos, was one of the centres, long ago, of the highest Greek civilization. We think of it now, however, only as the home of Sappho ; for it was in the city of Mitylene that she lived and loved, and taught and sang. Her birthplace was at nearly the other end of Lesbos, in the little village of Cresos, where the women seem to have been more beautiful than elsewhere, and the bread better ; and where, as in very few parts of Greece, the women, perhaps because they still make the same good bread, are now admitted to share the meals of the men. Sappho was favored in her birthplace and in her nurture ; but one likes best to think of her in her later abode of Mitylene, where she lived her true life. Here, in some grove of olive or myrtle, or in that marble house which she called the " Dwelling of the Muses," one finds her among the maidens and wives who had come from other parts of Greece to share her training. Anactoria is here from Miletus, Eunica from Salamis, Gongyla from Colophon. Erinna and Damophila are studying the difficult art of verse in the Sapphic meters ; Althis learns how to strike the harp with the plectron which Sappho invented ; some one else embroiders a sacred robe for the temple. Sappho corrects the rhythm of one, the notes of another, the stitches of a third ; then bids them abandon

their work to rehearse together some sacred chorus, or stop
to read a verse, or — shall one say it ? — to expose and
satirize a rival.   If Andromeda, the fascinating, draws
away Sappho's pupils to one of those rival feminine acade-
mies which extend as far as illiterate Sparta, then Sappho
may at least be allowed to remark, "and her language is
plain," that Andromeda does not know how to dress herself.

Out of the long list of Greek poetesses there were seven
women who, as the Greek anthology says, were "divinely-
tongued," speaking like gods ; and of these Sappho was
the admitted chief.   Homer was known to that nation as
"the poet," and Sappho as "the poetess."   She is believed
to have lived somewhere between the years 628 and 572
B. C., thus dating three or four centuries after Homer, and
two centuries before the time of Pericles.   Her husband's
name was Cercolas ; but little more than his name is known
of him.   It is supposed that Sappho early became a widow,
and that most of her poetic career was during her widow-
hood.   The story of her family records little more than
their names ; and of the facts of her own life history treats
so vaguely as to leave us in most unsatisfactory ignorance.
We do not even know with certainty whether she was beautiful.   Tradition represents her as little and dark ; but tradition says the same of Cleopatra, and we cannot put aside
as unimportant the crises in the world's story brought about
by small brunettes.   Plato calls her "the beautiful Sappho," and Plutarch and others use similar epithets.   The
loveliest thing of all was said of her, naturally enough, by
a man who loved her, — Alcæus.   He called her —

"Violet-crowned, pure, sweetly smiling Sappho."

The freshness of those violets, the charm of that smile,
the assurance of that purity, all rest upon that one line, and
rest securely.   The most remarkable intellectual association of Sappho's life was undoubtedly that which she held

with this same Alcæus; but there is not only no evidence
that she returned his love, but considerable reason to think
she did not. These two will always be united in fame as
the joint founders of the lyric poetry of Greece, and therefore of the world. There were no limits to the enthusiasm
felt in ancient times for the poetry of Sappho. A tradition
is preserved that even in her lifetime the recitation of one
of her poems so affected the great law-giver, Solon, that he
expressed the wish that he might not die till he had learned
it by heart. Plato called her "the tenth Muse."

Now why is it that over a woman so admired in her own
time some cloud of reproach has so long lingered? Modern
critics account for this by two simple reasons. First, because she had to endure the cruel criticism which mere con-
spicuousness in a woman always provokes; and secondly,
and more especially, because she was the scapegoat of a
quarrel between two types of Greek civilization. She
stood between the simplicity of the old Greek manners and
the luxurious culture of the new. In half-barbarous periods, like the Homeric, women enjoy the simplicity and freedom of a peasant life. And the poetry of Homer shows
that women were then held in honor. But as culture ad-
vances, the question comes up what to do with the women.
Sparta solved it in the old rough way, and said, "We must
exclude the culture." Softer, more polished Athens said,
"No, let us let in the culture, but exclude the women."
Lesbos and the Æolian colonies said, "Let us have the
culture and extend it to the women." They stood thus
between the two extremes, and their reputation and their
civilization were crushed in the process. The Athenians
thought the uncultured freedom which Sparta accorded to
her women bad enough; but when Lesbos gave to hers a
cultured freedom, it was intolerable, and those reckless pre-
Bohemians, the comedians of Athens, began to pick up mud
and stones to throw at the one woman who had most glori-

fied Lesbos.   An openly immoral Aspasia was tolerated at
Athens; but for a better poet and wit at Lesbos to be at
the same time an example of the domestic virtues was *not*
to be tolerated.

It is fortunate, perhaps, for historic justice that we have
within our reach an illustration of the way in which a whole
race of women may be misconstrued.   If a Frenchman visits America and sees a young girl walking or driving with
a young man, he assumes at once that she is of a doubtful character; just as an Athenian imagined that a Les-
bian woman who taught what in Athens no modest woman
was allowed to know must be no better than she should be.
An Athenian would no more imagine any difference between
Sappho and Aspasia than a Frenchman between Margaret
Fuller and George Sand.   If they saw any apparent difference, they imputed it to the additional vice of hypocrisy.
So they set the fashion, which future ages too long followed,
of writing Sappho down.   Ovid, himself corrupt, censured
her, and his censure has been echoed by Christian ecclesi-
astics.   But modern research and criticism have the honor
of giving us back our Sappho, "violet-crowned and pure."
Since the essay of the German Welcker (1816), the name
of Sappho has stood clear and honorable among nearly all
competent scholars.   Among her vindicators Bishop Thirl-
wall may be honorably mentioned.

As Sappho was widely distinguished as a teacher, and
trained pupils in music, poetry, and embroidery, her
time must have been fully occupied.   An account of her
academy, written by Maximus Tyrius, still remains to
us.   To be sure, one stout Scotch Presbyterian, Colonel
Mure, has taken up the cudgels against her as fiercely
as John Knox did against the fair Queen Mary; thus
showing, as Professor Felton says, the native antagonism
between Scotch Presbyterianism and handsome women.
But the position taken against Sappho by this latest of

the unfavorable critics is better accounted for by the essential impurity of Colonel Mure's mind. The argument against the purity of "the tenth Muse," which unkind ingenuity has wrought out from disjointed fragments of her poetry, falls to the ground when one considers the dramatic attitude which she first introduced into poetry. If one is to be called to account for having personally occupied every position one describes, it will go hard with the poets. Shall some forty-fourth century Colonel Mure so arraign Robert Browning, who depicts every conceivable variety of age, sex, and sin? Why, he could only be saved by the sheer impossibility of being indicted in any court for so many crimes.

The beautiful fragments which have been handed down to us of Sappho's verse fully explain the raptures of the ancients; and her one complete poem which remains, the "Hymn to Aphrodite," has, it is safe to say, excited more enthusiasm among critics than any verse of Dante, any sonnet of Petrarch's, or any song of Shakspeare. Hear a verse or two of it, and see how its subtile beauty survives even the hazard of translation. Suffering from the pain of disappointed love, she has summoned Aphrodite, love's goddess, whom at length she sees before her, smiling, with face immortal in its beauty.

"Asking what I sought, thus hopeless in desiring,
 'Wildered in brain and spreading nets of passion,
 Alas, for whom? and saidst thou, 'Who has harmed thee,
 O my poor Sappho?

"'Trust me, though he flies, ere long he shall pursue thee,
 Fearing thy gifts, he, too, in turn shall bring them:
 Loveless to-day, to-morrow he shall woo thee
 Though thou shouldst spurn him.'"

A love of external nature is one of the features prominent in the fragments of Sappho. She says little of her-

self.   She seems to have belonged to that class of enemies
of the human race who give out riddles to be guessed by
their neighbors.   Her excuse is that this art was in great
demand in Greek society.

Sappho never mentioned, in the fragments which remain
to us, the name of Phaon, supposed to have been her
lover; but she must have loved some one: what matter
whether he were Phaon or another?   Stern criticism also
pretty nearly does away with her Leucadian leap, and
leaves us uncertain as to how and where she died.   It is
certainly difficult to suppose that the most lovelorn lady,
living upon an island where every shore was a precipice,
should take ship and sail for weary days over five hundred
miles of water to seek a more available rock.   Be this as
it may, Sappho is gone, as are her music, her pupils, and
the city where she dwelt, — all, save the island she loved,
.and a few meagre gleanings from her words.   But this
woman, who lived twenty-five centuries ago, played such
a part in moulding the great literature which has moulded
the world, that the women of to-day have made little progress unless they do that and more.   Greece idealized
woman, and degraded her.   We have outgrown, in the
centuries which have passed since then, the theories of
an exclusively masculine social life, but we still make
our political life masculine only, and shall fail like the
Greeks, who rejected the hint furnished by the Æolian
school of Sappho, unless we learn wisdom from their
failure.

Miss Peabody agreed in the correctness of the parallel,
or rather the statement of points of resemblance, between
Sappho and Margaret Fuller.   She had supposed Aspasia
also to have been substantially vindicated, and was surprised to hear the censure upon her which had been

implied, if not expressed, in the essay. She thought the view of her taken in Landor's " Imaginary Conversations " the correct one.

Prof. GOODWIN of Cambridge said he had been surprised to find an ill judgment of Sappho so widely prevailing in former times. He had been brought up in the doctrine taught by Prof. Felton on that subject, and heartily agreed with the representations of the essay.

Mr. WASSON, liking much in the essay, disagreed with its concluding sentence. He thought the change from literary culture to politics was a descent, and that politics rarely improved those who dealt in them.

Mr. POWELL of New York was very glad of that last sentence; glad of the moral to be drawn for our life and times from the story of Sappho's; glad to hear afresh how far back the glories and achievements of woman dated, and to realize what encouragements were to be drawn from these facts for our present labors.

Mrs. CHENEY found in Margaret Fuller a beautiful instance of the individual power of character, leaving a great impression with but few writings. Sappho, she thought, may have been of this sort.

Mr. HIGGINSON said : " As to the differences between Margaret Fuller and George Sand, and between Sappho and Aspasia, if we could get at the facts, perhaps no defence would be necessary; but in the existing obscurity inferences will be drawn on both sides, and there is no help for it. It is well to hold on to all the representative women of the world; but happy is that cause whose representatives do not need to have allowances made for them. As to Aspasia and George Sand, it is very difficult to discriminate; the gentlest judgment must still find something to be explained away or apologized for. Margaret Fuller has written very well on that point, justifying Mary Wollstonecraft, but saying that such as she, though the prophets of a new era, could never be the parents of it. These last must be unquestioned and unquestionable persons. While there is much to discourage, there is much to encourage."

Miss HANNAH STEVENSON thought that character and principle, matters of the greatest consequence, were here involved. It was bad to have it supposed that one could be at once wisest, greatest and meanest, as was said of Bacon. Great principles are condensed in these controversies about individuals.

XVII.

ESSENTIAL CHRISTIANITY.

By MARY GREW.

THE founders of every system of religion, of every sect, of every school of philosophy, have been more or less misrepresented, and their teachings grossly perverted by their friends and followers. The more intense the interest excited by the system, the greater will be this misrepresentation and perversion. This is inevitable, for the conditions are the natural imperfection of the human intellect, the great number of interpreters, and the tendency of enthusiasm to intensify the diversity of interpretations when the opposing advocates meet for conflict. The religious element being the strongest in the human soul, religious controversies and wars have been the most bitter and deadly which the world has known; and in their process it is not strange that creed or theory, transformed into a battle-cry, should lose its original spirit.

One who is interested in Swedenborg, Luther, George Fox, or John Wesley must learn what they thought from their writings, not from the comments or the lives of their followers. Few thoughtful persons will deny that in a discussion of Christianity it is fair to claim that it shall be interpreted or defined from its founder's life and teaching, not from those of his followers. What, then, did Jesus Christ teach? What did he propose as essential to his religion and the eternal life of man? What did he say was the object of his mission? He answered these questions when he said, "For this end was I born, and for this cause came I into the world, that I might bear witness unto the truth." But what truth? It is with this inquiry that the mistake arose which confounds theology and religion, — the one a science, a schedule of propositions to be apprehended intellectually; the other an inspiration and a life. The question, What is Christianity? is but asking, What were the main ideas in the teachings of Christ? Surely these two, — the fatherhood of God, and the brotherhood of man. The ideal of God which he presented was that of a father, loving and tender beyond human conception; tenderest to those who most needed him. The duty toward God which he enjoined was reverent love and trust and obedience; the duty toward man, brotherly love and brotherly service. His religion was preached to the humble, uncultured souls of his time, and the common people heard him gladly; but no philosopher or metaphysician has ever evolved a system of ethics equal to that which he taught, or given to the world a rule of life so profound and so simple as his precept, " Whatsoever ye would that men should do to you, do ye even so unto them." He did not propound dogmas which required laborious intellectual comprehension. On the contrary, he only asked of his followers that they should trust the Father whom he revealed, and to this end he desired that they should become as little children. He would have them show love to God by love to man; by feeding the hungry, clothing the naked, ministering to the sick, and comforting the afflicted. Whether the dogmas which the Church presents us are true or false, they do not belong to the religion of Christ; whether good or evil in their tendencies, they are not to be charged upon him. If Christianity be interpreted by the words and life of Jesus, does it not command our pro-

foundest reverence in proportion to our development in
virtue, holiness, and love? We sometimes hear that certain ancient moral philosophers and religious teachers who
lived before Jesus was born gave to the world moral precepts similar to those upon which he has impressed his
name. But why is it, I ask, that his name, and not theirs,
is indelibly impressed upon them; and why has not one
of them taken such a grip of the world's heart, unless it
was that "never man spake like this man"?

The advocates of the religion of Jesus may justly complain that the leaders of the Church are responsible for
much of the criticism made upon that religion. One ob-
jector says, "I cannot be a Christian, because if I am I
must sanction slavery and war and the taking of oaths.
Those who expound Christianity find in it the sanction for
these things." The responsibility of such rejection as this
rests heavily upon the leaders of Christian churches. They,
not Christ, have piled upon men's shoulders burdens griev-
ous to be borne. They have constructed various systems
of doctrine and ritual which they have presented to men as
the embodiment of that religion, and taught that belief and
observance of these were necessary conditions of Christian
character, while their standard of morals has always been
little higher than that of the government under which they
have lived. The Antislavery struggle of thirty years in
this nation revealed most clearly the character of the
American church. Not only did it uphold that wicked
system, but the negro and his defenders were alike the
objects of the church's scorn. It fell into the grave error
of thinking creed more important than character. Of one
branch of the American church it was wittily said that it
was so occupied with "original sin" that it had no time
for the consideration of actual transgression. That the
church and the clergy have usually been in all ages the
opponents of moral reforms is the testimony of Albert

Barnes, a clergyman honored in the Presbyterian Church of America.

The fact is that the Church has fallen into the grave error of accounting the soundness of a man's creed and form of worship of more importance than his moral character. The churches, Papal and Protestant, bearing the Christian name, have forged fetters for human thought and practically sought to impose them. In the departments of religion, of science, of art, the Church has placed its spiritual detectives, who have stood trembling at the progress of thought, of discovery, of invention, and who have been prompt in the use of club and fetters. It was an extreme Protestant illustration of this fact which was recently furnished by the New York clergyman who announced that " science must stop, or religion cannot go on." Yet while this absurd declaration awakens the ridicule of the Church to-day, multitudes of its leaders are crying in alarm, " Doubts of our creeds and our rituals must be suppressed, or religion will die out of the land. Freedom of thought is dangerous to religion."

Upon the leaders of the Church who have thus slandered Christ and his teaching, I charge the responsibility of much of the rejection of Christianity.

The objectors to Christianity have often been intelligent men, yet they have made the blunder of taking their idea of that system from the followers instead of the founder. Instead of this we must look at the words and acts of Jesus himself, study his life, and judge of his spirit by that as well as by his words. Let us go back to that life spent in doing good; to that boundless pity; that tender love, which reserved its rebukes for prosperous hypocrites, and poured out its treasures on publicans and sinners. The fruit is not all, but by its fruits you know the tree. Christianity thus understood will prove attractive to many who reject it as now presented in the churches. Nowhere will they find anything more worthy their acceptance.

Christianity consists of —

1. Faith in God (not belief in a creed, but confidence in a Father) ;

2. The soul's consciousness of its intimate filial relation to God ; and

3. Love to God and the neighbor, co-existing with the faith above mentioned.

Out of these vital principles all true religion grows, and upon them Christianity is based. To them Jesus always appealed, referring his hearers for corroborative testimony to their own consciences. Facts of spiritual conscious-ness are our true foundation, not less than facts in the other departments of human life. Our highest ideal is God, whom we assume to be perfectly just and perfectly benevolent. We know that justice and benevolence are right in themselves, and we know also that they are suited to promote human welfare. We think no more of doubt-ing these facts of consciousness than of doubting the multiplication table. The very claim of the existence of internal evidence of the inspiration of the Bible is an admission of the existence of an adequate standard of judgment in our own minds by which that inspiration is to be tested.

The best foundation for a Christian character is the love of God and the desire of conformity to his will. The best illustration of Christianity is the life of Jesus. "Father," he said, "I know that thou hearest me always." Every one of us should understand and recognize this intimate rela-tion as existing also between ourselves and the Father. It is a low idea of God to assume that he communicates the knowledge of himself to Christians only. This assump-tion is the dictate of narrow bigotry. The Universal Father is mindful of *all* his children. He has not left him-

self without witness in *any* soul. His testimonies are
within us as well as around us. But his highest lessons
were taught us through Jesus, revealing the way to himself and the truth concerning himself.

The first speaker was Dr. BARTOL. He felt sure that all
present agreed in considering this essay a correct exposition
of what its author undertook to describe. Perhaps now
we might well go on to inquire, What was Jesus?

The loudest declarations of loyalty to him may be fur-
thest off from a real understanding of his character. Professions and compliments were no good test.

The great mistake about Jesus is to suppose that he
intended any system. He wished rather to show us a
method, to give us a spiritual impulse and motive. In
the mind of Jesus, so clear was God's truth that any dogmatic system would have been an offence to him. One step
of approach to him is the recognition that he taught *no*
system. Another step of approach to him is the recognition
that he did not look *down* only. He looked *up*, having,
no doubt, an ideal which he never reached, never realized.
Was he the embodiment of all those best things that he
conceived? We are told that he *grew* in favor with God
and man. Did he ever get his growth? Do we any of us
get our growth here?

What we owe to Jesus, more than to any other, is that
over him floated, almost visibly, the ideal of what man
should become. The great means of being in sympathy with
him is, like him, to look up ; like him, to strive toward the
highest. Unitarian or Trinitarian matters little. Is the
man himself upward-looking, at once abashed and exalted
by the vision of God? If so, be he Jew or Gentile, with
him Jesus would have fellowshipped. Jesus knew no boundaries. He knew none between God and himself, for he

said, "I and my Father are one;" knew none between himself and man: did he not call himself "The Son of man"? It was the infinity of his spiritual life which has made him the power he has been so long. Dr. Bartol thought that all would agree that in this method of Jesus there is something ultimate and final. He hit on a line of beauty, which must be recognized as something real and substantial, running through heaven and earth, through time and eternity.

Col. HIGGINSON spoke of Dr. Bartol's remarks as so fine that they prostrated and submerged criticism, and that after such an improvisation discussion seemed hardly allowable. All must admire the sweetness of tone and the spiritual appreciation of Jesus which Miss Grew has shown; but, like the anti-sceptical course of sermons given in this city last winter, she does not confront the real objection. She does not take a leading type of those who disavow the Christian name, like Abbot, Huxley, and Herbert Spencer. Mr. Abbot also goes to the record; but he takes all, and does not pick out the sweet and lovely things in the life of Jesus to make a character of. If we go to history at all, we must take all it gives. According to that, Jesus was not merely a spiritual teacher, but a Jewish Messiah, looking to rule in the new heaven and new earth, and announcing that he himself was to come in that very generation "to judge the quick and the dead." Belief in the second advent of Christ is still the overwhelming faith of the Christian Church, but the Church has extended the time. Jesus himself evidently taught that he was to come again before the men of his own day should be gathered to their fathers. He considered the teaching of the things here mentioned an essential part of his mission, and we must admit them into our estimate of him. Can any one read the Gospels candidly, and not see this? If Christ had taught *merely* the fatherhood of God and the brotherhood

of man, Mr. Abbot might have been a Christian. His
disavowal of that name is justified by his quotations from
the record. Whether such disavowal is the wiser course,
compared, for instance, with the position of Mr. Emerson,
— who is too busy to disavow, and leaves his attitude to be
divined from his works and defined by others, — may be
questionable. Mr. Higginson had always thought that the
word "Christian" had little more significance than the title
"Reverend." There was not much in it, but it was not
worth the trouble of disavowing. There are certain advantages in keeping the Christian name. It keeps one in
relation with more souls. Christianity is a historic and
secular word, as well as a religious one. Theodore
Parker, feeling all this, always called himself a Christian. To offset these advantages, if you do name yourself Christian, you are liable to be constantly called to
account for your opinions, and explain them, and smooth
over and pretend something that you do not believe. On
the whole, Mr. Higginson thought, there was a point of
view for the non-Christian side not represented in the
essay.

Mr. Sargent said that while he accepted and endorsed
Miss Grew's definition of Christianity as a practical system, yet the question must be bravely met, whether, after
all, Jesus was other than a radical of his time. The
assertion of miraculous works did not prove his divinity;
for some of the wisest men question the fact. Was he not
a great teacher, who was treated as all teachers in advance
of their time are treated? He *was* a great teacher; yet
he said to his disciples, "Greater works than these shall
ye do."

Rev. Francis Tiffany said the work of distinguishing
between the followers of a man and the man himself could
never be avoided, because no amount of explicit statement
and no amount of clear action can ever prevent a man

from becoming one of the greatest oppressors of human thought, from the fact that his works fall into the hands of narrow men. Neither Calvin, nor Luther, nor Theodore Parker ever claimed to be infallible; but he had seen followers of each of those men who had the spirit within them to burn another who differed from anything that one of those men had said. It seemed to him to be a waste of time to define words when they admitted of such a latitude of interpretation. It was very evident that the word "Christian" stood in the mind of Miss Grew for a line of beauty in life and character, and he did not believe that it could be overthrown by any man's protest.

Mr. R. P. HALLOWELL said: "The great objection we have to giving up the name Christian is from our education, which has led us to regard Jesus as a final authority." The worship of Jesus was really idolatry, false and dangerous like all other idol worship.

Gen. ARMSTRONG spoke vigorously in behalf of practical Christianity. He thought the true representatives of Orthodoxy were to be found, not among the clergy, but among the men and women who were quietly and unostentatiously doing the practical work of spreading Christianity; and he thought the system ought to be judged by the latter rather than the former. He related his experience in the Sandwich Islands, where his father was a missionary, and he spent several years witnessing such heroic self-sacrifice as he believed no other religion could induce. In order to replace Christianity he thought there must arise a system which should not only be logical, but generate enthusiasm. He liked nothing better than being enrolled under a leader, and he believed that Christ was the true leader of humanity. He thought that Christ was Catholic and not Protestant, and that he represents all that is good in Protestantism and Roman Catholicism and Mormonism and Radicalism, and that no one had any right to attempt to fasten upon him the name of a class.

Col. HIGGINSON fully appreciated Gen. Armstrong's admiration for the noble work done by the missionaries, but called his attentton to the fact that one had only to look a little wider to see the same enthusiasms, and that other religions have been equally effective. He fully recognized the value of having a leader, especially to the young; but, after all, there is an unspeakable value in the strength which comes when a man can see his leaders, one by one, take their position in the ranks of humanity, and still can see the personal relations which have grown between himself and them. One of the great forming sentences of his life was that saying of Emerson, that, once leave direct acquaintance with God and take secondary knowledge, as through St. Paul's mediation or George Fox's or Swedenborg's, and we begin to grow weak. He thought the vital worth of such a book as Plutarch's " Lives," or his " Morals," or the works of Epictetus, is that, while there is a certain charm in Christian works that you do not feel in those, there is in them a magnificent directness ; there is a feeling that here was a man who depended directly on God. You can wipe out all the religion of Jesus Christ, and all the Rénans and Strausses, and it does not affect these men ; and this quality of directness, he thought, gives to their work great value. While he knew a great many people who had been strengthened and encouraged by Jesus, he saw not less the weakness in some persons which comes from the habit of acting indirectly, the habit of acting outside of the inspiration of their own souls.

Mrs. CHENEY said : " The real life is the life of religion, and this truth agrees with what was said both by the essayist and by Gen. Armstrong. The life is a test of the animating spirit of the individual, but not of the form or the doctrine he holds. Jesus never used the word ' Christian,' and we may feel the just and inspiring element of loyalty whether we use that word or not. Each soul must find religion for itself. The Buddhist meets in the teachings of Buddha the fatherhood of God and the brotherhood of man; and the devout Mohammedan looks for them, not in vain, in the teachings of Mohammed. Let us seek to dwell in the large country of religion, where is hospitality for all souls."

Mr. TIFFANY inquired whether the Independents, like Mr. Higginson, did not merely take *new* leaders, — Plutarch, Epictetus, and the like, — when they proclaimed their freedom from old leaders. Complete isolation was not good for either soul or body. The lonely, independent men after a time degenerate, as Alexander Selkirk did. Our life is fed from external as well as internal fountains; and the more faithfully one applies himself to both, the better he will develop his right, real self, the estate God gave him to improve.

Dr. NEWELL said: "The successful religious teachers of all times are those who have patiently worked out some great idea in its application to life. Mere talk about religion is injurious, and a good deal of silence is needed to combat it."

Mr. R. P. HALLOWELL thought it was singular that, though Jesus' teachings were opposed to war, yet, when the country became involved in war, we found the Christians, not only going themselves, but urging everybody else to go. He inquired whether Gen. Armstrong's idea of Christianity would allow him to enter into fellowship with a man who showed by his life that he loved Christianity, and yet believed that Christ was a man.

Gen. ARMSTRONG replied that faith in Christ was a power which had been more efficient in the moral improvement of the world than any other influence. Still, he believed that a man could have the essential light of Christ without the doctrines of Orthodoxy. He thought that denominations in the Church are proper, right, and essential to its progress.

Dr. BARTOL said he believed Miss Grew's essay to be essential Christianity. The spirit which animated it was purely Christian. Christ, he thought, cared not to be worshipped; he did not wish men to crouch in lowly reverence at his feet. His purpose was to inspire them with the true feeling which should lead them on in the right way. The church which had been reared on his teaching, Christ never intended, he thought, as a finality. The Bible he deemed a Chinese puzzle, composed of parts which men were endeavoring so to marshal as to construct a map, a chart of heaven; and the reason why the puzzle had never been resolved was that the pieces were not made to fit. Jesus, he thought, holding all heaven in solution, came not to create a church, but to preach the brotherhood of man. Beautifully developed as his nature was, he had an ideal which he strove to attain, that was greater, higher, purer than himself. Men lived in imitation of him, grew closer to his nature, when they also, with upturned faces and earnest spirit, pressed nobly on towards the attainment of ideal truth and loveliness.

Mr. WHITTIER, who was unable to attend the meeting, sent with his apology for absence the following lines: —

HOW MARY GREW.

With wisdom far beyond her years,
And graver than her wondering peers,
So strong, so mild, combining still
The tender heart and queenly will,
To conscience and to duty true,
So, up from childhood, Mary Grew!

Then, in her gracious womanhood
She gave her days to doing good.
She dared the scornful laugh of men,
The hounding mob, the slanderer's pen.
She did the work she found to do,
A Christian heroine, Mary Grew!

The freed slave thanks her ; blessing comes
To her from women's weary homes.
The wronged and erring find in her
Their censor mild and comforter.
The world were safe if but a few
Could grow in grace as Mary Grew !

So, New Year's Eve, I sit and say,
By this low wood-fire, ashen gray ;
Just wishing, as the night shuts down,
That I could hear in Boston town,
In pleasant Chestnut Avenue,
From her own lips how Mary Grew !

And hear her graceful hostess tell
The silver-voicèd oracle
Who lately through her parlors spoke
As through Dodona's sacred oak,
A wiser truth than any told
By Sappho's lips of ruddy gold, —
The way to make the world anew,
Is just to grow — as Mary Grew !

XVIII.

RELIGION AND ART.

By ATHANASE COQUEREL.

ATHANASE COQUEREL belonged to one of those French Protestant families so distinguished by the talent and solid virtue of their members. His early ancestors were Jansénistes, and had settled in Rouen. From this city the Coquerel family removed to Paris after having embraced Protestantism. The father of the author of this paper was noted as an elegant and original preacher and a sincere lover of tolerance and freedom of thought.

His son, Athanase Coquerel, was born in Amsterdam in Holland during his father's residence in that country. He began at first his education in Geneva and finished it in Strasburg. At the age of three-and-twenty he was ordained minister, and was sent to Nîmes to take charge of a church there. In 1848 he returned to Paris, and was appointed almoner of the Collége Henri IV. In 1850, in spite of strong opposition to him on account of his liberal views, he entered upon his duties as assistant pastor of the Church of Sainte Marie.

During a period of eleven years M. Coquerel acted in this capacity, being re-elected every three years. His eloquent address, his learning, his generous character, winning manners, and broad opinions were all calculated to bring around him many warm friends; but, on the other hand, the conservatives were displeased to see the

growing influence which the young preacher was acquiring among his parishioners, and were never willing to grant him any more than the mere situation of an assistant.

At that time the Protestant theological school of Strasburg was creating a considerable stir by its liberal views, its critical investigations, and the freedom with which it treated the historical development of the Christian religion. M. Coquerel's open sympathies with this school, as well as his constant propaganda in favor of the freedom of religious teaching, were broadening the gaps which existed between liberal and orthodox Protestantism in France. When M. Rénan's " Life of Jesus " appeared, not only the Catholics but the orthodox Protestant clergymen thought it was their duty to attack the book with extreme violence. M. Coquerel on this occasion wrote an article in which, although making reservations in many a point of detail, he expressed his admiration for the work and its distinguished author, whom he called his " dear and learned master."

This was enough to break asunder the last barrier between him and his opponents. The latter, now completely roused against him, threatened him with nothing less than impeaching and convicting him of heresy. A commission was appointed to this end. After a fruitless attempt to effect a compromise, the accusation was brought forth publicly. M. Coquerel pleaded " Not guilty " in an eloquent address, in which he claimed for his own conscience the right of freedom of belief, and challenged the right of the Consistory to compel him to adopt certain dogmatic views which suited them. To this declaration M. Guizot, the celebrated historian and statesman, haughtily replied that the duty of orthodoxy was to preserve itself from heresy, and to prevent men's souls from being polluted by corrupted beliefs.

The dismissal of M. Coquerel was then voted by a majority of twelve votes against three, on the 26th of Febru-

ary, 1864.   Many were the protests raised against this
arbitrary decision.   Five thousand Protestants in Paris
sent a petition to the Consistory.   From all parts of
France an appeal was heard in his behalf.   But the orthodox party remained immovable and inflexible, being
positive that they were doing this for the great glory of
their religion; and twice, in 1864 and 1867, they rejected
M. Coquerel's candidacy for the office of pastor.   This
ostracism was not confined to him alone, but his friends
also shared a similar fate.

Athanase Coquerel is best known in this country through
his literary essays, admirable in form and thought, in
which he shows himself, perhaps, the sole legitimate suc-
cessor of Sainte-Beuve.   A few months before his recent
death, M. Coquerel visited our shores, hoping here to find
that sympathy with his views, and encouragement and aid
in his plans, which would enable him to erect a church for
the further promulgation of his ideas.

Among those gathered to hear M. Coquerel on the oc-
casion of his reading at the Chestnut Street Club were
Colonel T. W. Higginson, Mr. Alcott, Rev. J. F. Clarke,
Rev. Dr. Hedge, Rev. Dr. Lothrop, Rev. Phillips Brooks,
Mr. David Wasson, and Professor John Fiske.

M. Coquerel began by saying that he was not himself an
artist, but had during several years made the history of
art a special study, and had visited most of the public collections of art work, and many of the private ones, in all
the countries of Europe.   He desired to speak particularly
of the relation of art to Christianity, with the view of presenting some of the reasons which had induced him not to
put faith in the current dogma that art had flourished and
could flourish only under the protection of the Roman
Catholic Church.   In order to be an artist one must first be
a man if he can, must have something to say individually;

and in the next place must know the grammar of the language in which he would speak his thought, whether that language be architecture, sculpture, painting, poetry, or music. All art has an element of religion in it. It is the aspiration of the finite to express something of the infinite. Before the advent of Christianity this character of art was apparent not only in the Greek but in the ante-Greek types. The Doric temples expressed the simplicity, serenity, and permanence of the nature of the gods as conceived by the designers of these temples. When Christian art began it was blended with Pagan art, types of each appearing in the same picture or statue group, and it was sometimes impossible to distinguish whether a figure was intended for Christ or a heathen deity. The catacombs furnish many illustrations of this sort.

After the early Christian art, which had no complete development, came the Byzantine era. Byzantine art was simply no art. It had nothing to say, and wholly lacked that freedom and spirit of life which is the first condition of real art. It was stiff and formal. This continued its sway until about the year A. D. 1000, when there began to be a change, and the Gothic architecture sprang up. It typified the aspiration and prayer of a nation. All the best Gothic architecture was more Christian than Roman Catholic. Most of the cathedral-building was between the years 1100 and 1400. True art began about A. D. 1300, with a marked emancipation from the Byzantine school. Giotto is the representative of a school which did much to effect this. Both in the drawing and in the life and energy of expression of his figures there was apparent a power very far surpassing anything before known. After him came the giants Michael Angelo, Leonardo da Vinci, and Raphael. It is doubtful if there have ever lived their equals in individuality of character. The works of these men have given the Roman Catholic Church its prestige as the nursery of art. But they were not very devoted Catholics. Leonardo was in the habit of painting, in his landscapes, John the Baptist or Bacchus indifferently, and sometimes it was impossible to tell which he intended. Angelo's sonnets addressed to Vittoria Colonna, a Protestant, revealed how little of a Catholic he was. One of them would indicate that he was far advanced toward high Calvinism. Raphael was not an earnest or sincere man, and led an irreligious life, though perhaps not much worse than was usual with men high in the Church in that day. But the disposition of his mind is shown by the incident that in an allegorical picture representing Theology, painted in the palace of the Pope, he represented True Religion by a portrait of Savonarola, the martyr reformer; and this the Pope had to tolerate or get another Raffaelle to decorate his palace. M. Coquerel strongly insisted on the position that these men were in character essentially Protestants, and not devotees. Their religion was of a broad faith, such as is common to all races of men. After these were Correggio, Titian, and Domenichino, — great artists, and almost ranking with the greatest; but they were not really Roman Catholics, or at most were such only by a liberal classification. Then came the school of which Guido is the master, when conventionalism became the rule of art, and independent individuality died out. This was the end of Roman Catholic art in Italy.

The Catholic Church has pretended that it fostered art by governing it, laying down the rules of it, and giving orders for innumerable pictures. It has undertaken to say what are proper subjects for religious art, and even undertaken to prescribe particular rules for the treatment of each subject. The result is that we have galleries full of Madonnas, Annunciations, etc., repeated in tiresome succession without a gleam of inspiration or individual power.

One of its art inquisitors has declared that the Virgin should always be represented shod. A paper is published in Rome which undertakes to drill artists to conformity to set patterns. The Church has treated art with gross irreverence, spoiling pictures by clouds of incense, and ruining their effect by brilliant tapestry hangings. It is now a practice, when dampness is spoiling pictures, to take them away and place them in museums, which is the best thing that could happen to them. Their places are supplied by painted copies or mosaics which damp does not injure. The Greek Church has a council in St. Petersburg to sit in judgment on all religious pictures. The result is dreadful.

What was the effect of the Reformation? Luther was himself an artist in nature, and his best friend was a painter, who did great service in Luther's aid by illustrating for the common people the features of Luther's protest. Dürer and Holbein were also great artists. The latter did effective work against the Catholic Church by his satirical pictures. The satirical Passion is an example where the obnoxious characters are represented by the Pope and monks. War crushed this school, and during its long and fierce political struggles since, Germany has had no great school. The Düsseldorf school is doing some meritorious work, but it is not yet great.

With regard to the English school, M. Coquerel said he had never been able to like it. Reynolds's allegorical females seemed to him to be all made of ice-cream, and he sometimes thought he would like to hold a torch to them till they melted, so that he could discover where their bones were if they had any. He did not like to be troubled by anatomical preoccupation when looking at pictures. Gainsborough's works are better. The trouble with the English school was that its imagination had no substance of reality; it was all dream-stuff. He quoted a remark of

Ary Scheffer's to the effect that Shakspeare's most fanciful creations were but features of reality idealized. The
English painters proceeded by another method, and failed.
He thought the skeletons of Reynolds's women must be
unlike any ever seen. It was not generally known that in
the early days of the Reformation in France there was a
French school of art which was very complete and produced excellent work. Of these Androuet du Cerceau was
distinguished as an architect, Jean Cousin as a painter,
Jean Goujon as a sculptor, Palissy as a potter, and Claude
Goudimel as a musician. The latter wrote the music of
the French Protestant Psalms. Most of these artists were
the victims of Catholic persecution, and their works are
more celebrated than their names. Francis I., the Medici,
and others, flooded France with Italian pictures and
models, and true art soon yielded to conventionalism.
The Flemish school, at the head of which is Rubens, was
merely noticed. The Dutch school, with Rembrandt as
its representative, was dwelt upon at some length. Rembrandt himself was characterized as one of the boldest and
truest artists who ever lived. He was an inventor. The
Italians had seemingly exhausted the capacity of lines and
color in painting : he first discovered and applied the
element of light and shade. Disgusted with Dutch pictures of Italian skies, and Greek faces which the painters
had never seen, he tried to paint what he saw. In Holland,
the constant fog makes imperceptible the outlines of objects which are so sharp under an Italian sky. Rembrandt
painted everything in a fog, everything vague and unde-
fined, except the spot illuminated by a ray of light.

M. Coquerel would not deny that the Roman Catholic
Church had done much by demanding many pictures, but
its rules had strangled real art. The best work done for
the Catholic Church was done by men whom it influenced
but little.

With regard to art in America, M. Coquerel said he had only a slight knowledge of it. He thought, however, our country was now old enough to begin doing good work, and to American artists he would repeat what he said at the beginning. The two essentials of a good artist are that he should be a man having something of his own to say, and should as the first step learn the grammar of the language he desired to speak in. If he felt that these things were beyond his powers, let him turn his attention to something else.

Mr. SARGENT said he felt authorized to express for the whole company, as well as for himself, their gratitude for the very interesting discourse which had been given. He himself felt confident that there was an intimate relation between religion and the fine arts.

Mrs. HOWE suggested that, young as our nation is, its members have wrought some good work in sculpture and painting.

Mr. HIGGINSON found one thing unsatisfactory in the address, — its brevity. In regard to one point contained in it, he could not help feeling that Roman Catholicism was a positive epoch, and Protestantism a negative one, and thus not favorable to the highest artistic work. In the new time coming we might look for another positive epoch.

Rev. Dr. HEDGE thought M. Coquerel had shown conclusively that art, in its very beginning, was essentially Protestant. Protestantism he thought a return to primitive Christianity. The Roman Catholic Church was for a long time the only church, and Christianity could act upon art only through that.

The Church of Rome has furnished a mythology, — something absolutely indispensable to religious art. The nonexistence of this in Protestant art shows a deficiency on that side ; on the other hand, the realism of human life has freer scope in Protestant art. Dr. Hedge suggested the inquiry what was the relation of painting to the art of illumination, as we see it in the old missals.

M. Coquerel said : "As the spiral never returns, always goes upward, man always feels his relation to God, and his need to approach him. Aspiring to perfection is the rule in art as in morals and religion. Practically however, development is always unequal, one side in excess, the other deficient." As to the end of Protestantism, he thought there was no end to anything. Protestantism was a vindication of real rights, and thus a spiritual progress. As to the illumination of missals, that was an important work at the time it was done, and really great artists were engaged in it. Fra Angelico did some of the best work of that class, but even in him the Christian feeling was stronger than the Roman Catholic feeling.

Mr. Alcott quoted Aristotle, as saying that art was the reason of things without the matter. He (Mr. Alcott) thought the word " personality " would be a better expression of what M. Coquerel had called " individualism." As to high art, we must be flooded with divinity before we can have it. When we live superior lives, we shall have superior art.

Dr. Clarke expressed his full sympathy with the definition of art in the discourse, and the statement in regard to its historic development. " Artists and connoisseurs," he said, " do not make art. That comes from the existence of some great thing to be expressed, whence arises the impulse to express it. Very likely we do not see the art now existing among us. " Christianity came as a great inspiration to see truth and to do good. The Roman Catholic Church, while trying to do the good, forgot to see and insist on the truth, — a matter quite as important."

M. COQUEREL said he must adhere to his expression "individualism." He vindicated the word as well as the thing. He thought Protestantism by no means a negative matter. It protested because outrages had been committed against truth and freedom, and this was a positive as well as a most salutary work.

The charm of M. Coquerel's discourse — fluently uttered in excellent English, and evidently showing full acquaintance with his subject — had strongly impressed the company, who would gladly have heard more. The session, though long, was a delightful one, and all who heard the distinguished Frenchman on this occasion were charmed with him.

XIX.

HEART IN RELIGION.

By JOHN WEISS.

IF the heart, Mr. WEISS said, has any function to discharge in religion, it must be such an organ as is not described in the anatomy of the sentimental theologians. The so-called feminine virtues may be admirable, if the alloy of valor tempers them; but does any organic connection exist between moods of feeling and a condition of religiousness? Must a person rise to ecstasy, rush into the rhetoric of sympathy, dissolve in tender devoutness, grovel in self-opprobrium, before he can claim to lead a divine life? Mr. Matthew Arnold has lately given a definition of religion, which he says is " ethics heightened, enkindled, lit up by feeling: it is morality touched by emotion." Mr. Arnold says we made an application of emotion to morality " by dwelling upon it, by staying our thoughts upon it, by having it perpetually in our mind." But one might as well expect to become poetical by brooding upon a poet's subjects, or scientific by revolving the details of discoveries. Like poetry, emotion is born, and cannot be made or imitated. It is an affair of temperament, and may be absent in Seneca and Epictetus, although they dwelt upon ethical subjects with all the substantial conviction which Paul clothed in more magnetic language. Religion cannot depend upon a surplus of imagination and poetic sensibility. Its pivot is not a dread of sin, and it

is very inadequately expressed by language that is highly
charged with remorse. For religion is simply the recognition of the facts and laws of facts which constitute a universe. Such a recognition may of course include a sense
that all these laws precede us, are beyond our personal
limits, and that health and gladness depend upon our conformity to them. If we conform, our act involves the very
essence of religion, whether our temperaments are stoical
or ardent. To be well, within and without, is to inhabit
the kingdom of God. But in the expression of the mind's
consciousness of God is a whole gamut, which runs from
the low grumble of the materialist to the soaring note of
the ecstatic ; and it is a bad habit to estimate religiousness
by expression instead of by the state of health. Technical
religious experiences, accesses of emotion, no more alter
the texture and character of the moral law in individuals
than these or other states of sentiment alter the nature of
counterpoint and harmony. Set half a dozen musical
people to play the same piece, and each one will lend to it
the color of his temperament, the *timbre* of his voice, the
manifoldness of his nature : the result will be the presentation of half a dozen different styles ; but the style does
not alter the substance. Expressions of regret, remorse,
of lively conviction of unworthiness, find their way into
spiritual books ; but a person who uses them aptly is no
more religious than any plain, sober, just man, with little
ardor of speech, or any cool sinner who deliberately sets
about reforming his habits and resuming healthy conditions. If the kingdom of heaven is exposed to being
taken by the scaling-ladder of warm and strong expression, I think that the New Bedford negro would have been
the first to enter, for he distanced all previous saints by a
simultaneous appeal to the infinite heart and pocket. In
a revival meeting that was rapidly running to hysteria,
he jumped up and cried : " Come down, O Lord, into dis

meetin'! Don't scrutinize de expense; come down right frou de roof. I'll pay for de shingles!" When religionists use the word "heart," it seems to represent to them the traits that distinguish a type of nature called womanly.

It is useless to argue that birth and constitution largely secure the presence or absence of this tone, so long as the beatitudes stand printed in every New Testament, and lend the glow of the word "blessed" to moods which have the credit of being full of heart. Now, the beatitude of right-eousness leaps well through human veins, but its source is human integrity. No man hungers after righteousness who has not the structure which gives him a sense of jus-tice. The beatitude of mercy is the complement of this righteousness. No man can be merciful who is not abso-lutely just. Mercy is the quality which we enjoy latest in life, for it corresponds to the development of the judgment. An old man is merciful because he is old : if he has not thrown away his opportunities for knowledge, his age is a dispassionate state into whose equilibrium all that he ever heard, suffered, or inflicted has settled. But what shall we say of the poor in spirit, and of the meek, and of the peacemakers? How did the Teacher himself. illustrate these texts? No man ever lived who had a more exact appreciation of his own moral and spiritual condition than Jesus. He never pretended that he was not vastly supe-rior to the average run of men, nor did any scruples of modesty detain him when he reminded them of his gifts. How, in fact, *could* he illustrate his first beatitude, if Nature had made him incapable of it by furnishing him with a sumptuous soul which knew and exulted in his own powers? "I and my Father are one," he says; and he expects to judge the dead, and distribute eternal rewards and punishments. Fastidious critics try to manipulate the scene in the temple, where a scourge of small cords seems to have been wielded with considerable muscular Christi-

anity, if we may trust the report that both men and cattle
evacuated the premises with cheerfulness. Some preachers
try to maintain that the Master merely flourished the
scourge, but was too gentle to strike a blow. However
that may have been, it is certain that his tongue could
inflict a chastisement compared with which a whipping
would have been luxurious. To the Scribes and Pharisees
he showed a face flushed with indignation, and meekness
did not prevent him from declaring them a generation of
vipers, or saying, "Ye are of your father, the Devil." We
need not be at the expense of any scheme of atonement to
account for the crucifixion. Every nail that was driven
was a speech tempered and sharpened in flaming moments
of the victim. For no man ever burst forth into such a
clear resistance to error and to the anarchy of bad institutions as this man of sorrows. The beatitude on the peacemakers stands modified by the more daring utterance of
the one who says he came to set the members of families
against each other, and to make divine truth the motive
which should introduce foes into the household. The life
of Jesus preached a more vigorous and salient doctrine
than the beatitudes, when his virile arms came to close
grips with pretence and bigotry. His mildness appears to
be hardly more than class sympathy with workmen and all
the takers of rich men's contemptuous wages. "Blessed
are ye," he said, "when men shall revile you and perse-
cute you." He would have repudiated that weak phrase
of ours, when we say in praise of a man, "He has not
an enemy in the world." Miserable man! He does not
then deserve to have a friend.

The only heart which religion can organically claim is of
a quality to subserve its organic laws, — those, namely,
which sustain the universal health, and found society upon
equality and justice. This is something better than pious
consciousness of a God; it is embodiment of one, — the

Word made flesh. God is in all men. He retires behind overturned omnibuses and piles of paving-stones, and proves capable of a wrath destructive as his own earthquakes and typhoons. *Here* is God, — in the next man and woman, gaunt as a wolf with famine, on a strike in coal-mines and factories, cowering wretchedly in the gutter.

> "He is the green in every blade,
>   The health in every boy and maid ;
> In yonder sunrise-flag he blooms
> Above a nation's well-earned tombs ;
> That empty sleeve his arm contains,
> That blushing scar his anger drains ;
> That flaunting cheek beneath the lamp
>   He hoists for succor, from a heart
> Where Love maintains a wasted camp
>   Till Love arrive to take its part.
> This bloodless face against the pane
>   Goes whitening all the murky street
> With his own dread lest hunger gain
>   Upon his love's woe-burdened feet."

Rev. J. T. Sargent invited M. Coquerel to open the discussion. Monsieur remarked, with his French accent which gives charm and piquancy to whatever he says, that he understood English best when he spoke it himself. He found himself lagging behind often during the essay, — not quick-winged enough to follow through heaven and earth and all the universe. First, he had thought the lecturer's plan was to accuse heart, and he said, "No, we would not be dissected, and have our hearts taken away. Heart must defend itself." He thought next that injustice was being done to the beatitudes. We could not spare any of them. They must stand all together, as in the New Testament, and then they go through the whole range of life, and one is the supplement of the other. We had the mild and meek Jesus in the beginning, and the man of sorrows in the end. We have had much analysis, and now we want a little synthesis. When we find in monkish books an effeminate Jesus, we will not worship *him:* but we find the Jesus of the Gospels a *man*, and we like to see meek and mild Jesus able to use a scourge of small cords. Love for the poor and the lowly is the same thing as rage against tyrants and sycophants. One must be on the track of everything good, and then he will always see Jesus walking before him.

Rev. CHARLES BROOKS hoped that M. Coquerel would now understand how Americans feel when in Paris, listening to a French lecture. If he thought Mr. Weiss's discourse was rapid, he hardly knew how he would characterize that of a Frenchman. This created a good deal of amusement, as M. Coquerel had spoken with great fluency.

Mr. SUMNER, in answer to a call for his opinion, remarked that he had come as a listener, — had come from one of the outposts, and was glad to find himself among the leaders.

Dr. HEDGE said he had never listened to Mr. Weiss when he felt himself so much at one with him in sentiment; but he must entirely dissent from the speaker's definition of religion as recognition of the facts of the universe. Religion is not a recognition of facts, not a form of intellectual statement, but a feeling. It seemed to him a misfortune when Christianity was apprehended merely as a religion : it is more than a religion ; it is the divinely-appointed and progressive incarnation of God in society. Morality appeared to him of more importance than religion. The best that religion can do is to vivify morals, even as it is the inspiring soul of art and of patriotism. He had seldom been so pleased with a presentation of Christ as with that given this morning. But he did not think the

10

beatitude of the poor in spirit referred to those conscious of spiritual poverty, but to the outcasts of the religious world, the unchurched of that day and generation. Christ invites those whom the Scribes and Pharisees reject.

Mrs. HOWE said that the essay made her feel like asking Mr. Weiss with whom was his controversy. There was a martial spirit in it, and it seemed to her poetical without the peace of poetry. She was not satisfied with Dr. Hedge's definition of religion. Perhaps that was a man's definition; but, to her, religion was something more than a feeling of less value than morality, whose best work was to vivify morals.

Dr. J. F. CLARKE wished to endorse all that had been said concerning the masculinity of Christ. All paintings of him had failed to express him, through weakness. We are yet too far behind Christ to comprehend him. We shall have better pictures of him when the world catches up with him. For the "blessed" in the beatitudes he would substitute "good news." And he thought the good news was not for the "unchurched" alone, but for the sinners, for the utterly poor in spirit. He believed religion was more than a recognition of the facts of the universe: it was the aspiration of the whole nature toward something higher than itself, toward the highest of which it can conceive.

Mr. WASSON next expressed his approbation of the change from the minor to the major key in religion. Mr. Beecher, he said, had published the first volume of a Life of Christ, the frontispiece to which was doubtless the Christ of *his* admiration; but it looked like a discarded lover suffering the pangs of unrequited sentiment. He thought it was time to set forth the virtues of power and vigor, and to distinguish principle from emotion. In the last portion of the essay, it seemed to him, Mr. Weiss himself slipped into sentimentality. In one sense God might

be everywhere, — in grog-shops and slums and scamps ;
so He might be in the rattlesnake, which we do not hesitate to rap on the head.   He had a friend who believed
that God loves every man but a good man ; but to his
thinking the Divine Mind does not necessarily prefer the
evil, or even the poor.

Mr. WASHBURN followed with a word of sympathy for
the " churched" people.   If we recognize God in a hungry
highwayman, we must also recognize him in a well-fed
priest ; and he thought God was at a minimum in the
scoundrel, and at a maximum in the one man who seemed
to him, so far, the crown of humanity, — Jesus Christ.

Mr. AMES, from California, avowed a faith as wide as
the great country from which he came.   He believed, he
said, in everything and everybody.   Surely, neither Pagan
nor Christian could ask more.   There was yet need for the
word " heart," to express the provision of Nature for spiritual warmth.   Action was at present the glorious idol of
glorious Boston ; but we must not lose sight of the
warmth-giver, or cease our quest for the point of contact
between God and man.

Mr. POTTER thought that we needed a second essay to
balance this one, — an essay on the claims of the religious
sentiment.   It certainly had its place, and we can none
of us withhold a sympathetic admiration from the old
mystics.

Mr. WENDELL PHILLIPS wished, with great respect and
deference, to maintain that the character of Jesus was
no mystery.   " You need not analyze a lemon to find out
whether it is sour.   You speculate as to whether Jesus
was a masculine character !   Look at the men who have
learned of him most closely, — at Paul and Luther and
Wesley.   Were they effeminate? yet the disciple is but
a faint reflection of his Master.   The character from which
came the force which has been doing battle ever since

with wrong and falsehood and error was nothing less than masculine; but sentiment is the toughest thing in the world, — nothing else is iron.   And, in spite of friend Wasson, Jesus was right in pitying the poor in pocket, the burden-bearers, the takers of other men's wages. Compulsory labor *is* a curse — always has been."

Mr. WASSON protested against the injustice of leaving Mr. Phillips the last word; but the time was up, and it appeared

> " He heard a voice we could not hear,
>   Which said he must not stay."

XX.

THE PRAYER-GAUGE.

By CYRUS A. BARTOL.

DR. BARTOL'S subject was suggested by Prof. Tyndall's much-talked-about proposition to subject the
use of prayer to an experimental scientific test. "Does
prayer," asked Dr. Bartol, "make any difference? I think
yes, if the asking be genuine. Not by praying against
law. . . . This great world were an arrested development
but for the appearance on it of the human actor to dom-
inate the rest. He brings into existence new species of
plants by his fostering; he sails over seas; he is the exponent of the uses of the world, the illustrator of its
beauty. It is man who makes of pigments, pictures; of
marble, statues; he is a co-creator, and in the accomplishment of his designs he finds the answer to his prayers.
Luther was right, — to have labored is to have prayed. The
whole of Nature, from protoplasm to man, is forever climb-
ing higher; and what is this perpetual aspiration but a perpetual prayer? . . . Science cannot stop prayer, because
there is no final statement of laws; and the scientist is but a
provisional bishop, even in his own realm. Mr. Mill thinks
that not only morals but mathematics may be different in
some other world. We are cognizant only of phenomena.
There are no provable properties of matter without mind;
without seeing there is no light; without hearing, no sound.
The sun and moon are our servants, to be dismissed when we

can be better served; and our own aim at perfection is as much a law as the starry attraction, — our sense of duty a higher law, indeed a moral gravitation, to hold though the bands of Orion be loosed. Every struggle after purer living, to cleanse our own hearts, or to purify a State, is prayer. But prayer which is not a want, but a wish for private gain, not public good, is spent on the air, and must pass by God as the idle wind which he regards not. The real appeal to the Most High is no impertinent presuming on a violation of his statutes, which are himself in motion; it is a reaching toward Him, to flout which — on the ground of an everlasting title in the fleeting phenomena around us to be the recognized order of the universe — is the part of a shallow brain. No prayer-gauge can reach these deep-sea soundings. True prayer is an act of faith, which has warrant to act as much as any sense or organ. It is an experiment according to eternal commandment, which must succeed. Luther was right in saying, 'God, thou must hear me!' for prayer is a power which constrains God, were not his law his freedom. With prayer God has complicity; it is an address to the throne moved by the king.

"As to the experiment proposed in the hospital-wards, it is hard to see how it could be instituted, like a chemical one, under all the conditions requisite to an indubitable result. Can any philosophy ultimately declare the laws of health and disease so conclusively as to exclude the possibility that part and parcel of them may not be that mixture of divine and human will which we call prayer, though any attempt to appropriate or pervert its virtue to special, private use might be like the vain and impious offer of Simon Magus to buy the Holy Ghost? The Lord's Prayer has been as real a power in the world as that which raised the Alps or scooped out the bed of the Atlantic. Without consideration of the nature of the Being to whom we pray there can be no true prayer. 'Hath not the potter power,' said a Calvinistic mother to her free-thinking son, ' over the clay, to make one vessel to honor and another to dishonor?' 'Madam,' was the reply, ' God is not a potter.' Neither is he a trader, selling so much blessing for so much entreaty. No delusion is blessed. Fear of the truth is unbelief. In the ' Confessions of a Beautiful Soul,' Goethe writes that some champions of religion require examples of prayer actually heard. ' But,' says the Fair Saint, as Carlyle translates, ' how unknown to such persons must the true feeling be! I never returned empty when in straits and oppression I called on God.'"

The discussion which followed was quite an animated one. The Rev. SAMUEL LONGFELLOW thought that the prayer-gauge proposition referred only to prayer for physical results ; and this seemed not to be prayer at all to those who understood the word in its deeper meaning of spiritual aspiration. "We can each of us tell what prayer does for us, and we know whether or not it is a need of our natures. The truest prayer is that which offers ourselves as channels for the divine will."

A stranger present spoke with much feeling in favor of actual petitions for direct and recognizable ends. To disbelieve in the efficacy of such prayer would be, he thought, to abandon ourselves to fatalism. It should not be the descendants of the Puritans, who settled these shores that they might pray here in such wise as it pleased them, who should esteem prayer of small account. Had the men who had accomplished great things in the world been praying men, or had they not?

To this WILLIAM LLOYD GARRISON replied that the old notion of prayer seemed to him a libel on God, — as if he needed something to stir him up ; as if it were not enough for him to know our needs. He had never, in his long strug-

gle against American slavery, thought of praying to God to
abolish it: the task of abolition belonged to the American
people. If there is danger of fatalism on the one hand, is
there not danger of superstition and credulity on the other?
Is there anything uncertain in God, that we should ask
him to change his appointments? How dare the mother
pray that her child may live? Why her child more than
another's? Why not accept sickness, accept death, accept
loss, — this lesson to-day, another to-morrow, as seems
good to the Great Disposer? Assuming that God is infinitely good, infinitely wise, why not assume that, uncon-
strained by our entreaties, he will of himself do the best he
can? What have we to ask save the good-will, of which
already we are assured if God be omniscient and omni-
present? What is there of need or of desire which we can
communicate to him? Just in proportion as we sit in
darkness do we indulge in vain repetitions. If we have
already received the power of locomotion, do we need to
ask God to enable us to walk?

To this the Rev. E. B. WILSON made answer: "It is
vain if it pour, and my cup is bottom side up: with what
draught shall I quench my thirst? Prayer is my struggle
to get my cup right side up. And the mother's ' God
bless you!' and the friend's ' God help you!' will be, as
long as humanity lasts, the soul's instinctive cry to a God
in whose ability to hear and answer prayer it will never
cease to believe."

Mr. POWELL expressed his cordial assent to the belief
that prayer is a deep and, for the most part, silent communion of the soul with God, and related two or three
beautiful incidents illustrating the powerful influence of
silence; adding that it seemed to him the office of silence
in the Quaker form of worship found no substitute in the
much-talking of other religious sects at all comparable
with it as an agency for purifying the heart, ennobling
the aims, and strengthening the purpose.

Mrs. ABBY KELLEY FOSTER spoke of doing the Master's will as a means of coming to a knowledge of his attributes. Metaphysical speculations about the divine character have their place ; but she believed whoever went about among men, entirely devoted and self-consecrated to the work of doing them good, seeking the poor, the tempted, and the sorrowing, as Jesus did, would be more sure of growing into sympathy with God's heart and coming to an understanding of his will than by any other process.

XXI.

PANTHEISM.

By F. H. HEDGE.

PANTHEISM is a name of bad repute in theology, where it passes for something akin to Atheism, and a good deal more dangerous. The doctrine is of ancient origin, and many noble souls have held it boldly. In 1720 the English deist, Toland, in a defence of Pantheism, expressed his faith in a " God, the creative and ruling power of the universe, distinguished by reason alone from the universe itself." If this statement of Pantheism be accepted, we have in it a theory discriminated from Theism proper by the immanence in Nature of the Supreme Power, but not less widely separated from Atheism by the acknowledgment of a power to which the title of God is applied. Toland, so far as we know, was the first to assume the name of Pantheist, but he was by no means the first who held the pantheistic faith. Nor does his definition embrace all the varieties of views which might, with equal propriety, be designated as Pantheism. The Pantheist Schelling declared that the Pantheists, so far from maintaining, as has been asserted, that the sum of sensible objects is God, contend that the very reason of their being objects of sense is their privation of Deity. Giordano Bruno, unquestionably a Pantheist, distinctly acknowledges God as the author of Nature, which, he maintains, must have had a beginning and a cause. He calls Nature the mirror in which God is imaged. Scotus Erigena, that wonderful intellect which lighted the ninth century, is commonly regarded as a Pantheist; but he constantly and earnestly enforced the distinction between created and uncreated. Even Spinoza emphasizes causality in God, and distinguishes between the infinite and the finite. Pantheism is theistic, not atheistic, in its conception of cause and effect. It puts the universe as secondary, as effect; and God as primary, as cause. It confesses a God super-mundane, but not extra-mundane. And here comes in one principal point of difference between Theism and Pantheism.

The popular Theism supposes a God existing outside of the universe which he has made, — a Creator who once in time called a universe into being, and has been ever since a spectator and director of its on-goings, having no substantial connection with it, but only a providential and governmental one. The God of Pantheism is immanent, interfused, all-penetrating, the ground of all dependence, the life of all life. It is true that the view of many unquestioned Theists coincides with this pantheistic conception of Deity. But this is only one stage. That which really and fundamentally distinguishes Pantheism, as represented by Spinoza, from Theism, as usually understood, is not the doctrine of the *one substance*, but the doctrine of the *one sole agent*, — the denial of any other agency than that of the one God, as well in the spiritual as in the phenomenal world. Spinoza not only denies freedom of will to man, but denies to man substantial existence. He considers the human mind to be part of the infinite intellect of God; so that when we say the human mind perceives this or that, we say nothing else but that God, not in his infinity, but as explained by the nature of the human mind, or as constituting the essence of the human mind, has this or that idea. In other words, there *is* no such entity as the human mind or soul: what we call such is but a thought of God. We accordingly find it a marked distinction between Theism and Pantheism, that the latter does not at all recognize that attribute of Deity which Theism expresses by the term " Lord." The God of Pantheism is in no sense Lord, for he has no intelligent subjects, the mind or soul of man being only one of his own thoughts. But to the Theist godhead is lordship. Therefore it appears that, however the theistic and pantheistic conceptions of God in Nature might be harmonized, their conceptions of man and his relations to God must remain wide asunder. The one sees in man a moral agent, the other an irresponsible expression of divinity.

Spinoza is the typical exponent of Pantheism. His system, given to the world two hundred years ago, remains to this day the most thorough and complete of all pantheistic statements. His influence upon thought has been immense. To him Goethe owed more than to any other mind, and acknowledged his obligations with enthusiastic gratitude. Schleiermacher, in his discourses on Religion, bids us sacrifice reverently to the manes of the holy outcast, Spinoza, who was full of religion and of the Holy Ghost. Spinoza's ontology supposes a single and whole substance, comprising all that is, and of which all phenomena and all finite existences are modes and affections. Therefore he is said to have turned the Devil out of the world. There is no room for his Satanic Majesty in a universe which is all an expression of God. He says that in the nature of things nothing is contingent, but all things are determined from the necessity of the divine nature to a certain mode of existence and operation. You perceive this takes away all idea of the free agency of man, and, theoretically, all human responsibility. " Experience as well as reason teaches," he affirms, " that men believe they are free only because they are conscious of their actions, and ignorant of the causes by which they are determined." The great weakness of Pantheism, as expressed by Spinoza, consists in the relaxation of the moral sense consequent on refer- ring all action, good or bad, to God as the one immediate and direct cause of all. Its great strength is the quick- ened sense it gives us of the all-pervading and immediate presence of God. It has changed the divine omnipres- ence from a cold and unmeaning dogma to a fact of con- sciousness. Thus it has given to Nature a new soul. Wordsworth is the truest exponent of this sentiment among the English poets. In all Greek literature there is nothing which embodies it. Greeks and Romans painted no landscapes like ours, suggestive of mystery within and beyond. The soul of Nature is interpreted by Pantheism. But Pantheism and Theism are not of necessity contradic- tory terms : they should be complementary. Theism gives us the Holy Person, the providential care, the moral will ; Pantheism gives us the diffused presence, the all-pervading life, the divine nearness in the outspread landscape. To Pantheism belongs the world of nature ; to Theism, the world of spirits.

_____

Mr. WEISS endorsed Dr. Hedge's statement that the Greek mind did not know what a landscape was. The only pantheistic ideas of which we find any trace in antiquity were Egyptian. Their " Phanes " meant emanation, but it was an isolated idea in Egypt, and when it was translated into Greek it became Pan, merely a rural deity. To Socrates there was nothing in a plane-tree but its shadow. Before Theocritus, and thence down to Dante, you can find no such thing as the projection of human moods upon Nature. The Greeks vexed Nature with personalities, in- deed gave to every tree its dryad ; but they split with the prism of plurality the pure, white light of its unity. Music itself was only born into the world when Synthesis was born.

The sense of the interfusion of Nature with God is modern. Not only did Spinoza turn the Devil out of the world, he exploded also the old idea that long ago God packed into germs the potentialities of all that has happened since, and then withdrew himself into vacancy. Spinoza shows that the creative spirit is present every moment, — God is always in the process.

Mr. WASSON was glad to have Spinoza appreciated, but he himself had always felt a certain want in him, — a linear character in all his speculations. He did not know about so projecting God into all things that we left no margin for resistance. It seemed to him quite impossible to reconcile with our idea of God the direct derivation from him of canker-worm and cobra, or of all the evil which we see in ourselves and others. The opposition which has to be overcome by God is the real Devil, and Spinoza has not yet turned that out of the universe. Every organism in the world is a victory, and is assailed at ten thousand points by agents looking toward its destruction. There were always the struggle and the overcoming.

Mr. WEISS thought that there must be antithesis, and the Divine Mind conceived it in the first place; the struggle and the overcoming are part of the divine plan.

Dr. HEDGE said that a boy coasting down hill wanted a long hill. There must be history, and it must have length of days and years for its making. To the adequate idea of things there can be no evil.

Mr. WASSON thought that at any rate there was something to be overcome, and plenty to do.

Mrs. MOTT said she had been thinking of a remark made by Dr. Hedge very long ago, at a Unitarian Convention in Philadelphia,—that Unitarians must be true to themselves in the expression of their convictions. It was at a time when she had great need of the strength which would enable her to disregard the condemnation of others, — just after the

Hicksites, as they were called, had been cut off from their brethren. She learned then how fiercely people could do battle for words and formulas. The heathen make graven images: we make verbal ones, and we worship as ardently as they. Truth is one in all ages; and always the *listening* soul can hear the still, small voice. The trouble is that we do not listen.

Mr. FROTHINGHAM adverted to the general impression that Pantheism weakens the conscience and destroys the moral sense. The antithesis between good and evil seemed to him a necessary part of the education of mankind. One can do nothing without encountering obstacles. Let one's theories be ever so pantheistic, still the struggle will go on, and still the man of conscience will resist temptation. The good man will find stimulus for right doing in his creed, be that creed what it may. But if a man's conscience be lax, could anything more surely arouse him than the sense of the ever-present God, — the God not far off but near at hand, all in all? Pantheism is a religious idea. The great mystics have all been Pantheists, as the great poets are Pantheists. The great sweep of the affections toward God demands that he should not be a being whom we can measure — his outlines should fade into mist. Then you set him flowing in the universe, and all religions have windows which open to those all-governing skies. Americans are more pantheistic than other peoples, because their sympathies are more general and quicker.

Mr. LONGFELLOW said the essay had carried him back twenty-five years, to a time when he, with other students, used to walk into town to hear Dr. Walker talk about Pantheism. He remembered the doctor's saying: " What do men mean by calling those Atheists who believe in nothing but God? But if you ask me if Pantheism is less dangerous than Atheism, I answer, No, it is a great deal more dangerous, for it takes away the sense of moral responsibility."

But there is a pantheistic conception of God which brings
him so close that we feel him everywhere.   It is the ideal
tendency which inclines us toward Pantheism; and the
Americans incline to it more readily than the English, because they are a more ideal people.

WENDELL PHILLIPS hereupon protested against our judging men by their theories.   Theoretically Calvinism dis-
penses with works; but where do we find a higher standard of morals or better works than among the Calvinists?
While human nature is capable of a feeling of remorse —
as if, having a will, one might have done right and had
done wrong — we shall not be able to put aside a sense
of personal responsibility, or to turn the devil out of
doors.   Spinoza gives no theory which explains away the
fact of suffering, and he had seen suffering which he felt
sure was unmitigated evil.

The conversation closed with a final protest from Dr.
BARTOL against this notion of unmitigated evil.   He thinks
belief in any essential evil, in any fatality of everlasting pain, is philosophically inconsistent with our belief
in God; and he believes that human nature is incapable
of doing a thing which God cannot utilize for good.

XXII.

ECONOMIC LAWS.

By DAVID A. WELLS.

THE HON. DAVID A. WELLS'S essay on the relation of economic laws to public and private morality sharply opposed the present economic legislation of the country. The essay did not lack in stinging epithets wherewith to characterize what seems abominable in the opinion of the essayist. The grouping of thought is unusual, and covers a wide field of history, though the pernicious moral influence of statutes which violate economic laws is not a new conception. The distress of England pecuniarily and her rottenness morally, for the several hundred years she was under the system of guilds, apprenticeship, and navigation laws, was the theme of the first part of the paper, and the effect of internal revenue and tax laws in this country was the subject of the closing pages. What was said about our noble Revolutionary fathers, so exalted in modern esteem, must have surprised those who are not accustomed to think of them as chronic smugglers and law-breakers; but the facts show their human nature, and the listeners seemed to like the rascals (speaking, of course, as a royal revenue officer would have done) all the better for their contempt of law when it interfered with economically legitimate money-making.

Dr. HEDGE expressed dissent from the estimate placed on Adam Smith's "Wealth of Nations," and from the judgment that the Golden Rule, "Do ye unto others as ye would that others do unto you," has an economic significance, and that the full purport of the precept is not grasped till it is interpreted by an enlightened selfishness. When the selfish element becomes a motive, the rule ceases to be moral.

Next was Mr. WENDELL PHILLIPS, and before he ceased the clash of opposing doctrines and the earnestness of positive natures made the discussion singularly entertaining. Mr. Phillips stated first his disbelief in the free-trade doctrine, though he held that creed fifteen years ago. He had been misled by the theoretical arguments in favor of free trade, but had been set right by hearing the facts as stated by Mr. Henry Cary, the patriarch of political economy, to whose judgment the world listens. He had heard Mr. Cary say: "I had just finished a crushing reply to the New England tariff men, — one that I thought demolished their whole structure of argument. I went to bed delighted with my success in stating my case. Somehow I could not help seeing that, though the logic seemed perfect, it did not cover the facts. On paper it was all right; out in the world the facts were the other way. I lay awake all night, chewing on the contradiction, and arose the next morning a tariff man." Any one who listened from Cary's lips to the stern facts which converted him in that night of anxious, honest thought would never again be duped by free trade.

Nations are large enough, Mr. Phillips thinks, to be considered separately from each other. Internal industry should be diversified. Under free-trade rule our country would be wholly agricultural. Other elements must be considered besides the mere question of wealth. Should we lose our diversified occupations, we should suffer a great loss, though there might be a pecuniary gain. Nations might gain the whole world — that is, half the mate-

rial wealth of the world — and yet lose their own souls
and most of their bodies too. Theories are pleasing things,
and seem to get rid of all difficulties so very easily. One
must begin with abstract principles, and study them.
But wisdom consists in perceiving when human nature
and this perverse world necessitate making exceptions to
abstract truths. Any boy can see an abstract principle.
Only threescore years and ten can discern precisely when
and where it is well, necessary, and right to make an *exception* to it. That faculty is wisdom, all the rest is playing with counters. And this explains how the influx into
politics of a shoal of college-boys, slenderly furnished with
Greek and Latin, but steeped in marvellous and delightful
ignorance of life and public affairs, is wrecking the Republican party.

National lines — *artificial* lines — trip up fine theories
sadly. If all the world were under one law, and every man
raised to the level of the Sermon on the Mount, free
trade would be so easy and so charming! But while
nations study only how to cripple their enemies, — that is,
their neighbors, — and while each trader strives to cheat
his customer and strangle the firm on the other side of the
street, we must not expect the millennium.

From this point Mr. Phillips proceeded to state how
he would get protection without the arbitrary laws which
Mr. Wells denounced, and unfolded his well-known views
upon paper currency, by which money enough for business
can be borrowed for two or three per cent. Mr. Wells
asked him how it is that interest here is now seven per
cent, and Mr. Phillips promised to answer him a little further on, and explained his theory of using the credit of
the Government as the basis of the currency.

"The next presidential election," said Mr. Phillips, "will
turn to a great extent on the currency question. If the
South can be broken into natural divisions and brought to

behave decently, the currency will be the *only* great question. The next step of the Democracy will be to establish the greenback system."

"It will be worthy of it" [the Democracy], keenly interrupted Mr. WASSON, and his sally was received with laughter and applause by the unsympathizers.

"Yes," said Mr. PHILLIPS, "it *will* be the *first* work needed by a *true Democratic* party. For this greenback question only means whether we shall trust the Declaration of Independence — that all men are equal in money matters, as in everything else. Hitherto we have been Tories in money questions, and trusted the people only in other matters. July 4, 1776, said: 'The sober second thought of the *people* is the safest and best guide in all civil affairs, — personal rights, property, marriage, crimes and all. And we can devise machinery which will secure that sober second thought.'

"We have been living successfully and prosperously for a hundred years on that plan and platform, with one exception, — money matters. In those, capitalists, bank directors, and a select class have been thought to be the only safe guides. The people now claim that they can and will decide these as wisely and honestly as they do all other matters. This is the last fight between wealth and the people, — not between noble and serf, but between money-bags and the workingmen; between the men who create wealth and those who steal a living by the hocus-pocus of banking and the nonsense of coin. The people will now carry the Declaration of Independence into Wall Street, where it has never yet penetrated, and we shall have a more honest finance than the world has yet seen."

Mr. WELLS retorted, "We are the most dishonest nation on the face of the globe."

"No," said Mr. PHILLIPS, "not the most dishonest *nation*. Perhaps ours has been of late as dishonest an administration as the world often sees, — not the fault of the masses, but of the capitalists. Three times within a dozen years, capitalists, with their knives on the throat of the Government, have compelled it to cheat its largest creditor, the people; whose claim, Burke said, was the most sacred. First, the pledge that greenbacks should be exchangeable with bonds was broken. Secondly, debts originally payable in paper, as Sherman confessed in the Senate, were made payable in coin. Thirdly, silver was demonetized, and gold made the only tender. A thousand million dollars were thus stolen from the people. These are the crimes of capital: the people are honest enough if left to themselves."

To one who doubted this *popular* virtue. Mr. PHILLIPS replied: "Never expect heaven in Boston. I never said that a democracy was a *good* government. A thing may be the *best* we can get, and yet not be *good*. Democracy is not a good government, but it is the best we can get while we have only this poor, rotten human nature to work with. Governments created by the people have always been more honest and less corrupt than those originating with the aristocracy, and revolutions made by the people have generally been more merciful and less bloody than the victories of the upper classes. No student of European history can fail to see this."

Mr. Phillips's enthusiastic advocacy of his scheme of abolishing all coin, and issuing two thousand million dollars (an amount equal to the national debt), based on the thirty thousand millions of property of the country, so that interest should never be more than five per cent, was welcomed with much good-natured laughter, which betrayed no sign of a new convert to greenbackism.

Mr. WELLS replied to the so-called facts of Henry Cary, that he had once looked upon Mr. Cary as his Gamaliel, had been very intimate with him, and was brought up as a protectionist; but he found Mr. Cary's facts were no facts, and he became a free-trader perforce. He has repeatedly challenged Mr. Cary to public discussion, and has received only abuse in reply. More sparks were struck from each side, and Mr. Wells declared he hoped the question would go into the next presidential campaign, as Mr. Phillips said it would, and he wished that they two could meet in public discussion, and see which was right. He would be glad to meet Mr. Phillips on the platform.

So the warfare of words raged bravely and profitably, if public discussion for popular enlightenment shall be the outcome. A few other gentlemen spoke briefly, and the company dispersed, after a sitting of more than two and a half hours.

XXIII.

QUAKERISM.

By A. M. POWELL.

THE following is a synopsis of Mr. POWELL's paper:
The distinctive doctrine of Quakerism is the affirmation of "the immediate teaching and influence of the Holy Spirit" in the human soul. It has no elaborately-wrought creed, or articles of faith. Among Friends there is a general unity of belief concerning the immediate teaching of the Spirit, but a diversity of opinion in relation to other points of doctrine.

Inheriting a birthright-membership among Friends, I was early interested in their simple, humanitarian phase of religious life. But introduced in boyhood to the anti-slavery movement, and largely absorbed by it through the intervening years to the hour of its glorious consummation, I have had little interest in merely *sectarian* religion, except to relax its hold upon men and women. Added years only serve, however, to strengthen my faith in the fundamental doctrine which distinguishes Quakerism, and my admiration for the more important features of its historical record. The estimate of the human capacity which the doctrine of the "Inner Light" necessitates is an exalted one. It should be our business to lift all humanity up to the level of immediate, conscious communication and fellowship with God. This has been pre-eminently the mission of Quakerism. The capacity to receive the "im-

mediate teaching and influence of the Holy Spirit" is not
limited to the ministry or the membership of Friends, but
is as universal as human nature.   Acting upon this belief,
Friends have borne a most honorable and successful part
in almost every great practical missionary and benevolent
enterprise of the past two hundred years.   Even with untutored savages, where others fail, they have been enabled
to establish peaceful, harmonious relations.   Each in their
way recognize the common spiritual Fatherhood, and respect each other's individual rights.   Nearer, probably,
than any other denomination of professed Christians have
Friends, judged by their fruits, practically embodied the
Christian ideal.

One whose words are weighty in this circle somewhere
mentions Quakerism as " the lengthened shadow of George
Fox."   That this shadow has had more substance than
shadows are usually supposed to possess, I shall hope to
make apparent.   George Fox appeared at a time when the
reign of externalism in matters pertaining to religion was
well-nigh supreme.   He was born in 1624, at Drayton, in
Leicestershire, England.   Even in his minority he exhibited a gravity and staidness of mind "seldom seen in
children."   It was proposed to make a priest of him, but
he was finally apprenticed to a shoemaker, who was also a
dealer in cattle.   He often used in his dealings the word
"verily," and then kept so strictly to it that people who
knew him would say, "If George says 'Verily,' there is
no altering him."   He was remarkable, at eleven years
of age, for questions and conversation concerning religious
matters.   At eighteen and nineteen his mind became much
exercised.   He was greatly oppressed by the outward,
superficial, and corrupt type of religion which prevailed
among his associates.   He sought counsel of priests, but
only to become still more perplexed by what each clerical interview revealed to him.   Once he went to a distinguished

priest in Warwickshire, and talked with him about the ground of despair and temptation; but the only consolation the priest could offer was to bid him "*take tobacco and sing psalms.*" He sought still another, of great reputation, for light upon the problems which oppressed him, and this priestly physician, we are told, was for giving Fox some "physic, and for bleeding him." He had other kindred interviews and disappointments. After much striving with himself, he at last saw clearly, as he was walking alone by himself in a field on a First-day morning, that merely to be bred at Oxford or Cambridge was not enough to make a man a minister. Thereafter, greatly to the distress of his worthy and respectable family connections, he refused to go to church and to listen to the priests whom he had spiritually weighed and found wanting. He would go into the orchard or the fields by himself, and with his Bible seek the light which he had failed to get from others. There were at this time dissenters from the Established Church, but they also were equally powerless to afford him spiritual enlightenment. Again, as he was walking alone in the fields, he saw that though priests and people were wont to call their churches holy places, temples of God, etc., that "God, who made the world, did not dwell in temples made with hands, but rather in the hearts of his people." These were to him new, radical, important conceptions of fundamental truth. At this juncture his old family priest, named Stephens, became afraid of Fox, "*for going after new lights.*" Fox now had many more revelations. He dwelt much alone by himself, apart from his relatives and friends, that his mind might not be unduly biased and distracted. He passed many sleepless nights, and would spend whole days in solitary walks and sitting in a hollow tree, studying the lessons of the Bible and meditating upon the problems of life. After much tribulation many things which had

been obscure became clear to his understanding, doubts
which had perplexed him disappeared, and he became
filled with light, and possessed of a sweet peacefulness of
spirit inexpressibly precious. His work as a reformer
then began in real earnest. Of course he became a thorn
in the side of the priesthood, and shocked, as he would to-
day, both priests and church-people by his want of reverence for what they deemed sacred offices and sacred places.
He never joined any church, but gave himself to following
the "Inward Light." He diligently sought out the poor
and suffering, and did much to alleviate their sorrows. It
is somewhat singular to note, in view of the present prominence of the Woman's Rights reform, that one of the first
of the "odd notions," then prevalent in England, which
George Fox felt called upon to combat was that "*women
had no souls*"!

In some things he was doubtless narrow-minded; but
as his minor peculiarities are forgotten, he will be remembered in history as a far-seeing, comprehensive reformer.
William Howitt pays him a merited tribute in the "West-
minster Review," wherein he says: "On almost all those
great questions of civil and religious polity, which the
world is now coming to a late discussion of, he made up
his mind at once, and, as at one splendid leap, vaulted
across the broad morass of the errors and sophistries of
ages."

Quakerism had its martyr period. The legend of "Cas-
sandra Southwick," and more recently the "New England
Tragedies," have told the painful story in modern phrase,
reminding those who read of the great cost at which our
present religious freedom has been purchased, and teaching anew the always timely lesson of toleration. The
persecution was more wholesale in England, but, if possible, more violent in New England. Some idea of its
extent in England may be gained from Sewall's statement

that there were upwards of four thousand two hundred
Quakers, both men and women, crowded in the English
prisons at one time! Many of these had been grievously
beaten, or their clothes torn or taken away from them;
many were confined in dungeons indescribably loathsome.
Some of the prisons were crowded so full of both men and
women that there was not room for all even to sit down.
There were ear-croppings, burnings, and all imaginable
methods of torture, and hundreds of deaths in consequence.
But in this astonishing record of cruelty and persecution
for opinion's sake New England has a bad pre-eminence,
and Boston especially so. It seems incredible, to-day,
that Bostonians could ever have been so extensively
engaged in imprisoning, whipping, starving, and hanging
innocent, devout women and men. Think of a vagrant
law in Massachusetts, under which, if a Quaker was found
in Boston, no matter what the errand, — even if, as in the
case of Edward Wharton, to visit a sick friend, — he or
she might be arrested, imprisoned, and punished by the
lash on the naked body. Nor was this statute a dead letter.
For such a visit in this city to a sick friend Wharton was
arrested, and by order of Gov. Endicott was led to the
market-place, stripped and bound to a cart-wheel, and
punished with thirty lashes. So cruelly was the punishment inflicted that, as was testified, "peas might lie in
the holes that the knots of the whip had made in the flesh
of his back and arms." That was puritan Boston two
hundred years ago! Many others endured kindred sufferings, women not less than men. I need not more than
allude to the case of Mary Dyer, — a true and noble
woman, — whose only offence was pleading the cause of
religious freedom, and who was hanged in Boston by order
of Gov. Endicott. Her brave, serene death finds a modern parallel only in John Brown.

The New England Puritans were here themselves in

quest of religious freedom; but their cruel and murderous treatment of the Quakers illustrates how limited were their notions of religious freedom, and how effective was the more simple Quaker doctrine concerning matters of religion in disturbing and overturning sectarian bigotry here, as also in England.

To judge a tree, or a religious movement, by the fruit it yields is a safe rule.   Quakerism has produced few books; its literature is limited in extent; it has few Biblical commentaries; theological seminaries and ministerial colleges are to it wholly unknown: but its record in the sphere of good works, for the amelioration and improvement of the condition of mankind, challenges comparison.

On going forth as a religious teacher, George Fox indicated to the people that it was one of their first duties to deal justly and kindly with servants.   On the subject of Slavery, he was not led at once to announce the doctrine of immediate emancipation;   that was left for Elizabeth Heyrick, at a later date.   Such was the character, however, of the preaching in the early Friends' meetings, by Fox and others, that the slaveholders of Barbadoes, as early as 1676, moved by the slaveholder's shrewd instinct, were so much alarmed as to make a law to prevent the attendance of negroes at these meetings.

Clarkson, in speaking of his preaching against negro slavery in the West Indies, says, "Thus was George Fox probably the first person who publicly declared against this species of slavery."   Clarkson, who was not himself a Friend, also pays to Friends a most hearty, affectionate tribute for their faithful and generous help in the anti-slavery and anti-slavetrade struggle in England.   In our own country, antedating any other antislavery record here so far as I know, Elihu Coleman and other Friends in Nantucket, as early as 1716–20, and Friends in Pennsylvania at about the same or a little later date, commenced the preliminary labor within the Society which ended in making it a disciplinary offence for a Friend to own or hire a slave, and incorporated it as a standing counsel to Friends in the Book of Discipline to abstain from the use or purchase of anything wrought by the labor of slaves. In this struggle within the Society John Woolman bore an important part. His influence was felt also beyond the limits of the Society of which he was a member. When, in the future, the comprehensive history of the great conflict between freedom and slavery is adequately written, Woolman will be recognized as one of the most conscientious, effective, self-sacrificing, and morally heroic pioneer workers in the righteous cause. Benjamin Lundy, also a Quaker, rendered distinguished antislavery service, prior to and co-operative with William Lloyd Garrison, connecting the past with the distinctively modern antislavery movement in this country. He, too, was of the unpretending, self-sacrificing, morally courageous spirits, whose labors, in the important period of time covered by them, helped much to increase the current and swell the tide of successful opposition to the iniquitous chattel system. The modern, immediate emancipation movement, inaugurated here by Mr. Garrison, has been largely strengthened, as you are aware, by forces recruited from the Quaker ranks. There are associated therewith representative names of women and men which will suggest themselves to your minds without mention; as well as many others less prominent, but not less devoted, self-sacrificing, and efficient among Abolitionists. I do not forget that Abby Foster felt conscientiously constrained to disown her Society; that the New York Yearly Meeting dishonored itself by disowning Isaac T. Hopper and Charles Marriott because of their connection with the American Antislavery Society; that Lucretia Mott for a long time was but barely tolerated, sometimes bitterly persecuted,

on account of her antislavery testimony; or that many
of the most efficient Abolitionists of the Quaker stock
have done their work mainly outside and independent of
the Society. Of course I put forth no claim of exclusive
superiority on the part of Friends in the antislavery
struggle. It is safe, however, to say that in proportion
to their numbers they have furnished a relatively larger
quota than any other denomination of people in the effective working forces of that arduous preliminary moral warfare which preceded emancipation and made final success
possible.

George Fox was an early defender of the right of
women to speak in churches. At the outset of his itiner-
ant missionary labors this question — antedating woman's
rights conventions by two hundred years — came up.
Hearing of a great union-meeting to be held at Leicester,
wherein Presbyterians, Independents, Baptists, and Epis-
copalians were to unite in the discussion of religious topics,
George Fox attended it. During the progress of the
meeting, a woman started a question about some saying
by the Apostle Peter. The presiding priest, instead of
entertaining or answering her question, did very much as
it is probable Dr. Todd would do by Gail Hamilton or
Anna Dickinson under like circumstances; he said to her,
" I permit not a woman to speak in the church," though
he had before given liberty for any one to speak. This
so outraged Fox's sense of justice and propriety, and so
kindled his zeal, that he stepped up and asked the priest,
" Dost thou call this place [the Steeple House] a church?
Or dost thou call this mixed multitude a church?" But
the priest, Yankee-like, answered by asking him what a
church was; when Fox replied that " the Church was
the pillar and ground of truth, made up of living stones,
living members, a spiritual household, which Christ was
the head of; but he was not the head of a mixed multi-

tude, or of an old house made of lime, stones, and wood."
This caused such a stir that the priest came down out of
his pulpit, others came out of their pews, and the meeting
broke up in confusion. Many followed Fox to an inn,
where the discussion was continued, and several were converted by him to Quakerism, — among them the woman
who asked the question and who was forbidden to speak
in the church. Other women were convinced by his
teaching, and presently became themselves most effective
preachers. They shared with men, with quiet courage
and rare moral heroism, the fearful persecution and untold
sufferings in which all were involved by devotion to the
truth as it became known to them.

Another and yet more striking illustration of the beneficent influence of Quakerism, quite outside and beyond
the society limits of Friends, may be seen in their past
and present relations with the Indians. To the humane
experiment inaugurated on the Western frontier the present year among the Indians, official and authentic unofficial
testimony accords, though tried under very discouraging
circumstances and with embarrassing limitations, a large
measure of success. Just and humane treatment now, so
far as the Indians have been brought under its influence,
is restoring their confidence and transforming them into
peaceful neighbors, as did kindred treatment of their ancestors by William Penn and the early Friends. Fortunate will it be for the Indian and for the nation if the
experiment, so well begun, can be continued and enlarged,
until the Indians are peacefully settled upon permanent
homesteads, recognized and protected as citizens, to be
instructed and encouraged in agricultural industry, and
their children to receive education and training for a manhood and womanhood of citizenship.

Other subjects historically identified with Friends, treated
in Mr. Powell's paper, and which in this synopsis we can

but barely mention, were "Peace," "Capital Punishment," "Temperance," "The Poor among Friends," "Oaths," "Marriage," "Hireling Ministry," "Peculiarities of Speech and Dress," "Ceremonies and Titles," etc.

Each branch of the society, Mr. Powell said, presents its present rarest fruit in a living representative, both of national and transatlantic reputation, — the one a poet, the other a preacher. They worthily perpetuate for Quakerism the good repute won for it by George Fox and William Penn. Both are larger than the sect. In its merely sectarian aspect Quakerism is as uninteresting, narrow, timid, selfish, and conservative as is mere sectarianism under any other name. Too many Friends have little comprehension, apparently, of the meaning of Quakerism beyond a blind observance of the peculiarities of dress and speech, and the formality of the Meeting. Oblivious to the demands of the present, they cling to now meaningless protests of the past. They are as inaccessible to new conceptions of truth and as much afraid of following after "new lights" as was the priest Stephens, who was disturbed by and afraid of George Fox. To such Friends Fox himself, should he reappear among them, would be a "disturbing element" and a most unwelcome visitor. They have dishonored the important fundamental principle, and tarnished the Society's good name by subordinating it to narrow views of religion, to commercial selfishness, and the prevalent palsying conservatism of the outside world. The history of Quakerism in this respect is but the counterpart of sectarianism in other phases. Originally a protest against externalism, Quakerism, with too many Friends, has degenerated into a barren observance of its own peculiar formalities. With such, the letter quenches the spirit. Under their administration Quakerism, as a religious movement, declines in power and numbers, as it must. Having conquered for itself respectability and peace, after its hard-fought battle, Quakerism has lost its former aggressive character, and lives now too largely upon the accumulated moral capital of the past. The inheritance which comes to young Friends to-day has a value which, as simple birthright members, they but slightly appreciate, and therefore fail wisely to use. This will follow the law of all other inheritances, of which there can be continued possession only on the condition of judicious use.

The sources of spiritual strength for our contest, which so marvellously sustained the early Friends in their martyr period, and which have upheld kindred spirits in all time, are still at our command. That was a wholesome injunction of a venerable Quaker preacher who said, " We should so live that the garment which fits us to-day will be too small to-morrow." That will prove itself the best religion which shall stimulate mankind to unite with the clearest thought the most beneficent action.

Seeking the right earnestly, and striving alone, if need be, in field and orchard, turning confidingly to the "Inward Light," may we not all hope to realize

> " strength the evil to forsake,
> The cross of Truth to bear,
> And love and reverend fear to make
> Our daily lives a prayer " ?

Mrs. JULIA WARD HOWE thought we could not philosophize about religion without feeling our obligation to Quakerism. The limitations of that system were more æsthetic than moral. The maintenance of the right of women to speak freely in public was an instance of unsurpassed courage in the early Quakers. The individuality of inspiration was better and more practically taught by them than by the mystics. The privation of amusement, which they insisted on, materializes life and lessens its resources.

The usefulness of sect, with these people as with others, is only temporary. As to the revolutionary tendency which appeared in the first preaching of Quakerism, we must remember that Jesus was the most radical of revolutionists.

Mr. WEISS was glad to hear an account so clear and so candid as the paper had given. The radical error of the Quakers was that, believing in the inner light, they had undertaken to organize it into a system. He had been conversant with the best form of Quakerism during his residence in New Bedford, and had seen many of its members advance into radical Unitarianism. You find among these people a placid and equable way of meeting the losses and burdens of life. They know nothing of Calvinistic despairs, floods of tears, and outbursts of grief. You feel that the Spirit of God dwells among them. Yet, if you hear the Quakers in their meeting-houses, you do not find them satisfying or instructive. If their preachers are not " hireling priests," neither are they inspired. Many of them have fallen back into preaching " the blood of Christ."

A great moral sincerity is the prominent characteristic of Quakerism. They tell you your faults to your face. Other people praise this honesty, but they *do* it, and do it without arousing a hostile feeling in the person so labored with. This calm resoluteness is ingrained in the Quaker life. Socrates was a born Quaker. He recognized the inward light, in the form of a restraining voice within him. Theodore Parker also had this ; but in him it was more than a restraining voice, giving him an intuitive consciousness of right as well as of wrong.

WENDELL PHILLIPS said he had known the Quakers as intimately perhaps as Mr. Weiss had done ; and he might have said some things in criticism of them had not Mr. Powell so fairly covered both sides of the question. To him (Mr.

Phillips) Quakerism, like the earlier sects, showed the limitations of human nature. A religious genius arises, and bears the precise testimony needed by the world at that time; but if he tries to organize or perpetuate himself, he fails. George Fox was a great religious genius. William Penn was a trimmer, who, if he had lived in New England in our time, would have been a dough-face.

The decline of Quakerism began earlier than our friend has represented in his essay. Josiah Foster in that denomination was a pope. Elizabeth Fry was a noble woman; but in religion was a narrow-minded bigot, who would not stay in the house with Lucretia Mott because the latter did not believe in the Trinity. George Fox was motion. When he ceased to move Quakerism, it fell back. It has not continued the aggressive attitude which he took. Quakerism has taken care of its own poor, but has never combated pauperism in the community at large.

Fox shows us how little we owe to colleges. The great religious ideas of modern Europe all came up from the people. Intellect led by scholars opposes progress. If Fox were here among us, he would be as radical now as he was then, and would be again imprisoned as a disturber of society.

At first, the plain dress showed a spirit of self-denial and reform. Afterwards it became, like a monk's frock, only the uniform of a sect.

As to the persecutions practised by our forefathers, — though Mary Dyer was a glorious apostle of truth, many of the Quakers who came after her were really a nuisance, and needed a restraining force. This should be kept in mind as a palliation, though it does not excuse the manner in which the Quakers were treated.

Rev. SAMUEL LONGFELLOW said he had hoped to hear some good silence, as more appropriate to the theme before them. It was true, as had been said, that some Quakers by birthright were making progress beyond the bounds of the denomination. One of them had told him that his daughter attended a Unitarian chapel, though he himself felt bound to continue the protest against a hireling ministry. Mr. Longfellow thought they might properly reflect that the hireling *spirit* was the thing to be opposed. The Quaker self-control and tranquillity were admirable in aged people, but more spontaneity seemed desirable in the young. The doctrine of immediate inspiration was a very precious one ; and precious also was the Quaker faith in the power of testimony borne against wrong, the simple saying of how it looks to your conscience, and a firm persistence in this testimony.

Dr. BARTOL remarked : " The doctrine of immediate inspiration existed long before Quakerism. This *is* religion. This makes religious books, made the prophets, made Jesus himself. If we think Jesus a special exception, we mistake. He, like us, heard an inward voice speaking to his soul. There can be no such thing as religion, or a God, without a speaking of that God to the soul, and the soul knowing that it is God who speaks. We must not only hear a voice, but know what voice it is. We hear his voice, and he hears ours. Instead of one Son of God only, there is an innumerable multitude." Dr. Bartol had heard it said of Father Taylor, who taught the possibility and the duty of being perfect, that, on being asked whether any one else had ever been as good as Jesus, he had answered, "Millions !"

Mrs. CHENEY then gave a brief testimony, saying that, though Quakerism is a very great phenomenon in religious history, its ignoring of art and science, and consenting to neglect so many of their gifts, is a serious defect. Its method is always to cut off, without constructing anything or adding anything ; and a tendency to morbidness of conscience is manifest not only among them but among those who have come out from them.

Mr. FRANK B. SANBORN said that to him Quakerism seemed an English institution, springing up at a time of great mental activity among the English people. There was a decided and absolute difference between the first Quakers and the Quakers of to-day, although both held the doctrine of immediate inspiration. The light seen by George Fox and James Naylor was identical with the cases of spiritual illumination which have been known in all ages and countries. Socrates, however, was not a Quaker, and had little in common with the fervor and the energy of destructiveness shown by the founders of that sect. The English habit of mind crystallized the doctrine of the early Quakers, and tended to perpetuate just that thing without variation. Yet if we class our Quakers with the early ones, we shall confound things essentially different. If George Fox should now come among us, he would sympathize rather with the Methodists than with any other sect. The Quakers of our time shut themselves up in a corner, and seem content with a small part of the field of human nature.

RICHARD P. HALLOWELL said that Quakerism seemed to him a reaffirmation of what Jesus said and taught. The original Quakers believed thoroughly in the inspiration of the Bible, in the atonement, and other Calvinistic doctrines. The decline of the Society had proceeded largely from its sectarianism. The committee supervise the preachers. The majority of Quakers of the reformatory and progressive sort not only hold to the doctrine of immediate inspiration but sympathize with the Free Religious Association.

Mrs. ABBY KELLEY FOSTER said that Quakerism had now no high moral or religious principle to distinguish it from the other sects. It had not only made no valuable attainment of late, but had even lost its original spirit of reform. She had been brought up in the Orthodox branch of the Quaker Church, but while there she was a doubter, even an atheist, living without God and without hope in the world, with no anchor for her soul. When the living work of the temperance movement and the antislavery movement began, inspired by the doctrine of love to God as a Father and love to man as a brother, — the doctrines enforced by Christ, "Love thy neighbor as thyself," "He who loveth not his brother whom he hath seen, how can he love God whom he hath not seen?" "Whatsoever ye would that men should do unto you, do ye even so unto them," — in these doctrines she perceived and embraced a living Christianity, a Christianity of work. Therefore her life had been devoted to labor for the world's uplifting. She came to this meeting in one of the brief intervals of labor for the still oppressed black man of the South. She had no time to theorize, had never been able to understand the theological speculations of the Orthodox Church, her only idea of salvation being salvation from the sin of trampling on God's moral laws. She had no leisure for speculations or æsthetics. While Lazarus lies at the gate, who can sit at speculative study in his library or revel in the cultivation of his tastes.

Mr. LONGFELLOW said it was a comfort to know that in all these sects, crystallized as they might be, there was a movement party and a progressive wing.

Mr. SANBORN said that John Brown spoke well of the Quakers, and found them helpful to him.

Mr. POWELL said the great fact of Quakerism was that it was a working, practical religion. It seemed to him that the Free Religious Association needed that vigorous working spirit which the best of the Quakers had shown. He doubted if the Methodists were now the most progressive church. The experiment of the Quaker Commission among the Indians was working most satisfactory results, exercising a restraining force upon the savage people, and making some of the whites realize the disgracefulness of cheating them. Quakerism is not an English, but a human institution, and its lesson to people of other sects is that they should work as well as enjoy.

Rev. WILLIAM H. CHANNING had unfortunately missed the reading of Mr. Powell's paper, but he owed thanks to Quakerism for its testimony to an ever-present Spirit of Truth, and its free communication with human beings. This let him into the heart and life of "the beloved Son." Fox and his friends reaffirmed that doctrine of the abiding of God in the human soul which has wrought such wonders in modern society. Angelina Grimké was a product of the Quaker Church, and her faithful testimony against slavery while it was strong and prosperous was a manifest work of the indwelling Spirit of God. The Quakers see with perfect clearness the equality of woman with man in regard to rights and duties. Another cause of gratitude to them is their constant inculcation of the doctrine of peace. We must never give up the doctrine of the abiding of God in the individual soul. If he were a Quaker, Mr. Channing said, he would preach it more confidently than ever.

XXIV.

EVOLUTION.

By EDWARD S. MORSE.

DESPITE the many technicalities inevitable in the treatment of the subject of Evolution, and the unfamiliarity of literary people with its details, no one who has heard Professor Morse lecture will need to be assured that, in presenting this branch of science to the Chestnut Street Club, he was able to hold closely the attention of his hearers. His happy power of translating scientific terms into familiar language, with his remarkable skill in blackboard drawing, rendered his treatment at once easily intelligible and fascinating. As he so rapidly and skilfully executed with both hands his illustrations, Dr. Bartol remarked that it seemed as if the chalk had been transmitted from Agassiz's fingers.

The essayist endeavored to show that certain of the groups into which the animal kingdom is divided, though widely separated at advanced stages of development, converged at earlier periods, so that they came very near each other in some instances, and in others seemed to have a common origin. Birds, he said, had always been considered a closed type, that is, a group of which any member is at once recognizable by characteristics common to all. Reptiles, on the other hand, are known to partake of the distinctive features of other groups. He then undertook to prove that the latter class runs into the former, thus overturning the old theory that classified birds are a distinct and complete type. In illustration he gave representations of a bird and reptile in embryo, which he said so closely resemble each other at this stage as to be undistinguishable. He then traced them from the point whence they diverged, showing how they developed, stage by stage, their distinctive characteristics. Thus he argued that birds and reptiles have a common origin, and the same truth holds in regard to insects and worms.

Professor Morse then went on to speak of men and apes. He pointed out certain peculiarities in the formation of the skull, which, in all the human species of to-day, he declared, never vary except in the smallest degree. He showed their marked difference from the corresponding parts of the monkey. Yet he asserted that these very parts in old skulls — and by old he meant those of 30,000 years ago — had no similarity with the identical portions of the human skull of our time, but did exactly resemble the corresponding features of our monkey. These facts, the speaker urged, must be by every one regarded as significant and suggestive; although a thorough knowledge of the details of the anatomy of animals was necessary to a complete understanding of the principles involved in the question of evolution.

The members of the Club felt some delicacy about venturing upon a discussion in the face of the last statement, recognizing that with Professor Morse as the advocate of evolution, a debate in regard to his scientific position would be altogether too one-sided. They were unanimous, however, in expressing their interest in the essay and their pleasure in having so important a subject clearly set before them; and in this way the Club slid half-unconsciously into expressions of opinion upon the topic of the paper itself.

Rev. James Freeman Clarke then stated, that, having read several books for and against Darwinism, he was still unprepared to say where the burden of proof rested. Indeed, he thought the question was yet hypothetical. A great many scientific men, he thought, had accepted the theory because they did not believe in spontaneous creation; and, on the other side, the many persons who did put faith in the theory of instantaneous generation would not listen to that of gradual development. His own religious views, he continued, were no stumbling-block to his recognition of the plan of evolution should it be fairly based upon proof.

The conversation soon drifted away from questions of anatomy to the relations of human nature to that of the lower animals. Some one remarked that the likeness to animals, sometimes very marked both in the appearance and character of human beings, might be considered as a token and proof of their descent or ascent from a former order of being. The opinion was expressed that there might be an evolution downward instead of upward; at all events, it was plain that individual men deteriorated, losing their spiritual qualities and acquiring beastly ones. It was suggested further that a soul which had been thus degraded might be reintroduced to life in the form of an animal.

In this way the general subject of the transmigration of souls came into discussion, and many interesting things were said, — those participating in the talk becoming so much engaged that efforts to find an opportunity of introducing Mr. Clemens (Mark Twain), who was present, were unsuccessful, as he was obliged to leave at an early hour. Mr. Clemens had been hovering upon the outskirts of the audience, closely watching Professor Morse's skilful manipulation of the crayon, and apparently much interested. A friend who accompanied him relates the following incident of their homeward walk from the meeting of the club.

"As we passed out," he writes, " Mr. A. joined the party, and while the rest of us were chatting briskly about the incidents of the meeting, Mr. Clemens was silent until we got up into Beacon Street, when he spoke out in a serious way, saying, as nearly as I can recall his language: 'Well, that was an extraordinary meeting! How that chap did draw on the blackboard! I never saw anything like that. I'm sorry we had to come away, for I was mightily interested in the talk going on, and wanted to say something myself. When Mrs. Sargent asked me if I would speak, I did n't want to do it at all, but I thought it would n't be polite to decline. I did n't care much about evolution, but when they struck the doctrine of metempsychosis, I got interested. That doctrine accounts for me: I knew there was something the matter, but never knew what it was before. It's the passing off on a man of an old, damaged, second-hand soul that makes all the trouble.'"

XXV.

LAW.

By SAMUEL LONGFELLOW.

THE subject was " The Idea of Law," treated mainly in reference to religious thought and feeling. " The idea of law," said Mr. Longfellow, " holds a large place in modern thought. The laws of Nature, the laws of society, are phrases familiar in all our ears. We hear also of the laws of trade, of supply and demand, and the like ; indicating a sense of a certain order of events taking place beyond the control of individual wills, something inherent in the nature of things, making them to be what they are, and to go on as they do. This idea of law is everywhere taking the place of the notion of accident, or of arbitrary will, in the carrying on of the world ; indeed, Mr. Huxley, the English physiologist, thinks it will soon banish the notion of anything like spontaneity in the universe. But the idea of spontaneity and the idea of freedom, which we believe in because we feel them in ourselves and must needs ascribe them to all spirits, are not necessarily opposed to the idea of law. For by law we mean the orderly and continuous method according to which a force operates ; and a force may be spontaneous in its origin even though it must act under fixed conditions. We need not be afraid that we shall lose our freedom because we are under law. There is more freedom in order than in lawlessness. It would be foolish, under the notion of enjoying greater freedom, to try to see with our ears, or to hear with our eyes. So in the domains of the mind and the heart. True freedom of thinking is found in thinking logically and consecutively, not in thinking at random. True freedom in loving is found in loving wisely and chastely, — not as passion's slave, but as passion's master. We mark the progress of civilization by the gradual substitution of a government of laws for the arbitrary power of despotism. As intelligence progresses, the autocrat gives way to the limited monarchy, and that in its turn to the republic.

"We hear much complaint of the evils of popular liberty, and, clearly, such evils exist; but the benefits of liberty greatly exceed these evils. A monarchist has said that there is no sentiment of loyalty in a republic. This, however, is a great mistake. The love of country is better than that of a prince, who may require much idealization to make him worthy of love; and we find — have found in the history of our own nation — loyalty to country a stronger and deeper sentiment than loyalty to any king. Our delight in law is a delight in order, — physical order, or beauty; moral order, or justice. Statute law is venerable only when coincident with justice. So too in science. The scientific observer cannot rest contented with a new fact till he brings it under a general statement, sees in it the expression of a law. We all find a crystal more beautiful than a clod; and we delight to know that each mineral crystallizes invariably into a special form. Out of the same materials of earth, air, and water, the rose will always form roses, the apple-tree apples. What security as well as delight we have in this presence of law in outward Nature! It is the sense of order, of the omnipresence of law, which makes scientific men so unwilling to accept the idea of miracle. Even conservative theologians are beginning to speak of miracles as the operations of a hidden law; but when a miracle is acknowledged to be the result of law, hidden or other, does it not cease to be a miracle, and become simply a rare event? All changes, all eccentricities, must be classed under law before we can be satisfied with them."

Here Mr. Longfellow referred to the remarkable fact of a lecture by Rev. Dr. A. P. Peabody, entitled "The Sovereignty of Law," — a lecture expressly claiming this doctrine "without limit, interruption, or exception," and also expressly specifying under it God's answers to prayer, and the phenomena called miracles in the Old and New Testaments, — having been delivered in the course popularly known as the "Anti-Sceptical Lectures," delivered in Boston winter before last, and since published in a volume entitled "Christianity and Scepticism."

"The truly religious man must see God as much in ordinary things as in extraordinary. Order, to him, is perpetual Divine presence. To the devout mind the order of Nature is far more sacred, far more divine, far more full of God, than any interruption of order could be. Is there more of God in a fig-tree withering than in a cherry-tree blossoming? For myself, miracle, a deviation from order, is a hindrance to religious belief. I do not say that the order *proves* God any more than the miracle would. In outward Nature we find no proof of God, and we had better cease looking for it there. In the soul alone, in the human spirit, the conscience, the affections, the will, the ideal imagination, — in these lies that primal sense of God which is its own proof. But when in the soul we have met and known God we look abroad, and the universe becomes full of illustrations of him, and our research into his ways in the world of matter throws light upon his ways in the world of man. We must learn not to think of the law of God for us as the arbitrary utterance of his will, but to look for it in every one of our conditions, physical, moral, and spiritual, and so to respect our natures as the revelations of his purposes for us. All deep experience awakens, deepens, and confirms our sense of God's presence.

"The hymn of Cleanthes to Jupiter, from which Paul, speaking on Mars' Hill, quoted to the Athenians the declaration, 'For we are also His offspring,' contains many just and elevated sentiments, such as are commonly thought to have originated with Christianity." Mr. Longfellow read a translation of portions of this beautiful poem, and added that Cleanthes, who gratuitously taught philosophy and religion, was himself, on the complaint of an enemy, once brought before the tribunal of the Areopagus, charged with having no visible means of support. The sentence was, after hearing his defence, that he should receive from the State a hundred pounds of gold yearly!

"The cxixth Psalm has much to say of 'the law of the Lord' and 'thy law.' But by law is here meant *statute* law. The scientific idea of law is very different. The law of a thing is found in its nature. We need to substitute the idea of inward principle for that of outward enactment. We should recognize the law of God in our own native constitution. We want to recognize that what we call sin is but the perversion or misuse of some faculty or passion or propensity which in its right use leads only to good. We want to recognize that the Love of God, and the Justice of God, and the Truth of God, and the Providence of God all work according to their law. Not that God is Law, or Law is God: law is not a power, but only the orderly method by which a power acts. The love of God is a spiritual force, working in an orderly method. So his *will* is a perpetual principle of good, working in and through all things by a regular method.

"We see how a distinct conception of God's operation by law would modify our relation to him. We should seek abiding faith in the rectitude of law, and strive for personal conformity to it. Obedience to law is our only safety, spiritually as well as physically. The recognition of this truth will not interfere with our use of prayer, which is an opening of the soul upward, an exercise of reverent trust. From this attitude of the soul we may derive great advantage, if we do not abuse it by petitions for external things. The love of God, to which we thus voluntarily open our hearts, is not an individual interest, but all-embracing. It is not indulgence and cosseting; it seeks not our ease, but our welfare. This love, acting by law, is the strength which bears us up in trial. The providence of God is neither special interference nor general superintendence, but perfect saving presence, — saving still, through all seeming destruction and loss.

"It may be objected that in this estimate of providence we make no allowance for accident. Some one has said that in the universe of God there are no accidents. What he *meant* by that is strictly true, and yet the coincidence of two events, as the undesigned intersection of two trains of cars, may bring about an accident. When we consider how manifold are these intersections, we shall find ample room for as much of this element of chance as we need to explain life; and we may also remember that to an immortal soul the safety of the body is not a matter of the highest importance.

"Religious teaching commonly represents some arbitrary punishment as assigned to sin. But the justice of God, viewed in the light of law, loses every shade of implacability or arbitrariness. It is the justice of cause and effect. It accomplishes precise and full retribution. The thought of God's justice should be a comfort and delight to us, instead of a terror. Justice, in his hands, is a perfect law, tending to bring all men back to obedience. Transgression is bad, because it is disorderly. God's law is not external to us, but internal. This is our judge, not on some one appointed future day, but now, and every day.

And it is not our judge only, but our redeemer. Every moral truth of which we once had vision; every thought and purpose of good; that which we are capable of being, however faithless we have proved; the ideal of our life, — it is that to which we shall be held until it be accomplished."

Mr. WEISS said that one point of exception to the essay occurred to him, — the statement that external Nature did not suggest God. He thought that the conception of the Infinite *did* proceed from the observation of order in the universe. The idea of unity is the fragrance of the soul, the topmost blossom on the tree of life. Having that idea, you find the perfection of development and of symmetry in everything. We cannot know deity till we know unity, and until then there can be no such thing as intelligent worship. One of the finest contributions to the idea of law is, that the advocates of miracles are beginning to ascribe them to a deeper law, not seeing that they thus cease to be miracles.

Mr. LONGFELLOW explained that what he had said was that Nature did not *prove* God.

Mrs. HOWE thought all expressions on these subjects must be inadequate. As to special providence, if we discard the idea of it, how else shall we name that divine presence which accompanies us, which makes all things work together for our good, and allows no accidents?

Mrs. LIVERMORE was inclined to feel that no accident was possible in God's economy. All things were arranged to a good end.

Rev. Mr. BLAKE remarked that perhaps our idea of accident comes from our not being accustomed to follow law into its minute ramifications. That final step in synthesis which can comprehend our own union with the

13

Infinite can never be taken by a finite mind. He never had found anything happen to him which did not prove afterward to have subserved a good purpose. But, as a good woman once said to him, "You stand an excellent chance in life of getting a great deal that you don't want." Mr. Blake expressed his satisfaction at the ground clearly taken in the essay, — that the law was not God, and that God was not the law.

Mr. LONGFELLOW said that in physics law was often confounded with force.

Dr. BARTOL said : "Though we cannot prove, physically or metaphysically, the existence of God, we are not less assured of it; and in this faith men may not only willingly but gladly accept any form of death or affliction." He related an affecting story of a deep grief which had befallen one of our own members, — the story of two who loved each other and were about to marry. The wedding-dress was made ready, the wedding-house was prepared, and the bridegroom — his heart beating high with hope and pride — was suddenly taken out of this world. Accident we will not call this blow — providence shall we name it? It is harder to explain than railroad collisions or steamboat disasters. But the remarkable thing about it was not the providential appointment nor the human disappointment, but the quiet acceptance of it by the recipient. He found the bereaved soul, not complaining, not lamenting, but just *taking sides with God*, and accepting his work. The noble soul is the one that does not take note of its personal affliction, but hears through its stillness the voice of its God, and is not afraid. And this arises from the perception of unity to which Mr. Weiss referred. When the soul is *unselfed*, then we are convinced of immortality; we heave in sight of that great country on the crest of the wave which carries us up. You may call this deep sense of unity faith, if you choose ;

it is a wide-spread faith. Huxley and the rest of the scientists investigate because they are sure beforehand, — sure they shall find order, full of faith in law. A good Episcopal clergyman said: 'We may talk of the beauty of holiness, but hardly of the holiness of beauty.' Did that man quite understand the divine unity in which holiness and beauty are one?"

Mr. McCauley believed in no such special interventions of divine power as were called miracles by the mediæval Church. Life is the real miracle; God is a reality: all else is either natural or supernatural. But the method of God's action is above our comprehension.

Dr. Bartol said: "We cannot do anything *fatal*. Of sin as well as of sorrow we must say, it never can be fatal. Griefs and sins are a part of our salvation, and we should hardly be willing to part with their fruit in our hearts."

Mr. Gannett said: "If God is in one thing, he is in everything. What we call cause and effect are one series of relations; but *all* things are related to each other, though we cannot explain how. If man can triumph over Nature and accident, God surely can."

Mrs. Livermore expressed her gratification at Dr. Bartol's statement that there was nothing *fatal*. We must learn to exercise such patience as God does. As to herself, she had come to feel by experience that there is no such thing as accident, though her life had been modified against her will by what were *called* accidents. "Somehow," she said, "I rest in God as a safe guide and friend, never to be lost or alienated. All is planned by him, all is just as he intended, and so I rest resigned in him."

Dr. Bartol rejoiced in *our* unity as well as in the unity of God. As to prayer, — sometimes it seemed to him that God prays to us as well as we to him. He begs us to do right.   But whatever of him may be unknown, one thing, as Whittier said, we know : —

> " We know not where His islands lift
>   Their fronded palms in air ;
> We only know we cannot drift
>   Beyond His love and care."

And with these consoling words the session ended.

XXVI.

SELF-OBLIVION.

By CYRUS A. BARTOL.

I KNOW not what divinity or divination, according to the Orientals, is in dreaming. I dreamed of being in a convocation discussing Jesus, till, as the air grew somewhat vexed with the battledoor-and-shuttlecock passing to and fro of his name, he himself, in my vision or dream, rose, and said to the assembled company, "Touch me not." What was meant originally by that seemingly rude repulse? Was he a ghost the hand would pass through? Did he reserve his first greeting for another? Or did he go on to say rather, "The God I ascend to is yours as much as mine. Let me alone; the time to dote on me is past." This was the topmost round of Christ's character; one step above self-sacrifice on the cross, self-abnegation after the crucifixion. Not that he would disparage his aim. He knew and asserted that he was a showing of God, but, having shown him, would retire. What appearance on the stage could match such self-withdrawal? He was a medium whose virtue is to display the object, if I may take so trivial a figure, like the window in a house you pass by in the evening, where no window, nothing but the entry-lamp is to be seen. You cannot see the Master, whose mastery is perfect to reveal, behind, within the all-informing soul; as you do not notice much the man who unveils a picture in some great cathedral, to

be the valet of its beauty the business of his life. This
temper of self-renunciation Jesus hinted not at the close
only, but throughout his career, resenting being called
good, — willing anybody should speak against *him*, but
not against the Holy Ghost. As the absence of his statue
brought Brutus to mind, Christ was manifest less in his
advent than his exit. His arrest of us is — paradox of
beauty — his refusing to be stopped with. We have Jesus
only in being passed on by him ; and to worship him or
abide in him as a Finality, if it be orthodoxy, is nevertheless infidelity and rejection of Christianity, the fetichism
he abjures, and flat contradiction of his own bidding. To
make him an idol is to lose him altogether.

With that sublime soul to put one's end above one's
self, then, is the method of character. Do your work,
and divert attention from your hand in it. The fine actor,
— what makes him, but to be lost in the personage he
represents ; orator in the theme of his discourse ; singer
in the melody he chants ; poet in the verse he writes ;
every artist, builder, agent, in the business Heaven sends
him on? What does Michael Angelo know of bending
his neck out of joint painting the ceiling of the Sistine
Chapel? What does John the Baptist resolve himself
into but a voice in the wilderness, as Garrison did in the
land Slavery was making a worse desert? Why did John
Brown think the sovereign State of Virginia and the whole
South no disproportionate antagonist, but that his cause
was more than Union or nation? The best work everywhere is that of those absorbed in it, like the silk-worm
in the cocoon it weaves for its shroud ; the bee lost in the
heart of the flower it sucks, and then, as my honey-mer-
chant told me, like other devotees, killed, suffocated for
his pains ; the coral insect, continent builder, in the rocky
reef. To be great for a man is to note and hit the distinction between being a tool and an instrument. What

is the captain with his plume, the general, president, king, Bismarck in Germany, Grant in America, but that? Self-oblivion is God's remembrance. The glass of admiring eyes is a fragile preserver, service of your kind a safe the last fire will not crumble. "That is a Raphael," we say of the picture on the wall. Is Raphael in it at full length? No: figures of others, — the Holy Family, angels that stoop, or cherubs that peep. "That is Beethoven," — 't is an orchestra playing his symphonies, till his bronze fades from your misty eyes. "That is Shakspeare," — yes, most hid when most revealed; less apparent in the self-referring sonnets than in the disinterested plays, all the *dramatis personæ* but the lines and angles to measure his immense personality, — a dwarf in the incidents of his biography, a seraph that soars and sings in his immortal lines. If you know how fine you write, you are second-rate. You have no business to be so smart; the great author never reflects on the grandeur of his page. So Jesus says, "Not me, but my purpose, my method, my direction, my affection for God and man, — in these my mission is fulfilled. The New Jerusalem has many avenues: arrive at your station how you will, I am content."

Jesus would have us not for his servants, but for his friends; whither he is gone we *can* follow him. His was the ideal method; but are we bound to his ideal? Rather, is there not one ideal for him and for us; and are not society, state, church, the household we live in, as well as stars that shine over us, members of God? By the laws of life we reach him, over every causeway that is portion of himself. "I put myself," says one friend, "outside of Christianity." That were to be, so far as Christianity is anything, outside of God? There is no such thing as a "Come-outer." We are all Stay-inners, and in some sense Christian; we are inside of all human life. Purely individual we cannot be. In every man is an Ideal greater

than any man, and than all men. This vision, let me protest, is not for show, like the gilt pipes on the old organs,
but for use. The soldier in our war had it, who, burning
and perishing with thirst, refused to touch the officer's can-
teen, lest the blood from his wounded lip might spoil it for
the other men. When the English collier, in his bucket with
the broken rope, cries " From under ! " to those at the bottom ; when the French soldier begs the surgeon to keep
his ether for those worse wounded, and stifles his own cry
of pain with his bloody handkerchief; when the American
acrobat, dying on the stage to which he has fallen, is the
only man who looks out for the safety of the trembling girl
left on the trapeze ; when the conductor runs forward on
the track of a Western railroad to save a little child,
clears death by a hand's-breadth, and goes on punching
tickets, — each one saw, with more or less clearness, the
something higher than mere living. Relinquishment is
possession ; and Death can mortgage Life eternal.

God can take care of his property ; but Calvin's God is
Saturn over again, devouring his own children. 'T is the
beggar with whom the seeker after the Holy Grail shares
his crust. When it was proposed in a convention to resolve Christianity into love to God and man, it was objected
that this is the end to which Christianity is the means.
But as we learn to vote by voting, walk by walking, swim
by swimming, so one learns to love God and man by loving them. Immortality is present. We are not going to
be immortal unless we are so. We were shocked at Chief-
Justice Taney for affirming from the Supreme Bench that
the negro in this country had no rights which white men
were bound to respect. Yet what was his decision but
part of the larger decision that mankind has no rights
which God is bound to respect ; that he would be justified
in purely arbitrary dealing with this corrupt race? Nay,
we have claims on Our Father which he will own and

never deny. Has the child yonder there in his cradle no
claim on you because he is ignorant and weak? Reverently, but firmly, I ask God to justify to me my existence
and my nature, to compensate me for loss and console me
for grief; and he who did not resent Job's expostulation
will not condemn my demand, but in time or in eternity
will satisfy me that his creation was wisdom.

Mr. WEISS said: "I think sometimes that the pure intellect of a man — or perhaps it would be safer to say his
understanding, which makes deductions from experimental
observation — is tempted to conclude that the struggle
for life, on Mr. Darwin's principle of natural selection, subsists in this matter of immortality. One of the legacies of
modern science to man is that surmise which infests him
every now and then that the best livers, the most thoroughly
rounded people in every sense, are those whom Nature picks
out to survive the death of the body for a purpose not yet
known, but existing in the divine intelligence; and there is
a certain feeling that the divine economy conspires with
that, such as we perceive prevailing in the present aspects
of all things. We are cajoled into fancying for a while that
that analogy passes, by some aerial pontoon, the abyss of
the grave, and furnishes some future hopes of good by
means of the most veteran minds, and that the rest fall off;
that thousands and millions of years of barbarism, which
succeeded to the reign of the mammoth, thus fell off into
nonentity and annihilation; and that the Divine Mind
throughout all those epochs, by tentative processes, was
slowly feeling its way towards that race of men and women
which should embody that aboriginal idea of natural selection and furnish him with his souls. I will tell you what ex-
tricates me from that idea, for I consider it to be an idea
which is fatal to the development of mankind, fatal to the de-

velopment of the most insignificant as well as the most glorious of God's creatures, utterly destructive to any sentiment
of paternity or personality of the divine intelligence, fatal
and arrogant, and threatening to establish a hideous aristocracy of intellect and virtue.   One recollects what Abraham
Lincoln said, who had a very rare intuitive ability, — for
I must insist on continuing to use that word ' intuition,'
though I believe in experimental observation, — that rare
intuitive, sometimes called metaphysical, ability.   He was
asked one day if he believed in the immortality of the soul,
and he pondered, and turning, simply said, ' All, or none.'
And that, it seems to me, is just the redemption of mankind ; it is the salvation of men and women to believe
that.   I don't care what you call it, whether you call it
an induction from a long series of experimental facts, or
whether you call it the original form of mind, or an immediate touch of divine presence.   I think if we cling to that
fact, to that intuitive sense of the divine meaning in making men and women, we shall find that we extricate ourselves from that surmise derived from modern science by
the help of the principle of that paper which has just been
read to us, which contains so many points, which was so
bristling with fine turns and delicate phrases — like ' Self-
oblivion is God's remembrance '—that we hardly know
where to take it up ; yet out of the whole of it comes
that perception that the totality of a person's character is
equivalent to personal immortality and the proof of personal continuance, and that we are just as likely to find a
thoroughly rounded and symmetrical soul in some heathen
proximity and neighborhood as we are in this room.   And
anything short of that is going to undermine, faster than
science can work above ground or underneath it, our faith
in man, and our faith in God, and our *raison d'être*, our
reason for being here at all.   Anything short of that makes
it impossible for you with all your intelligence to account

for the fact that you sit in this room, and that we feel each other's presence across the room, and that by having come here to sit together we flow instantly though invisibly into a very fine and deep perception that our presence is nothing but the outpost of God in the room, and that when our intuition speaks to us of personal continuance for all or none, it is God furnishing us with his countersign; and we pass to and fro across that frontier which science declares to be impassable, — we pass to and fro as a bird crosses a hedge or goes through the densest thicket without touching twig or bole, by that fine intuition of flying which causes him to escape all obstruction and to come through again into the clear air. So it seems sometimes as if one would not come out on the other side of the jungle through the thick-set growth existing within, and as if there could not be another side to it and the light and air beyond, — yes, the sun and the moon, and a heaven full of stars beyond the jungle. I say, in our high moments, when we recover ourselves from the arrogance of petty facts which seek to limit us and restrain our personality, and free ourselves from the idiosyncrasies and conceits which make us nothing better than a herd of chimpanzees with their domination over us, we resume ourselves, and pass that jungle without knowing it, by that feeling which comes down out of heaven. Yet I know that it is *here*, not elsewhere; it is not that *jenseits*, — the *other side*. But it is all that divine perception which is made up of observation and of intuition, that irresistible, far-reaching, and personal consciousness which is our perception of the divine. And character serves as a proof of this because it is totality of living. It is not knack or talent; it is not your capacity for making a statement; it is not my capacity for thinking an argument; it is not Bartol's exquisite capacity for those nice and fine comparisons; it is not your preference for the struggle of entering

into a great reforming issue: it is that fact which makes
all those things possible when the time comes and the man
or woman comes; it is that part of the most despised, humblest, modestest soul now breathing in six-and-thirty States
which makes God's heroism through him possible, perhaps,
if he may be elected.   The elements of personal character in a thoroughly rounded individual start from a
supremacy of a natural sense penetrating all talents, reforming and reconstructing the inside and the outside of a
man, so that it is possible for God to make use of him as
his postern into the finite.   This is the way I extricate
myself from that film or nebula which the vast accumulat-
ing facts of science throw around my mind.

Rev. CHARLES LOW wanted to say a few words because
there was so much in the essay which met his own feelings.
Dr. Bartol had wisely dwelt on the danger of putting
Jesus in the place of God, — the means instead of the
end.   The essay, commencing as it did with a dream, had
reminded him of another dream, — Jean Paul Richter's, —
in which the dreamer, appalled at the danger of this same
substitution of Christ instead of God, dreamed that he
saw Jesus wandering through the universe in search of
the Father; till at last he went into the churchyard, and
the little children rose and crowded to his knees, crying
sorrowfully " Where is He?" and Jesus answered, " We
are all orphans, I and you."   But, because it is fatal to put
the means in the place of the end, we should not fall into
the other danger of losing sight of the means altogether.
Christ *is* the best means of showing us the Father; and
while we need a guide, a leader, surely it is well to receive
our direction from the one who is best and highest.

Mr. POTTER thought the great power in character to be
personality.   Our life is not in our surroundings, or in
what we inherit from others, but in personal quality.   If
he might criticise Dr. Bartol at all, he would note what

seemed to him a defect, — that of so presenting the character of Jesus as to make him seem passive, the medium of a force which passed through him, instead of originated with him. We have looked too much at the feminine side of the character of Jesus. It has a masculine side, a force and power and tremendous energy of which it is not well to lose sight. Two men, above all, came to his mind as representing in this age the moral force of Christ. Thomas Garrett used to meet, unarmed, slaveholders armed and angry, and quell and abash them simply by the moral power of his presence. Isaac T. Hopper was of this kind also. The divine spirit does its work, not through human passivity, but through personal will and energy.

Dr. BARTOL assented to this, and disclaimed any intention to represent Jesus as merely passive. Without personal force he would have been no illustration of the personal force which moves the universe.

The Rev. SAMUEL LONGFELLOW felt that the doubts of science were answered when character was accepted as the true key to unlock spiritual knowledge. The doubter finds himself silenced by his own highest moments. The scientific explorer in theology is bound to accept the experiences of saints as the very facts on which he must base his deductions. But we must verify spiritual truths in our own experience before they are true for us. It is always the pure in heart who see God, — hearts purified from self-seeking as from slavish fear.

Mr. POWELL expressed his delight in the essay, which he had come from New York to hear. We are moved to-day by the thought of Jesus, as men were moved by him when he was on earth, because he was so largely endowed with a divine personal magnetism. More than other men Jesus drew near to God; but the knowledge of God was not his prerogative alone. He had stood lately beside the coffin of Thomas Garrett, and had realized there the power and force of character. Seldom in this country had such a tribute been paid to private worth as was the assembly which gathered together to do honor to this man, who did not write or speak, but only lived. Thomas Garrett had passed through stormy scenes. Dwelling just on the border between slavery and freedom, he had assisted more than two thousand slaves to flee from the one and find the other. When he was sixty years old, Chief-Justice Taney sentenced him to pay for this work by a fine so heavy that it swallowed up every dollar of his property. A few years ago he stood at Wilmington, alone, as the opponent of the slave-power. Even the Quakers, to whom he belonged, withdrew from him. But he did not falter, and late recognition of his worth crowned his bier. For more than two hours a strange procession filed in and out of his house to look at the calm face of this conqueror, who had at last gained the victory over death. Slaveholders were there as well as Abolitionists, colored persons, rich and poor, grown men and little children, hundreds and thousands. The great personal magnetism of his character drew them.

Mr. WASSON said that it seemed to him there must be an eye in the soul which is the supreme eye of the human intelligence. Darwin considers what we call the instinct of birds the result of their long ages of experience as a race. When a bee constructs a cell, his work is the growth of half a million, perhaps, of years. But neither busy bee nor swallow flying south could tell, even if he had the gift of speech, why the cell is built in such a manner, or the flight is so timed. Man, summing up in himself the experience of all the ages, has come to an intelligence of which the record is character. Shall he regret all this, and say, " I am going to put away all the results of the past, and stand alone, on this bank and shoal of time " ? Verily, bird and bee might pity his poverty.

Dr. BARTOL thought we were conscious of that in ourselves which must have duration; but he was less impatient to know our destiny than our origin. That we came from God seemed to him the primary truth; and if he must believe only one of two things, — either that he drew his being from an infinite source, or that he himself should endure forever, — he would choose the former, and, so choosing, be sure of the latter.

XXVII.

MARRIAGE.

By HENRY JAMES.

THE memory of the last essay by Henry James, Sr.,
was so fresh in the minds of all the members of the
Chestnut Street Club that they assembled with unusual
punctuality, apparently determined not to lose one word
of the paper which everybody felt would be so truly
valuable. Mr. James announced that he should endeavor to set forth the true or philosophic grounds of
marriage in human nature, and show the reason why the
marriage bond has always claimed, even in its imperfect
civil form, such a ruthless divine sanctity; and the result
of his effort was an essay as remarkable for the orthodoxy
of its spirit as for the heterodoxy of its form.

Mr. JAMES began his essay by remarking that the *literal*
or enforced sanctity of the marriage tie appeared to be
dying out, and this at a day, too, when its sanctity as a
free or *spiritual* bond between the sexes seemed to be very
much enhanced. He thought this change was incidental
to the nature of marriage, which was much better understood at present than it used to be, when it was maintained
in the interest of the family bond among men, or regarded
as merely legitimating a man's offspring. The reproduc-
tive instinct has never been honored for its own sake in
men. It has always been felt to be a mere survival of
the animal in man, and as men grow in refinement of

nature its tendency is more or less to die out. Accordingly, the instinct is nowhere so luxuriant as it is among the poorer classes, in whom animal want is still very tyrannous; so that the uncultivated negro of our Southern States and the uncultivated Irish of the Northern cities rightfully dispute the dubious honor of being designated as "the American *proletariat*."

This explains why marriage has always been held necessary to legitimate the procreative instinct in men. It is as if the creator of men had said to himself: "So long as men are base enough in imagination to identify themselves with the animal in them, instead of looking at the animal as a mere negative stepping-stone to the human form, I will take care that their propagative instinct shall at least be presided over by a ritual which shall indicate that the ultimate or accomplished form of human life is not a gregarious, but a *social* one, capable of reconciling the most pronounced antagonisms of temperament in its subjects, and producing harmony out of the most abounding discords." Such, at all events, has been the practical function of marriage, — to lower the brute-material force in our nature, and educate its divine-human force. While the constant effect of it in a large, general way has been to put an ineffaceable stigma upon the animal in man, it has practically developed his rich interior *human* nature or quality as no other influence could; and the way it has done this is as truly marvellous (or miraculous) as anything in history. Marriage has effected this capital service for the race in commending the wife to her husband's affection as personating exclusively the real, objective, or race element in humanity, — its *neighborly* element, so to speak, — while the husband himself has been restricted to personating its phenomenal, subjective, conscious, or *personal* element. In this way of utter submissive wifehood and motherhood woman has

14

been an absolutely unmixed blessing to man throughout history. Being cut off from all ridiculous rivalry with her husband by her religious and civic identification with him in marriage, it has been the wife's good fortune to avoid provoking her husband's jealous self-love ; and she has, accordingly, been able to quicken in his heart a flame of chaste, interior, spiritual tenderness, such as no other sexual tie would ever have evoked. Any more carnal tie than marriage between the sexes would have left men more than ever a prey to every selfish cupidity, jealousy, and revenge ; so that the heart of man, instead of being gently opened, as it has been by marriage, to the access of the social sentiment, would in course of time have been relentlessly closed against it.

Here, then, according to Mr. James, is the inappreciable boon conferred by marriage upon human kind, — that, out of selfish, it has made the isolated individual heart of men social, by taking advantage of woman's superior spiritual quality, and promoting every way her spontaneous subjection to man. But now that this immense result has been secured, and man's innate selfishness and savagery have .been thus softened and socialized by the unselfish ministry of the wife and mother, it is impossible and contrary to nature, the lecturer thought, that the marriage institution itself should not reflect the surprising resurrection, in becoming *spiritual* out of *literal*. For example, Mr. James thought that a man at this day who should be inclined to insist upon his wife's legal or literal — that is to say, her voluntary or enforced — subjection to himself in marriage would be spiritually no man, but an abject, imbecile cad, who ought to be denied a marriage certificate, and relegated back to celibacy. Subjection on the wife's part, we all know, has been the immemorial letter of the marriage law. But we also very well know that the letter of a law has notoriously no other use than to minister death to its obedient subjects, while the spirit alone gives them life. And now that woman has revealed our better and diviner nature to us, in her long, uncomplaining servitude as wife and mother, any man must be a downright fool, in all spiritual regards, who should still invoke the deceased letter of the law in order to excuse or justify himself in disowning or flagrantly violating its living spirit. No; the literal dispensation of marriage has now given place to the spiritual dispensation: and spiritual marriage consists in making woman henceforth the supreme object of the bond, and man its free, spontaneous, devoted, even adoring subject. Where these conditions do not exist, accordingly, marriage in any divine or spiritual sense does not exist, but only and at best a legalized conventional concubinage.

Free-love finds no advocate in Mr. James. For, looking as he does upon love as constituting at most the fickle, perishing earth or ground of marriage, he naturally looks on the latter in its turn as constituting the essential heavens or eternal home of love: so that free-love — or love not inwardly attuned to marriage — is, in his estimation, an absolutely inhuman pretension, and can only legitimately mean a crude protest of love against the tyranny of *literal* marriage, and its prayer to be raised from the grave of the senses to which every such marriage consigns it, into that higher, chaste, and immortal form which spiritual marriage alone confers upon it. The partisans of "free-love" are doubtless for the most part sincere and honest men, as men go; but they are, at least, extremely unintelligent men, for they pretend that the most selfish and rapacious of the passions — that which has done more, when left to its own independent devices, to harden the heart and brutalize the manners of men, than all other causes combined — is now ready to supplant, in the esteem and affection of mankind, a tie with which the very highest dignity and interest of human life are indelibly associated.

XXVIII.

TRAGEDY.

By CHARLES CARROLL EVERETT.

THE subject of Dr. Everett's paper was "The Tragic Element in Literature and Life," and he illustrated his theme very aptly. The Orestes, Antigone, and Œdipus were the examples which he selected from Greek literature as showing that type of tragedy in which the actors are the mere instruments of eternal law; he chose King Lear to represent the blindness which seems an inherent part of the characters in tragedy, and Victor Hugo's Marion de Lorme as a play in which the inevitable retribution of sin is well set forth. Turning to history, the essayist went on to show how Socrates, the most subjective of all the Greeks, was slain by the will of the most objective of all States, because he advocated principles which, if carried out, would have caused its destruction. In the same way, the essayist argued, the Jews killed Jesus because they saw that his teachings would lead to the destruction of Judaism : he atoned for his words with his life; they atoned for their acts with the destruction of their city.

For a more modern instance, Dr. Everett selected the example of Napoleon, who atoned for his mistaken trust in England's chivalry by imprisonment and death on a desolate rock ; and England's atonement for her want of magnanimity to him in feeling the scorn of all generous souls, until at last she was glad to yield to the prayer of his people, and allow his bones to be removed from their dreary island sepulchre. All tragic forces, like all natural forces, were pronounced good by the essayist, in whose estimation the principal source of all trouble lies in suffering lower forces to act through the medium meant for a higher. He then touched upon the tragedies arising from radical differences of character in persons thrown together either by kinship or marriage. The end of all tragedy, he said, considered as strife is repose, either when one is successful or when one is defeated. The calmness of success is evanescent, that of death permanent; so that the thought of it as a symbol of the highest rest becomes inspiriting. In closing, Dr. Everett spoke of those who, although they cannot change facts, yet use them for their own advancement, — as Jean Valjean, in Hugo's novel, uses his early career as an incentive to more earnest effort in later life. Freedom does not beget freedom, but moral necessity; and in free, pure personal liberty all tragic conflicts find at last their solution.

———

Dr. BARTOL spoke of the universality of tragedy considered as a struggle, and said that great was the joy where a tragedy was enacting, as in a home where a fire burns brightly on the hearth. As good historical illustrations of tragedy, Dr. Bartol pointed to the lives of Daniel Webster and Abraham Lincoln; the former, yielding to the temptations of the lower law, was killed by the higher; the latter, resolutely following the teachings of the higher law, was killed by the lower. "Perhaps," said Dr. Bartol, "those who hear me have found some tragedies in their Unitarian, Universalist, Baptist, Methodist, Episcopal education before coming here."

Mr. HIGGINSON began his remarks by speaking as Dr. Everett had done of the grand, majestic mask worn by Greek tragic actors, but gave the preference to the mo-

bile human face. Modern literature, he considered, had
a finer grasp than ancient, as, instead of the mask of
the universal, it gave each individual a mask of his
own. Margaret Fuller, in criticising " Elective Affini-
ties," had pointed out the fact that in painting a villain it
was necessary to know the justification which he makes to
himself; and the best test of truly artistic literary work
was, that in it there would be found no wasted villains.
" I wish," said Col. Higginson, " that our friend Wasson
were here to act as *advocatus diaboli*, and put in a plea for
the epic theology. Some say that the antagonism between
good and evil is going to be eternal, and not ending
so easily as Prof. Everett and I think. Nothing is so
conspicuous in Nature as the economy of tragedy. It
was a compensation to Dr. Livingstone for having been
shaken by a lion, — certainly, a compensation to us
for his having been shaken, — to know that the apparent
torture is really a blessing, as it stupefies the victim.
Drowning and freezing are easy deaths; gunshot wounds
cause torpor; and I have been on board a steamboat
freighted with the wounded from a battle-field, and heard
no more noise than I heard here while Prof. Everett
was reading. Dr. Channing assured me that in all his
practice he had never seen a person who was afraid of
dying. So that those accounts of death-bed agonies which
are found so useful at prayer-meetings and revivals may
be fairly considered as unworthy of confidence."

Mrs. CHENEY said a few words concerning the manner
in which Dorothea in " Middlemarch " puts aside the tragedy
which seems almost inevitable in her life by calm persistence in well-doing, and Romola retains all that is best in
her existence by self-renunciation. In " Elective Affini-
ties " Charlotte retains, by simple calmness, the happiness
which the other characters, although far more brilliantly
endowed, lose by rashness and selfishness.

Dr. BARTOL spoke of the sublime happiness which evidently filled the soul of Ottilie at the moment of perfect self-renunciation.

Dr. MINER seemed inclined to the opinion that the real battle of life was from the struggle of certain opposing qualities in human nature, rather than from any conflict between man and the law of things, and that the struggle generally resulted from a lack of insight and foresight. In all trouble, it is said, there is educating power; God serves us kindly by using us roughly. We do not know how short is the road to the repose of heaven, but I hope it will not be so long as some sad ones think before it is all open to the light.

Mr. WEISS, in his usual very quiet manner, proceeded to testify to his dislike of the idea of a heaven full of repose, and declared that in his opinion it would be contrary to the whole cosmic plan to suppose that an immortal soul was going to be satisfied with sixty or seventy years of fighting. The Spiritualists, he said, are given to speaking of heaven as the Summer-land. Their idea of it seems to be a mush of universal indolence; a paradise of sugar-candy and gingerbread, in which everybody has a flower-bed and a garden and a house with a verandah. As for marriage, it is evident that in that relation it is the intention of Providence to bring together two persons who never can, by any possibility, agree.

Dr. MINER inquired if Mr. Weiss would believe in a divorce on the ground of incompatibility.

Mr. WEISS replied that he should not, as that would put an end to the discipline. It would not do any good, either, he said, because, if the parties married again, the trouble would begin once more. Recurring to his first thought, he went on: "We are the same persons as ever, when at the end of our sixty years of life we enter another world, stocked with men of different races and eras. There they are, in hordes and clans and crowds and epochs and generations ; and we have to live among them, and cannot shut ourselves up in our little Pedlingtons. I never thought of tragedy as a slur on God, and I hail it, not for art, but for immortality."

Dr. Miner asked whether, when freed from earthly limitations, we might not see things with more clearness, and not be so prone to engage in contests.

Mr. Weiss declared that, rather than be at rest, he would prefer to accept the pantheistic theory of indefinite absorption into the Absolute.

Dr. Bartol agreed with Mr. Weiss that freedom of life really ended when the struggle was over ; it was time then to call the sexton and make your grave.

Mr. Higginson said that in this world there was an obvious limit to trouble, since, being only able to learn of such false reports as were repeated to us personally, or as we read in untrustworthy weekly journals, we could only quarrel with a limited number of persons *per diem*, while by and by we can fight with myriads and æons contemporaneously.

Some general discussion now ensued, in which Mr. Longfellow and Dr. Bartol joined, and Mr. Higginson defined the theory of everlasting conflict as the gospel of eternal discussion. Mr. Longfellow asked why it might not be possible that, as we went on, the elements of conflict might disappear from our lives, while the energy which they had generated remained ; and Mr. Higginson assented, saying that it might also be possible that we met and conquered evil in higher and higher forms. For instance, he said, Prof. Everett and Dr. Miner devoted their lives to a struggle of a certain sort ; probably there were not many desperadoes or cutthroats either at Cambridge or Tufts, but still the gentlemen had as good a chance to work themselves to death, and deserved as much honor, as the teachers in a school-ship or a reform school, and it was not right to exalt those who fought a lower form of evil at the expense of those who fought with a higher. When Mr. Weiss declared that he adhered to his original theory of eternal conflict, and expressed a willingness to have the steel in his nature refined to its utmost capability, but wished that it should never lose its point, Mr. Cranch wanted to know if the things which Mr. Higginson called quarrels and Mr. Weiss antitheses did not result for good. Mr. Weiss thought that the lively time caused by his bomb-shell proved that point, and asked what kind of a Radical Club Mr. Higginson meant to get up in heaven without any quarrels. Mr. Temple wished to know what sort of music that would be in which there were no dissonances that needed resolution, using this analogy to prove that quarrels gave zest to life; and Mr. Powell told an anecdote of a Quaker lady, who, while lying in a cateleptic trance, felt as if her soul were severed from her body; while in this state she was conscious of an ability to will her spirit back into its earthly tenement, and did so by an effort. This, in Mr. Powell's opinion, showed that the soul was always in a state of action.

Mr. Abbott said that he had been listening with interest to the discussion in the Halls of Valhalla, but it was too much for his avoirdupois, and he had to come down to earth. He thought Socrates was the best illustration of the absolute elimination of tragedy, and that in him that element found a solution in a pure personality. Man was really dead when he gave himself up to evil, abandoning the ideal.

XXIX.

CONSTANCY TO AN IDEAL.

By JOHN WEISS.

ALLUDING to the saying that "God is on the side of the strongest battalions," Mr. Weiss said that undoubtedly God *is* on the side of valor, foresight, self-control, and perseverance. He referred to the way in which the Dutch nation were prepared, in the providence of God, to struggle effectively in the maintenance of civil and religious liberty. Beginning in a marsh, where their utmost efforts were needed to preserve life and a standing-place, for centuries they seemed to be only building and repairing dykes; but they were really gaining the qualities needful to fence out bigotry and tyranny, and their education in physical defence blossomed into noble traits of moral and spiritual life.

The will is the directing impulse of all the powers that the human being possesses. All the labor of human hands and brains is resolved into simplicity and elemental identity by the spiritual chemistry of the Creator. He is happy who can pass through Circe's den, not only unsullied, but a liberator of his comrades.

One great danger which threatens us is that of being content with our arrival at any given point. He did well who burned his ships that his party might be compelled to move onward. The true way to deal with our attainments is to use them as stepping-stones to something higher still. The men in best condition to move on are the men likely to be most demoralized by waiting. When a man is disposed to view his course with complacency, and remark even to himself, "How well I have done!" he is in danger. His only safety is to burn his ships, and pass on to further achievement. Men are not made for such conceited reveries. God has always more work laid out for us.

Nevertheless, there come inevitable periods of discouragement, and these form a trial intensely severe to those persons whose physical and moral constitutions seem to be the culmination of generations of one form or another of careless or vicious living. Here Mr. Weiss drew a most vivid picture of the condition of one who has inherited from several ancestors the results of reckless indulgence of appetite, or the habit of avaricious accumulation. Even such, however, are not forsaken of the Father. For them too there is a continuance of the divine opportunity upon the earth; they must burn their ships, reject the past, and press resolutely towards a better future.

We inherit a portion of the divine imagination, and no society is corrupt enough utterly to extinguish it. Mankind is expressly built to perpetuate God's pure intentions. Heaven is never in despair, and a new progeny is constantly coming forward to execute its purpose. It is a blessed thing that parents, however they may desire it, cannot decant the old wine into the new bottles.

The essay closed with a description of the fervency of Bernard Palissy in sacrificing all things else to the attainment of his ideal, and a representation that thus only could the greatest successes be accomplished.

Mr. CHANNING spoke first of what all seemed to feel, — the fertility of thought and tropical luxuriance of expression in the essay, which made it difficult to select a point for comment. It was also, he said, a solemn sermon, in which each hearer must find himself brought to judgment. Happy is he to whom the Spirit says distinctly, According to your measure of power you have been true to your ideal. His ideal, Mr. Channing said, had always been a city of God on earth. Our business is not to be singly perfect, but to form, in intimate connection with our brethren, an image of God in humanity. He, however, had had no occasion to burn his ships: his idea had always been to pursue, to advance. God is great, and very slow in his processes; and he asks of us steady persistency in the course which appears right. Sometimes we are accosted by veiled angels, sometimes by veiled tempters. We are sure to meet with difficulties, yet we should never yield to discouragement. A city of God on earth! Has God indeed given to men free opportunity to build one? Some of us once tried the experiment at Brook Farm. Much merriment has been made over the result of that experiment, and it may seem a great practical joke of Providence that that establishment ultimately became a poorhouse. Ludicrous as the seeming failure was, Mr. Channing thought that the attempt had had its uses. The state of England was in many respects very unlike our own; yet when he went to England, Mr. Channing said, he found numbers of people there interested to try the intermediate steps between our present imperfect state and the complete establishment of the city of God on earth. All the evidence still goes on to show that this work must be effected through that sublime word of peace, "co-operation." The facts coming to light ever since have proved the correctness of what we said at Brook Farm in 1846. We, stigmatized at that time as visionaries and Utopians, were right. Co-operation *was* the real tendency of that time. The real battle was between capital and industry. It was first fought out on the Slavery question, and has since proved its reality in other forms.

Our work on this continent is to build God's city of peace. Those in Europe who study the course of events here think that we have an eminently favorable opportunity to become ideal men and women. We must be worthy of the better birthright that has come to us through the civil war. We must build the city of God in each township, in each home. But we cannot build this city with the hands of men alone; our sisters must do their part towards it, and they know as we do not what their proper work should be. Mr. Channing closed with a fervent eulogy upon Margaret Fuller, from whom an influence had come to him nobler than from any other human being.

R. W. EMERSON, who was the next speaker, said he had highly enjoyed both the text and the comment. Every temperament, said he, has had its sect in the Church. Once Calvinism, the Church of the bilious temperament, ruled in the world; since then, every variety of temperament has found its appropriate sect. As a result, there has come a vast difference in the character of the preaching. Formerly, human affection had no voice in the pulpit, or only in rarely exceptional cases; now, an improved method very generally prevails. With regard to Brook Farm, so far as Mr. Emerson knew, none of the people engaged in that experiment considered it a failure. All have rejoiced that they were there, considering it a rich experience and a useful part of their education.

Mrs. HOWE had been much gratified, both with the subject chosen for the essay and the profoundly sympathetic treatment of it. In its language, music had found a complete expression, and the comment upon it had given us history and prophecy. She agreed to the truth of what Mr. Channing had said of our special opportunities and duties in these days; and she was glad also to hear him say that the city of God was not to be built of separately perfect people. The Brook Farm experiment had not been useless, for even the scattered stones of that edifice were seen beautiful and useful in all the situations where they have since distributed themselves.

Rev. SAMUEL LONGFELLOW was glad to be so eloquently reminded of the claims of the ideal, and rejoiced in the conviction that every attempt to follow ideal excellence would bring its own reward. He wished to ask, Was there no way of preventing that war which, it had been said, impended over us? It seemed sad that peace could be expected only through war. He had hoped that we had reached the beginning of the foundation of the city of God in the mutual co-operation which was beginning to be practised in various ways; but whether the desired end were to come early or late, we must still work on in hope.

Mr. WASSON had not been quite satisfied with the statement that the impending war was to be between industry and capital. So far as his experience went, labor was quite as much demoralized as wealth. The working classes were no more moved than the rich by an appeal to disinterestedness. The new future will not open upon us until both classes, the indigent and the wealthy, remember the vocation of man to the highest. If, while we talk of human rights, we go on putting power into the hands of men who abuse it by taking every possible advantage, we shall continue to find new complications of disorder. The abolition of Slavery was more God's work than ours. We may well ask ourselves whether some new understanding of the laws of social life be not necessary. A demoralization now going on and growing worse in our country is a fact; and our road to the realization of God's ideal is likely yet to witness some terrible contests.

XXX.

ORIENTAL RELIGIONS.

By MRS. A. H. LEONOWENS.

MRS. LEONOWENS began by speaking of the great antiquity of the Rig-Veda, as indicated not only by the assertions of those who believe in its sacredness, but by the evidence of an astronomical record which is included in one of the early books. She read a most gorgeous description of the ancient city of Ayodhya, the modern Oude, and then left the subject of the antiquity of Hindu sacred books and Hindu civilization, and went on to present the claims of the former to the admiration of Christians. By way of doing this, she read several passages from the Rig-Veda and the Mahabharatta, dwelling particularly upon the fact that the Deity is constantly called Father and Mother, by which compound epithet the universality of his nature is recognized, and also drawing attention to the monotheistic spirit of Brahmanism. She quoted some of the Brahmanic definitions of the Deity, saying that she doubted if all the so-called development of the human mind had added anything to them, and then spoke of the coincidences between the meaning of the Hindu names for natural objects and the discoveries of modern science concerning them.

Mrs. Leonowens then went on to say that the more one studied the more firmly was one convinced that the Hindu religion. had, by migration, been carried all over

the world, and become the parent of all other forms of
faith.   She dwelt particularly upon the coincidence between the Christian idea of the Trinity and the Hindu conception of a Deity formed of Brahma the divine cause,
Krishna the preserver, and Siva the divine spirit, argu-
ing that this proved that the younger religion derived its
idea from the elder.   She spoke of the Vedic chivalry of
feeling towards women, saying that the modern tendency
to give them their rights and their proper place was but
a return to the ancient standard.   The essay closed by
a comparison between the universal sacrifice performed
daily by all Brahman priests and the sacrifice of the mass,
which, in Mrs. Leonowens's opinion, are not only similar
in ceremonial but in significance.

The Rev. JOHN T. SARGENT then spoke in commen-
dation of the essay, and said that he thought it must
be conceded that modern forms of religion had added
little to some of the noble ideas of which Mrs. Leonowens
had spoken.

A. BRONSON ALCOTT remarked that all present must feel
that a wider horizon had been opened by what they had
heard.   All Christians were beginning to feel that they
must, even while reverencing those things which they held
sacred, extend their hospitality to the religious ideas of
other races, remembering that all truth has not been revealed exclusively to us.

The Rev. SAMUEL LONGFELLOW evinced a decided preference for the Christian Scriptures, and remarked that
there was an immense mass of stuff in the Brahmanic
sacred books which was unfit for reading ; he also ventured
to contradict an assertion made by Mrs. Leonowens that
Christ and Krishna were identical in meaning, and said

that whereas the former word signified "anointed," the latter meant "black."

Mrs. LEONOWENS explained that Krishna really meant "dark blue," which was the color of the robe worn by kings at their anointing, and also the hue of the sky, which was the anointing of the earth.

Mr. LONGFELLOW expressed his pleasure at learning the real meaning of the name.

Dr. BARTOL then spoke on prayer, enunciating his favorite theory that the soul which is nearest to God does not like to speak of him, and does not need to speak to him, but merely listens for his word, content to do his will. The speaker also dwelt at some length on the dissatisfaction which he considered that every one must feel with a day in which he had not toiled and suffered.

Mr. SARGENT said that he supposed it was the modern opinion that there was no efficacy in prayer, except in its reaction upon the petitioner.

Dr. BARTOL said that prayer was a realization of the unity of the soul with its source, not a carrier pigeon sent out to ask for aid, nor a cable reaching from a wreck to the shore.

Mr. ALCOTT followed this up, saying that the earnest desires of our hearts are our real prayers, and that the Friends truly appreciate this when they sit in silence and wait for the Spirit.

This series of remarks drew forth an earnest speech from JAMES FREEMAN CLARKE, who asked why we prayed if we did not long for something, and did not hope to receive it by praying. "I cannot," he said, "agree to the theory which would make prayer a mere reaction. If I thought so, I would call it meditation. Why should I pretend to ask God for anything if I do not expect an answer? Am I so cut off from the Infinite that he cannot hear my petitions? Am I so far from him that, while I can ask a man for anything and receive it, I may pray to God

15

in vain? When man asks God for help and opens his soul to receive it, in order that he may do his will, real help comes. My friend here says, ' To labor is to pray ; ' but suppose there is no life, no heart, no love in you, and there is a vast work for you to do, and no help but that of the Spirit, what then? That is the time for prayer. Then is the time to put ourselves in the place where the work is to be done, and without undue solicitude to open our souls to God, and help will certainly come. He will give his spirit to us if we ask for it, for he is more ready to bestow favors upon us than we are to heap them upon our children. I feel this so deeply," Dr. Clarke concluded, " that I am relieved from all sense of responsibility, and know that all I have to do is to open my soul to God. Year by year my creed has grown shorter ; now it is only ' From God, for man,' and I cannot leave out either part."

A little burst of applause followed Dr. Clarke's remarks, and, as it died away, Mr. SARGENT said that the sunshine of God was all about us, and our error was in not opening our hearts to it.

Dr. BARTOL said that he should not object to anything which Dr. Clarke had said, but he thought we must be at a distance from God, and not united with him as we should be, before we could ask him anything. He gave before we could ask.

Dr. CLARKE commented on this by saying that he thought that even the childish babble of her infant was sweet to a mother.

XXXI.

RAPHAEL AND HIS CRITICS.

By TITUS MUNSON COAN.

DR. COAN contended that there was too much indiscriminate and conventional praise bestowed upon the works of the great painter. He thought it had been as little the fashion to criticise Raphael as Shakspeare, and the consequence is that the general impression has prevailed that Raphael was faultless.

Dr. Coan considered the limitations of Raphael's genius. The first of these which he mentioned was the fact that the artist seemed to see beauty in the human form, and not elsewhere, being in this respect like all the artists of his age, none of whom studied Nature. Raphael sometimes fell so far short of truth in the portrayal of some minor objects as to cease to produce decorative pictures, thus falling below the requirements of even the German critics, who have not, as yet, decided that ugliness is really desirable in art. To illustrate this point, Dr. Coan criticised the frescos of the Loggie of the Vatican, and pointed out that in these Raphael had curiously erred in the representation of the horse, the ass, the camel, the sheep, and of flame and water. In regard to composition, also, these frescos were pronounced defective, monotony being very common. He then entered upon an inquiry as to Raphael's probable view of art, questioning whether he regarded its mission as simply decorative, or considered that it should be ennobling, and quoted Ruskin as an advocate of the former and Taine as an expounder of the latter view. The essay closed with a glowing tribute to the artist, who, Dr. Coan declared, while he had faults which the honest critic could not ignore without self-abasement, was yet the guardian of the highest in art, and had produced the noblest pictures which had yet appeared in this shining world.

Mr. CRANCH spoke in defence of Raphael, saying that landscape and animal painting hardly existed in his time.

Mr. SARGENT suggested that possibly he fell into his faults from subordinating all other things to the presentation of the sacred personages whom he painted.

One of the guests accused Raphael of inaccuracy in drawing the human figure, and seemed to think the artists of the present age had advanced far beyond him.

Mr. GANNETT asked if more importance should not be given to the nature of an artist's mistakes than to their number, and suggested that as Raphael only failed in minor details, his errors were less grave than if he had looked at his subject in a narrow, unartistic spirit. If the artist's conception is grand, we may overlook some faults of execution.

XXXII.

THE BIRD AND THE BELL.

By C. P. CRANCH.

IT was the first occasion on which a poem had been substituted for an essay, and of course the innovation
gave rise to some speculation. "What will there be to
discuss in verses?" asked one and another; but the result
proved that themes for subsequent discourse were not
wanting. Mr. CRANCH's title was "The Bird and the Bell,"
a real bird and a real bell, which symbolized, as the theme
grew, the clear music of natural religion and the brazen
clangor of dogmatic theology. The poem opened with a
description of an early morning of early spring, in Flor-
ence, in which, waking from sleep, the poet heard the
carol of a bird, so clear and fresh that no heart could hear
it and not rejoice, — a carol of youth and hope and
spring. Upon this music broke the clamor of a brazen
bell, "joined in a moment by a hundred more."

> "Oft have I listened in the dead of night,
>   When all those towers like chanting priests have prayed,
> And the weird tones seemed tangled in the height
>   Of palaces."

While this "incessant peal filled all the air," the sweet
bird-music was drowned and ceased, and the clanging bell
seemed a symbol of the church of many burdens griev-
ous to be borne, which drowns with the monotonous
echo of its creeds and formulas the glad, spontaneous cry

of the recognizing soul to its God. Here followed a long
apostrophe to the mighty church, — the Church of Rome,
"old, but still adorned with jewels of her youth." Mr.
Cranch saw in this "wrinkled bride, affianced to the blind,"
the nurse, not the mother of art, — an unwise nurse, always
cramping and fettering the children in her charge, while
these great souls looked over and beyond their prison-walls,
and caught from the earth below and the skies above new
splendors for Rome's tarnished crown. Still addressing
this cruel foster-mother, he cried : —

"Is there a daring thought thou hast not crushed ?
Is there a generous faith thou hast not cursed ?

. . . . .

"Dark Sorceress, whose Circean cup bereft
Man of his fair proportions and large hope,
Thy throne is built on darkness !

. . . . .

"Art thou our mother, truly ? None so bold
As lift thy veil, and show how hard and cold
Those eyes of tyranny, that mouth of guile,
That low and narrow brow, the witchcraft of that smile,
That subtle smile, deluding while it warmed."

A picture followed of Italy struggling for her freedom ;
then of Italy made free, while

"The nations greet her as some lovely guest
Arriving late, where friends pour out the wine.
Ay, press around, and pledge her in the best
Your table yields, and in her praise combine !
And ye who love her most, press near, and twine
Her locks with wreaths, and in her large, dark eyes
See all the sorrowing Past, and her great Future rise."

Mr. Cranch thinks that this church of darkness can do
little to-day, when the sun of progress is risen. But we
of to-day may not boast ourselves, unless

" We are, indeed, so sure our faith is best
   That we can dare to leave it large and free,
Nor fear to bring the creed to reason's test,
   Scorning intolerance toward all who see
      With other eyes."

Striving thus, through trust in God and man and toleration toward all sincere believing, for the truth —

" The music of the soul can ne'er be mute.
   What though the brazen clang of antique form
Stop for a hundred years the angel's lute ?
   The angel smiles, and when the deafening storm
Has pealed along the age, he sings again,
Clearer and sweeter, like the sunshine after rain."

It seemed to Dr. BARTOL the great test-question about
any truth, " Can it be sung, can it be set to music? " The
words of Jesus were of themselves rhythmical ; they were
a song of hope, a chant of courage. But this test would
make sad work of dogmatic theology. We should have
trouble to sing Calvinism. Election is not musical, nor is
everlasting punishment melodious.

Mr. JOHN DWIGHT spoke of Bach as the singer of Calvinism,— some of his compositions go into all the literal
details of the crucifixion. But he thought it made no difference about the creed of Bach ; there was something beneath the creed, and the creed was only a moving power.
It was only the true thing which can be sung or printed ;
false things do not last.

Mrs. HOWE said that the poem to which we had listened
seemed to her the truest and the best word she had ever
heard about Italy in connection with the subject. She
thought that in Mr. Cranch's poem there was a new
point of presentation ; and she was reminded by his name
and this suggestion of another and earlier Christopher, —

Christopher Columbus; and she thought that Mr. Cranch also belonged to the discoverers in his discovery of new thoughts.

Mr. SAMUEL LONGFELLOW followed this with a word about the other side; he said there were plenty of persons who could speak on the other side, or the ecclesiastical side, if they were present, but it seemed to him that Nature must eventually win over ecclesiasticism. He then illustrated this by a pleasing incident which had come under his own observation in one of the Italian cities. He saw a little child dancing on the pavement of the church interior with perfect abandon and ease, who presently approached the altar and dropped upon her knees with the rest, said her little prayer and danced out. Here was a touch of Nature which seemed to offer such contrast with the old forms. He then spoke of John Hay's poem of "Jim Bludsoe," with its fidelity to Nature, which fact had made it so universal in acceptance and appreciation. We must hold fast to everything natural, he said, whether in church or out of it.

Mr. POTTER, referring to what had been said about Calvinism, — that it could not be sung, — wanted to know what we would do with Milton's "Paradise Lost" then. A good many people found it rather hard reading now, but no one would deny that Milton was a great singer.

Dr. BARTOL again spoke of the man being greater than his creed, and therefore singing above it.

Mr. ALCOTT believed that everything true and high set itself to music. All men and women who influence mankind are idealists. The sentiments harmonize and become melodious. The New Testament itself was a poem; so were the utterances of Jesus.

CHARLES G. AMES alluded to the isms of the day, and said that all the isms had a mission; Calvinism he declared to be the greatest ism of all. He believed in Cal-

vinism, with Calvin and the ism left out. He believed
that Catholicism, too, was of greater importance and
meaning than we thought. It fitted into history in a way
we do not understand. He could not believe so great
a power could spend itself as an evil force. Other forces
are to play upon it, and eventually work it to its will.
Why cannot we fall into some way to harmonize with all
beliefs? "I do not belong to the church," he said, "but
the church belongs to me."

Mr. GANNETT said in reference to what seemed to be the
central point of the discussion, Calvinism, that he thought
Calvinism *did* sing. Life is the highest expression, and
what great musical lines were in that life! He thought we
should accept all things; and he quoted from Mr. Emerson,
"I accept the universe." He thought that was significant
of a broad belief.

Mrs. HOWE begged to say another word just here, —
that it was *not* Emerson who had made that statement, but
Margaret Fuller. She said she did not know that the universe was ever offered to Mr. Emerson.

A general laugh ensued here, and Mr. AMES, catching
the spirit of it, in his happy manner said that he thought
the universe was offered to us all; that we were all here
for that; and he, for himself, had always felt like one of
the largest stockholders.

XXXIII.

FATALITY.

By JOHN WEISS.

MR. WEISS treated in the most delightful manner the subject of "Fatality," which he illustrated by the Greek story of Œdipus. The Greeks were in the habit of considering every calamity as the punishment for some especial sin; but in this story they embodied a feeling that besides Fate there was also Fatality in human life, — something in the regular sequence of events which could not be referred to violations of divine law, though it might be due to ignorance and weakness; something unfortunate as well as retributive, which deepened the Greek reverence for the closeness of the invisible world. We often say of a person, "It is just his luck," not blaming him, but recognizing the fact of his being, so to speak, born to misfortune. Now, Œdipus seems to have been pre-eminently born to misfortune.

He was the son of Laius and Jocasta of Thebes. Exposed on Mount Cithæron by his parents to forestall the fulfilment of a prophecy that his father would lose his life at his hands, left there with his feet pierced through and tied together, he yet lived to be called Œdipus, — a word which means "swollen feet," for he was, though comely and well-proportioned, a trifle halt and uncertain in his movements from this early exposure. A shepherd finds him, and carries him to the palace of Polybus and Merope, at

Corinth, where, by that royal couple, he is adopted and brought up.

For a long time he supposes himself to be their son, but learning by some chance that he is not, he repairs to Delphi to consult an oracle. He is cautioned by the oracle to beware of meeting his father and his mother, for if he should meet his father he would slay him, and if he should meet his mother a yet more direful disaster would ensue. Still half believing that Polybus is his father, he will not return to Corinth, but takes the road to Thebes. Now this was about the time of the ravages of the Sphinx, and Laius, the real father of Œdipus, chanced to be on his way to Delphi to consult the oracle. Father and son met in a narrow passage, where some trouble about passing each other grew into a quarrel, and Œdipus killed his father.

Arrived at Thebes, he found the whole country agitated by the presence of the Sphinx. She had propounded a famous riddle, and refused to leave the place until it was guessed; but every one who attempted to guess it and failed she devoured, — a practice not conducive to Theban cheerfulness. The Thebans in despair proclaimed that whoever would guess the riddle should become their king and the husband of Jocasta, the widowed mother of Œdipus.

The Sphinx propounded her puzzle to Œdipus, as to his predecessors, — "What animal is that which walks on four feet in the morning, on two at noon, and on three at night? It has but one voice, and when it has the most feet it is the weakest." You are not surprised at the Greek mind's guessing it — a modern school-boy could do that. What animal is it? Why, man, of course, answers the awakening Greek: and he himself, the answer, is the greatest riddle; for though he crawls as a babe, walks in the noon of his manhood, and declines upon a staff at night, he has but one voice, and that is the inspired, inspiring soul.

Not many years had Œdipus been seated upon the throne of his father, with his queen, his own mother, by his side, when a pestilence broke out to ravage the land which he had freed from the Sphinx. Of course, instead of searching for a natural and physical cause for this visitation, he betakes himself to an oracle. The oracle tells him that the murderer of King Laius yet lives among the Thebans. At once Œdipus resolves to become the dead king's avenger. At last he finds out that he himself was the murderer. Jocasta thereupon understands the whole complication of events, and kills herself. Then Œdipus, horror-stricken, snatches the golden buckles from her robe, and plunges and replunges them into his eyeballs. " Let me go sightless into Hades," he exclaims, " for how can I ever behold my father again?"

Lame, blind, gray in a moment with the shock of his misfortunes, he is thrust forth by the other members of the royal house, and totters into exile, invoking upon his own head the Erinnys of his mother. But the very Fates are softened towards him, and the gods make him their care. His children grow up to be his comforters. His daughter Antigone, the loveliest woman of all literature, waits lovingly upon his footsteps. Even his death is an unaccountable, painless fading out of sight.

Round this immortal story Mr. Weiss spun the golden threads of his eloquence.

Mr. EMERSON broke the momentary silence after the essay. He thought it well for us to sit upon the riddle of the Sphinx; and he had very much enjoyed Mr. Weiss's suggestive paper. Those old tragedies and stories were full of human significance. We could not have a better definition of the Greek chorus than that it was the voice of humanity throughout the play. We should need a wide

generalization to reconcile all the speeches of the Greeks
on the matter of fate; but a poet is not bound to reconcile
what he does and says with everything else which he has
said or shall say.

Col. HIGGINSON remarked that it seemed to him the
Greeks were simply more daring than we in recognizing
the cloudy aspects of existence. They played freely with
these vast conceptions of fate, and the like. The modern
tendency is to analyze and explain, and rather to put out
of sight what cannot be reduced to system. Aristotle
asked questions boldly and baldly enough; but before his
day if the Greeks must suggest an interrogation-point
they did it grandly, as in the case of the Sphinx. Among
the moderns, Hawthorne, indeed, wrote with a certain
grand mysticism, — gave sublime hints, after the manner
of the ancients; but the Greek idea of fate belongs to
the cloudy region, and it is difficult for us to treat it satisfactorily.

Mr. FROTHINGHAM said that a man living in New York
saw little of Greek philosophy, though a good deal of certain kinds of fate. He never touched a Greek tragedy
without feeling that it included everything; but we did
not always get, as we had this morning, an interpreter
who could bring to light all the shades of meaning. There
seemed to be nothing to take us out of the dilemma between optimism and despair until we came to the poetic
view. The old Greeks were happy, fated to be happy,
and so bequeathed happiness to the world; and we feel it
in going back into their atmosphere. It is not merely for
the cultivated, but for simple human nature. Imagination is above dogmatism.

Dr. BARTOL expressed his thanks to Mr. Weiss as well
as his interest in every sentence of the essay. But he felt
that if fatality be the last result of fate, fate itself is but
a voice, as its derivation shows: the speaker is behind.

Law did not make the world. Fate is the gesture and
voice of the Infinite Person, who is Love. Goodness is
the first idea. We may not see till we are nearer to the
light, but we must believe. He should be sorry for us to
date from Fate, or believe ourselves Fate's children, instead of the children of God.

Miss GREW thought the age which produced the Greek
story could not have produced the interpretation which
Mr. Weiss had given. He had drawn from it more than
its framers knew was there.

Mr. POTTER said the history of the universe is a Sphinx,
— intelligence striving to develop itself into individuality,
or force into intelligence. The history of each individual
is the history of a struggle between spirit or moral force,
and this blind fate or circumstance the background on
which we are developed.

Col. HIGGINSON observed that the two poles of our lives
must include all the wide range of inherited tendencies and
causes with which Dr. Holmes has dealt, as well as their
opposite, the individual will. What was grandest in Thoreau was his conception of a man's power to ennoble his
own life. He, himself, had no fear of science. It gave
even to poetry much more than it took away. We do not
see Dr. Howe enumerated among the literary men of America; but few things were written which thrilled him as did
Dr. Howe's reports. They were as noble and inspiring as
any Greek tragedy; and while reading them one understood how science is coming to the aid of art and poetry
and religion. We are yet to work into our own lives all
which the Greeks knew of excellence and of beauty.
About a thousand years hence we shall have very nice
times.

Mr. POWELL wondered if distance does not lend some
enchantment to the Greek view. He fancied that to-day
humanity is nobler than ever before. We do not need

to dwell apart from the natural world in one of imagination, because the most beautiful pictures are strictly true. We are only on the threshold, as yet, of the unexplored world of spiritual forces. They are indicated by all history, and are everywhere at work; and we ought to look more at life from that side.

Miss PEABODY thought the point of the tragedy of Œdipus to be that he who had unriddled the Sphinx knew nothing of himself. While that ignorance exists, the Sphinx must tear men in pieces. Œdipus states the truth intellectually, but is not saved by it. The tragedy of life is that everybody drifts. We perceive, and are not helped by our perceiving. There is truth enough in the world to save it, but it is not saved. The story of Œdipus illustrates this. What the oracle says shocks him, but does not hinder him from rashness; and such is the always recurring tragedy of life.

XXXIV.

IMAGINATION.

By CHARLES CARROLL EVERETT.

PROFESSOR EVERETT began by saying that he had noticed a tendency at the present day to repress, and even to disown, the imagination. The imagination is simply the faculty of imagining. This simple power is of more importance than we often think. If we could learn to see, to look accurately and take in all that we see, and then remember what we see and reproduce it to the eye of the mind as it existed for the eye of the body, life would be a new thing for us. This was the real end of education, and in this the training of the imagination held no small place. But this is only a small part, indeed the smallest part, of the functions of the imagination. Not merely does it reproduce for the mind that which the eye has seen: it goes beyond, and separates the elements of that which has been beheld, and recombines them in new forms. It goes even farther: it introduces new elements, creating for the mind that which the outward senses could not discern. In all this it keeps true to the lessons it has learned, and keeps true to Nature even when it changes the nature which has been beheld. The imagination and the fancy might thus be distinguished. The imagination follows the lines of Nature: the fancy works more independently, forsaking the intent of Nature and adapting ends of its own, combining the elements of Nature arbitrarily and artificially.

The fancy brought together the parts of the man and of the horse, and created the centaur : imagination created the Apollo. The world of fancy is a world apart by itself, while the world of imagination may be more natural than that of Nature itself. Tyndall recognizes the fact that the imagination is an instrument of science itself. The grandest discoveries of science were made when it had left the regions of the seen and the known and followed the imagination by new paths to regions before unseen. Newton, watching the fall of the apple, began dreaming of the movements of the stars. His imagination leaped to a conception which embraced the universe. The discoveries of science become to the minds of most men hard, cold, prosaic facts. It is forgotten that when they first dawned they came as poetry, and were the outgrowth of the imagination, — the poetic faculty. Nowhere to-day is imagination more active than in the realms of science. The theory of development was as truly a creation of the mind as the fables of Æsop. The fable may be more fanciful, but the theory is more imaginative. Not only is the imagination thus efficient in science, in the practical affairs of life it fills a place no less important. The man of affairs is largely dependent for his success on the powers of the imagination. It is less by a process of conscious reasoning than by the flash of intuition that he lays his vastest plans. Here, as before, it is the imagination of the trained mind that oftenest does its work successfully. There is a genius in affairs as truly as in literature or art ; but it is imagination, and not fancy. The man of fancy also dreams dreams and risks his money on their truth, but has left only the memory of his wasted means and of his palace in the clouds. The poet or student, living largely in the regions of the imagination, wonders how life is possible amid its cold, hard realities without the play of the imagination. He is right in this, but wrong in supposing

16

that the imagination is excluded from these so-called
practical affairs. It is looked upon by its masters as a
good servant if well-trained. But is the imagination
merely a servant? To whom does the world rightfully
belong? As it exists for us, it is the creation of the
imagination. She lends it to science to study, to analyze,
to reason about. She lends it to business to work or to
play with. But when, because she is thus helpful, she
is treated as a servant only, she may well assert the right
of sovereignty. Art and poetry are the methods of the
imagination, and these complete the world. Art gives us
the ideal man, life, and Nature. As we look upon them
we feel that this is the real man, the real life, the real
Nature. The perfect man is the ideal man; the perfect
life, as yet largely a dream life, the ideal life. It is the
goal of humanity. I believe in all that the botanist tells
about the flower; but if he sees nothing more in the flower
than his analysis can show him, then the little child who
claps its hands in delight at the beauty of the first blossom of the spring sees the flower more truly than he does.
The whole is more than the sum of its parts. The ideal
is more real than the actual: it destroys the actual that
it may fulfil itself. The oak which the little sapling
became is more real than the sapling, for the sapling
yielded to its power and became the oak. The imagination, first the explorer and then the poet of the race,
became at last its seer, its prophet, and its priest. The
senses give us only a confused series of sensations; the
understanding gives us only lifeless fragments; the imagination gives us the universe in its wholeness, and trans-
forms it into the living garments of divinity.

XXXV.

THE NEBULAR THEORY.

By BENJAMIN PEIRCE.

THE speaker distinguished four general periods in nebular evolution, — chaos, nebula, star, planet. How
this subject takes hold on infinity may be imagined from
Professor Peirce's statement that, incomprehensible as the
duration is from chaos to planet, with its unnumbered
millions of years, it is possible that there may have been
many chaotic periods from the beginning to the present
time. There was at first, speaking of our present system,
a collection of matter in a simple, inactive state, not necessarily infinitely diffused. It may have been the remains of
old stars which have retained the resultant of their former
motion, and so the harmony of the universe now may be
the result of a previous harmony, and may be transmitted
to the end. The division which has occurred in matter
must have had its beginning in the original chaos, or
the organized system could not have come from it. The
plan must have been in the system from the beginning, as
the plan of the eagle is in the egg. To the idea that there
was in the beginning a system without a plan Professor
Peirce is resolutely opposed, as to any other absurdity in
the minds of unthinking men. The original chaos must
have been invisible. Luminousness is evidence of living
force. Yet we can imagine what chaos is from what we
see about us. The grains of sand, the cold planets, and
dead suns may be potentially chaos.

But as soon as there is light we come to the second stage, that of the nebula. Seven periods are recognized in this epoch, — nebulosity, the nebula proper, the cluster, the annular nebula, the spiral nebula, the Milky Way, and the Magellanic clouds. This classification approaches that made by Sir William Herschel. Nebulosity shows the slightest diffusion of light which can be perceived by a telescope. In almost every point of the heavens there is some light to be found. The nebula proper has more distinct boundaries than the nebulosity, and the intensity of light in it is unequal. Sometimes the variation is very marked, and sometimes very faint. In the former case several nebulæ are supposed to be connected. When these nebulæ are concentrated they form clusters, but the approach to this condition from the single nebula is made gradually. Next comes the annular nebula, which, in its simplest form, is a mere ring. This is found in all parts of the universe, and the arrangement of matter in circular form is thought to be under the very same law which determines the arrangement of molecules. In the case of dumb-bell nebulæ the outline is filled to a full circle by telescopes of high power. It is thought that some of these nebulæ may be annular, with the side presented towards us.

A little episode in the address at this point was noticeable, for a subdued applause greeted the speaker's heartfelt earnestness. He spoke of the identity of the controlling law in the nebula and the child's top. The same force goes through its period in a hundredth part of a second in the child's top which completes the precession of the equinoxes in long ages. Then he said: "It seems as if the divine truth loves to nestle in the arms of little children. Who dares to say, in the face of such facts, that there is no love in Nature but in this cold, selfish heart of man?"

The spiral nebula, first noted by Lord Rosse, is not

limited to that one case, but is found in a great number of instances. The Milky Way was studied closely by Sir William Herschel. He thought it was nothing but a nebula in an advanced stage. Magellan's clouds we do not see. They are found in the southern sky, and appear as clouds of light. They are an immense quantity of stars, double stars, clusters, and nebulæ, of all kinds known. It appears to be a wonderful system.

Herschel came to the conclusion that it is impossible to draw any line of demarcation between the different stages of star development. His conclusion was proper and natural, — that the very appearance of the periods running into each other is only an indication that they are different stages of the same thing. He compares the development of the stages of plant-life. In these successive stages we can read the ideal history. The question is, "Is it true? Is Nature a false witness, or can we believe her?"

Five stages mark the star epoch, — the round nebula, the nebulous star, the star proper, the double star, and the solar system. The round nebula may have no concentration at the centre, but usually it does. In proportion as it is round, is there a concentration of light at the centre. A nebulous star is one stage forward. What appears a star under a low power of the telescope will appear as a nebular star under a higher power. So the development proceeds till we come to the stars which show no nebulosity under a telescope of the highest power. But some stars without a nebula are known to be connected. They are seen to revolve about each other. No line can be drawn between these stages of change; and so the nebular theory has arisen, — that in the mass of matter there is a disposition to concentrate, and that this concentration is continually going on, and that heat is given out by the compression of the parts upon each other, and the mass is heated till it becomes more and more luminous. The compression goes on, and finally the particles come into such connection that the action of chemical force is possible, and the gases appear. Then deposits are made in the mass, — solid substances, which give a very different kind of light from the gases or the nebula. This can be distinguished by the spectroscope; but Herschel did not have means to make the distinction, and hence he doubted whether there was any real nebula. The spectrum of a star has continuity, but the spectrum of a nebula has not. Yet the spectra of of nebulæ differ among themselves so they can be distinguished from each other. The variety of nebulæ in form is so great that Professor Peirce thinks it is impossible for the mind of man to conceive any possible kind which is not actually found in the sidereal heavens.

Of solar systems we know but one, yet there are probably many in the universe. The characteristic is a self-luminous body surrounded by bodies not self-luminous. We cannot expect to see other solar systems, because the amount of light reflected from the satellites is so small. The new telescopes are not likely to bring out this small amount of light. Professor Peirce at this point dropped some casual remarks, which, very comforting to Cambridge, may be profitable to ambitious telescope-makers. The telescope at Cambridge, he says, is probably richer in results than the larger one at Washington or the one in the West. With a larger glass the magnifying, which greatly influences the twinkling of the stars, will be increased. With the Cambridge telescope there are only two or three nights in a year when it can be used, and the professor avers that he would rather work with a glass of ten or twelve inches than with a larger one. A good night for the Washington telescope cannot be expected more than once in three or four years. For larger telescopes they must wait a length of time proportional to the magnitude of the telescope, and, perhaps, get one night in a century.

In the solar system there are about one hundred and eighty small planets and eight large ones, all moving around the sun in the same direction. The satellites of the planets generally move in the same direction also; but the partial reversal of the movement in the case of the outer planets, when fully explained and understood, does not interfere with the nebular theory, but rather sustains it. These satellites also rotate on the axes in the same direction as their motion, and it is infinitely improbable that this coincidence could have happened by chance. The planets are nearly all on the sun's equator, and have their own equators in nearly the same plane. These phenomena were brought forward by La Place, in the beginning of the century, as evidence of the nebular theory. His proof was the result of remarkable mathematical logic, tracing back the course of physical power. The wonderful uniformity of motion and position prove a great plan behind, and an intelligence to execute it.

Seven stages mark the planetary epoch, — the frozen star, the inorganic period, the organic, the planet proper, the satellite, the comet, and the chaotic mass.

As the planet concentrates, it comes to have a solid exterior. On the question whether the centre or the outside solidifies first, probably no reasoning is better than that of Dr. T. Sterry Hunt. Solidification must begin at the centre. He has shown that solidification of particles would take place on the surface, and these masses would sink to the centre; but some substances — water, for instance — solidify first on the surface, and we do not know how far the process continues. We may have a solid centre and a solid surface, with a liquid mass between, and Professor Peirce is inclined to accept that view. Sir William Thompson thinks he has proved that the earth is solid to its centre, but Professor Peirce does not regard it proved by any means. Thompson's proof by the precession of the equinoxes is not convincing.

When the planet is solid on the exterior it is in the inorganic period. When it has cooled down so plants can live,
it is in the organic. A very pertinent illustration of the
proof of original heat was given by the speaker from his
loaf of brown bread. Fresh from the baker's, it is warmer
on the inside than on the outside. On the second day,
warmed over in his oven, it is warmer on the outside. So
a body which is warm on the inside must sometime have
been equally hot on the outside. Now the earth is hotter
in the interior than at the surface. Then it is cooling off.
The heat of the interior could never have been greater
than it was sometime at the surface. Scientific men know
at what rate heat will pass through the strata at the surface of the earth. They know how long it would take for
the heat to disappear wholly. As we descend toward the
centre of the earth the heat increases one degree Fahren-
heit for every fifty feet. This continues to be the ratio so
far as our knowledge extends. Sir William Thompson
estimated the time for cooling down to the present condition at a hundred million years. This period has been
reduced by Tate to twenty millions, — a time altogether
too short for the phenomena of the organic world as they
are observed.

How did organic life come into the world? Professor
Peirce will not undertake to say; but he thinks no scientific man will deny that if any planet should be subjected to
the same changes as this, animal life would appear upon
it, just as it has upon this. The professor maintains a
firm belief in the action of secondary causes in the work-
ings of Nature, and that God intrusts the outworking of
his plans to them. By secondary cause only, he says, is
science possible, and in that way alone can intelligence
have any meaning in its application to the physical
universe.

Are there inhabitants in other parts of the universe?

In considering this question, the Professor spoke first of
the moon. In its long days and nights it is alternately so
heated and cooled that either extreme must be destructive
to all organic life. In the case of a self-luminous body,
like the sun, after it had become sufficiently cool to permit
animal life, the opportunity for such life could not last more
than fifty of our days at the extreme, judging from the
rapidity with which in the night-time heat from our own
earth passes off into the starry spaces. Life is to be expected only on a planet. There must be an atmosphere to
maintain an equable temperature, and there must be a sun
to give warmth. So far as evolution is concerned with
these conditions, there can be no evolution without some
outside action.

The other planets of our system were next considered.
Mercury is probably not in a state fit for animal life. Neptune and Uranus are so remote that their temperature must
be very low. Jupiter and Saturn are so heated that it is
not likely that animal life could exist upon them. Mars
is thought to be much like the earth, but a recent English
observer doubts it very much. He thinks that what are
called snow-caps on the poles are but clouds of vapor. It
is probable that Mars is not yet cold enough for animal
life. Only Venus and the earth are left as probably fit for
animal or intellectual life.

What is all this for? The Professor asks the question ;
and his answer is, that the universe is a vehicle of intelligence to intelligent beings, and we are made to study the
universe. There is a plan in the earth, and we should
study it. The greatest facts of our comprehension rest
upon the laws which first attract our attention, — those of
gravitation and motion. Why do these great laws come
down to the smallest matters? Only one answer is possible. It is absurd to say it is the result of an unintelligent
evolution of Nature. It may be that evolution is the

machinery to which the working out of the plan is submitted; *that* the Professor believes as firmly as he does the law of gravitation: but there must be a plan behind it. The idea of design which he himself has cannot be explained unless there is a Designer in Nature.

As the address closed there was less desire than is generally the case to venture theories or criticisms, though the lack was fully made up by expressions of regard and indebtedness to the speaker of the hour.

Mr. Weiss affirmed again his belief in the imagination which is the source of all imagination; and Mr. Wasson questioned in regard to secondary causes whether there were not points where the theory of evolution is not adequate to explain the phenomena. Such points, he suggests, may be the passage from the inorganic to the organic periods, the development of sex, the passage from the organic to the mental, and the passage from the germinal cell to the adult form. He questions whether the form of every living thing can be accounted for on physical principles.

Prof. Peirce, appealed to, preferred to leave those questions to the naturalists, and the company then dispersed.

XXXVI.

BUCKLE AND CARLYLE.

By WILLIAM J. POTTER.

THOMAS CARLYLE says, " The history of what man has accomplished in this world is at bottom the history of the great men who have worked here." Henry Thomas Buckle says that in the history of mankind, as in the physical world, " all is order, symmetry and law; " and that it is the business of the historian to show that " the movements of nations are perfectly regular, and that, like all other movements, they are solely determined by their antecedents. If he cannot do this, he may be an annalist or a biographer or a chronicler, but is no historian." These two statements represent two quite opposite, though not perhaps irreconcilable, ways of regarding human history. The one emphasizes and magnifies the importance of *persons* as leaders of the human race; resolves history substantially into personal character and volition, makes it the sum of the dispositions, energies, and acts of the men who have shown conspicuous ability in human affairs. The other seeks primarily to discover and trace that kind of law and method in human affairs which is behind and antecedent to the character and actions of persons; regards persons as merely the instruments in the unfolding of events which they have little or no power in producing; conceives of humanity in the mass as being pervaded, shaped, and developed by an intel-

ligent force and purpose, which may be called divinity
or destiny. On the one hand Carlyle, himself the most
brilliant illustrator of his own definition of history, gives
us the life of Frederick the Great as the history of Germany
for the eighteenth century; the letters and speeches and
acts of Cromwell for the history of Puritanism and England's civil war in the seventeenth century; glowing pictures of a few leading persons, and of events happening
under their leadership, as the history of the French Revolution. And in this Carlyle but carries to the extreme
what may be said to have been, until quite recent times,
the general theory of history-writing, — namely, the chron-
icling in their proper connection and order of the deeds
of great men, and the transactions of communities and
nations under the guidance of great men. On the other
hand, in opposition to this theory, Mr. Buckle and the
new school of historical writers agreeing with him give us
histories of human progress, and even of specific national
affairs, in which the personal influence and existence of
individual men, however great and active, are lost sight
of almost as if they had never been. These writers endeavor to trace the progress of events to the progress of
impersonal ideas and tendencies working in human society
in the aggregate. They follow the movements of nations,
civilizations, religions, back to certain primary dispositions
and sentiments of the human mind, and attempt to show how
the development of these, under the various conditions of
migration, hereditary law, mixture of race, climate, natural
surroundings of all kinds, action and reaction of nations
and ideas upon each other, has produced all that variety
and steady progress of human affairs which we call history.
They claim that both events and ideas have been developed
in a certain necessary sequence which personal volition has
no power to break or change; and that even the great men
who seem to lead, are, with all their capacities for thought

and action, the product of past general conditions of human development, and have not so much moulded society as been moulded by it.

Of these two theories of history, the latter is evidently getting the ascendancy. A disposition is gaining ground everywhere to believe more in the steady progress of *law* in human affairs than in the fitful, arbitrary power of *will;* to trust the logic of events rather than the authority of persons ; to follow the lead of ideas rather than the beck of the hero.

More and more with every generation do events seem to follow the average thought and tendencies of a community or a nation, and less and less to be controlled by the dominating power of a few great minds. This was strikingly illustrated in America by our late war. It was most emphatically a *people's* war. It did not produce one single man of transcendent, overmastering genius. Abraham Lincoln became most truly the nation's leader by closely watching and following the national mind ; but we criticised him freely while he lived, and only canonized him after his tragic death. Secretary Stanton, with his iron will, and heart all aflame with patriotic devotion, showed more than any other the power of a strong personality ; but his power arose from the fact that he was a true representative of the courage, patriotism, and love of justice in the heart of the nation.

Looking abroad, we see that Gladstone and the Reform party follow rather than lead the English people. Italy misses Cavour to this day, indeed ; and the cause of German unity would be seriously endangered by the loss of Bismarck's sagacity and energy : but these men have been leaders only because they have incarnated, for the time being, in their own persons the *souls* of their respective nations. It begins to be seen that thoughts lead, rather than persons ; and thinking people are perceiving that this must apply to all phases and departments of human progress, religious as well as secular; that all history is a tracing of certain impersonal forces or laws in the operation and progress of human society, rather than a collection of personal memoirs and biographies. This theory eliminates the miraculous element from religious history, and hence comes into accord with the scientific thought of modern times. It shows religion at bottom to be allegiance to certain naturally-revealed principles of intelligence and rectitude rather than to supernatural personages, and seeks to explain how the belief in such supernatural personages has arisen out of these natural and universal religious sentiments.

The theory of law in the domain of morals is pushed to its extreme by the statistical school of moralists, who maintain, on the authority of carefully-gathered tables of statistics, that there are laws which govern the most trivial as well as the gravest acts of men; that, whatever individuals may do by way of stemming the current, there must be just so many crimes in a given population in a given time. Now, the human mind makes a natural protest against these sweeping assertions. One very important part of human nature feels itself overlooked when the operations of human society are reduced to mere machine activity. And against this extreme the Buckle theory must be guarded by adapting to it a very important element from Carlyle's statement.

But, first, let us glance a moment longer at the merits of this theory of the agency of law in the world's history. Of course, ecclesiastical Christendom quarrels with it, — must quarrel, if it would save its traditional schemes of theology. For this theory would have us study Christianity from a different point of view than that of theology, — regard it not as a new creation, but as a growth, the natural result of what had gone before. This theory of history is making a harmonious adjustment between religious philosophy and progress and the new knowledge which man is gaining in other directions. It points to the way of reconciliation between religion and science. All religions, traced backward, show marks of near kinship. The very sign of the cross, which more than any other symbol is identified with Christianity, was in use among the Phœnicians, the Romans, the Etruscans; entered into the mythology of the Brahmaic religion in India, and was familiar to the Aztecs in America, and even to the ancient Maya race who preceded the Aztecs. On the hammer of Thor, the old God of Thunder, Baring Gould finds the cross; and nations whose very names are lost in antiquity left it sculptured on the urns in which they put the ashes of their dead. The view of Buckle and his sympathizers is the grand democratic view of history. It lends dignity to human nature; for it makes all men necessary, and tells us that God does not and cannot incarnate himself wholly in any one person, but must have all humanity for his organs. He works through the whole.

But this theory becomes dangerous and detrimental when it is pushed to the extreme of denying altogether the agency of personal volition and personal responsibility. It then violates both facts and philosophy. We *must* allow for the element of personal power for which Carlyle pleads. The two theories are to be reconciled in a higher synthesis which shall grasp and unite both agencies, — the agency of law and the agency of persons. That which we call law in the universe becomes in human persons vital, self-conscious, self-active. Both characters and events must be referred back to one train of causes. And what are these impersonal forces, laws, tendencies, ideas, which this scientific view of history brings into such prominence, if not what religion must call the living presence and potency of Divinity itself? Thus the old doctrine of Divine

Incarnation, superstitious as a specific dogma, but most true and beautiful as an ideal aspiration of the race, becomes a veritable realization. Infinite intelligence, energy, love, clothes itself in the form, activities, and life of humanity.

_____

Dr. BARTOL spoke of the essay as a fair and judicial statement of a great question, which is growing more and more important. The question seems to be, What is the personal quantity of the universe? Is there any quantity or power at all but the personal? But "personal" is only a word, behind which we must hunt for its meaning. "Person" meant originally a *mask*, through which the actor's voice sounded. And what is every soul but a mask through which a great power speaks? Yet we are conscious of will and of individuality, of some likeness between ourselves and the universal Nature.

Rev. JOHN CHADWICK referred to the importance of having both sides of a question brought out, as in the essay. He was afraid of saying anything which might be a signal for polemics, yet he could not help saying that, in speaking of the cross, the essay did not show them that it had been in those old times the symbol of self-sacrifice, of which it is the symbol in Christianity.

Mr. HIGGINSON said that he did not think the essayist meant to shoot his arrow quite so high as those who had criticised him. The interest for him was largely in this, — that it taught lessons of the distribution of ability in human beings, and therefore of the proper distribution of power in human beings. He thought some persons, as they lived longer, tended to see a concentration of power in individuals, and others tended more and more to look away from leading individuals to the whole of humanity; some people, as they lived longer, saw more and more brains in themselves and their friends, while others saw less and less in themselves and more in the people at large. The question was whether Deity incarnates himself in certain great leaders or in the whole of the human race. For himself, he held the latter view, and said that Emerson had shown how the leader was fed from all sources, and all other times were constantly pressing upon him. The longer he lived, the more weight he attached to the general voice. He never was on a committee without finding that the humblest member of it had something to say, some word of his own which could be of use to all the rest. But when history is written we see more and more in the leaders and less and less in the followers. It is the tendency of history to concentrate itself on leading minds; but he pitied profoundly those launched on the Carlyle sea, which sweeps out of thought and consideration all but the very few whom some chance of merit or circumstance has raised upon the safe height of memory and observation.

Mr. CHADWICK said that the great man comes always as Jesus came, that the thoughts of many hearts might be made plain. Those failed to comprehend Jesus who did not see that he blossomed as a rosebud does from its stem, out of the fulness of the time which had prepared all things for him.

Mr. ALCOTT said that great men were always the prophets of an age to come; the world has to be educated up to them. Through the great minds the revelations are made to the multitude.

Mrs. CHENEY thought that while the last part of the essay indicated fully the reconciliation of the sides which exist in history, the method of treating history by personalities did not get quite so fair a representation as the other side. Carlyle, the extremist, was put forward as a representative of one, and the very best of the other side as the representative of the other. She thought there were much happier instances of the first method of treating history than Carlyle, brilliant as he is; and that our own country furnishes very powerful evidences of this in Motley's " History of the Netherlands," where William of Orange seems to flow all through the history as a beneficent father.

Rev. SAMUEL LONGFELLOW said that our own individual interest in the matter under discussion to-day is that we may be able to rescue our own individuality from the absolutism of law. We cannot be satisfied without feeling that our individual wills are powers and centres of powers; that we are not merely passive but creative. The greatest teachers do not desire to be idolized, and would rather show us how to think than think for us. It is indolence which makes us accept their teachings unquestioned; it is so much easier to worship than to work.

XXXVII.

DARWINISM.

By NATHANIEL SOUTHGATE SHALER.

PROFESSOR SHALER said: "It is the present belief of most naturalists that man comes from the animals below him, not necessarily by natural selection, but
still through some simple genetic way. It may be that the
ape mother bore a child which was a marvel to her loving
eyes, so far did it go beyond its kind; still it was her
child, and she, though happier than her race in its greatness, was still its mother. On this matter of the genetic
connection of animals, students are of more accord than
upon any other broad question; natural selection, however, seems to me not the god of the human race, but
a most important, though not the only agent in creating
and perpetuating the differences among animals. Probably the most notable influence which can be exercised by
any pure science is brought about through its power of
modifying our conceptions of life. If science has done no
more for man than to expand the notion of the dependence of effects upon causes, of which the untutored man
has only a trace, it would still have given an inestimable
force to his sense of duty. Who can measure the influence which astronomy has had on the conception of life?
When Science took the heavenly bodies from the unsteady
hands of heathen deities, or the blind rule of aimless Fate,
and placed them in the government of immutable, benefi-

cent law, it gave a basis for confidence in the destiny of
the universe and all its parts, which did not exist before.
Who can reckon how many lives have been broadened
and brightened since those heavens have been lifted, —
since the crystal arch which was always ready to fall
upon an unhappy world has given place to boundless
space and infinite creation?   When Science, with other
means, gave us the earth on which we stand, not as a
plaything of yesterday to be destroyed in cruel sport to-
morrow, as the infant man had fancied, but with foun-
dations from all time and an architecture so contrived
that decay but brings new creation, — when it peopled
it with purposes, and made it the throne, not the grave,
of man, there was indeed a new heaven and a new earth.
In the beginning the world was veiled with the common-
place to its savage denizen.   When he began to seek for
a determining cause for the things which stood out promi-
nently against the background of dark fatality, it was
natural to attribute them to something like himself, only
bigger and stronger, — a method to be commended for
its simplicity.   This anthropomorphism was a merciful
padding, keeping him from bruises against those stern
laws, which, though they come to be friends by and by,
are at first sight implacable and severe.   Polytheism gave
man company in that dreary time when else he would
have been lonely as the babes in the wood in this wilderness of things.   But when man came up to abstractions
he brought with him polytheistic habits.   Little by little,
to be sure, the gods of old were put away to live in marble,
and the world given in charge of more puritanical personalities.   Man would follow his reason in remitting all else
to the operations of law; but *he* was apart, and for himself.   Force might make or unmake the world, but he
was the pet of the supernatural.   True, he was not a god
now, but he had been in the beginning; and it was only

some ugly mischance, some game played on him by snake
or woman, that had dragged him down. In his sombre
fits he was degenerate, fallen, — a poor worm, but still a
fallen god, held down by the Devil. Soon he was to be
lifted to the purple royalty of his birthright. Yet, poor
man, what mattered it if the heavens were raised, the
earth broadened, the past made a vista of providential
events, the future secured while suns endure, if yet he
stands among them the only accident, the only fallen
thing, — stands, while the universe moves on? This night-
mare which held him spell-bound is gone now; he, too,
joins the great procession, reaching back into an illimita-
ble past, and forward to a future aglow with hope. When
man took the beast for his kinsman, empty heads laughed;
but there can be no doubt that when he chose to come up
from the worm, rather than down from the god, there was
the basis laid for a moral revolution which exceeded any
that our world has seen. When we come to believe that
our race is the last of a series of determined steps by
which life has climbed up from inorganic matter; when
we see that through the space of a hundred million years
' one increasing purpose runs,' — the building of man, —
then he becomes more to himself than he has ever been
before. Man could not seem thoroughly respectable to
himself so long as his future was at the mercy of an impending millennium; he was a creature under sentence,
and awaiting execution. When he links himself with the
animal series, all this is changed. The wonderful certainty
of that evolution gives a logical certainty of greatness to
the future, and its hope is immense; it cannot fail to illu-
minate life with something of the glow of religious faith.

" This doctrine of genesis gives us a new sense of kinship with creation, a new sense of duty to the life below us;
and this is the greatest addition to our moral code since
the days of Christ. There has been little trace of this

feeling before the beginning of this new line of thought, while now it grows apace. We have societies for the prevention of cruelty to animals; of modern knights, who go about redressing the wrongs of these helpless ones, as the knights of old went forth in defence of women and children. It is true that other races, long ago, have stumbled upon a certain kind of reverence for the brute creation; but it was another form of self-love when the Hindu refrained from injuring an animal because it might be inhabited by the soul of one of his kindred, and to this complexion might he, too, come at last. It is a different thing, this kindly gratitude with which we look upon the creatures who once carried our lives, and left them higher than they found them. The man who feels this is a patriarch, and round his tent cluster kinsmen of every degree, — none so humble but they may claim share of his high estate, part in his strong protection. In this view sin becomes a relapse into lower forms of being, — a spiritual malformation, to be healed if it may be, restrained if it must be; but in any case, understood and pitied, not scorned. The comprehension of our alliance with the past shows us the future in our own keeping. Races to come must ban or bless us, as we make the most or the least of our opportunities. Already man has taken himself out of the struggle for existence. The law of natural selection no longer has power over him. The weakly no longer die from weakness alone, but too often live to transmit their woes to a plentiful generation. Better, indeed, that the race should suffer the loss of giving its best to the weakest of its children, than take the moral damage which would come from the regulated infanticide which has sometimes been recommended. But the race will not improve to its uttermost capacity until at least as much sanity rules over human reproduction as over well-organized stock-breeding. The progress of a nation is not to

be estimated by its census, but by the quality of its individuals. We must come to the knowledge that to bring
a mortal into life without a chance for insuring its physical
and moral welfare is a wrong to the creature who is to
suffer, and to society which must bear the burden. Let
those only be parents who can transmit qualities worthy
of being handed down, and the race will speedily distance
the centuries which have gone before. The conviction of
this duty is penetrating thoughtful minds already. Is it
too much to hope that by-and-by its leaven will spread
through the race? It consecrates many lives to a living
martyrdom, indeed; but will not a strong soul suffer as
much and as willingly for the sake of a sublime duty as
myriads of fanatics have suffered for a delusion or a
dogma? No features of the world have been so difficult
to reconcile with the instinctive conception of the justice
and utility which rules the universe as pain and fear. But
suffering, in the light of these new ideas, loses the sting
of injustice. The old must pass away, that the new and
better may come; the individual, the species, the class,
the very scheme, dies that it may grow. The jaw of the
shark and the lion's claw are rude tools of physical and
intellectual culture.

"Will the belief in immortality be weaker or stronger
for the evolution of these ideas? Scientific proof of immortality there is not, and is not likely to be; and perhaps no greater evil could come to mankind than to find
such proof. Hope goes out when certainty comes in, and
it is doubtless best for the race that its crowning question should be left to that faith which comes most surely
from a high, pure life, and the broadest study of Nature;
for, to my thinking, the study of Nature is full of immortal hope. Shall future waste give the lie to the economy
of all the past? Must it not be, rather, that when the
sun itself shall grow dim with countless ages, this life

of the soul, to which all the ages have rendered tribute, must go on, with ever-increasing powers, to a future of glory beyond our present poor conception?"

———

Dr. HEDGE thought that one of the best things religion has given us is reverence for lower orders and forms of life, and that the Hindu reverence for animals did not grow out of the notion of the transmigration of souls, but was the offspring, not the parent, of consideration for animals. The Hindus, long ago, had hospitals for sick animals; and this sense of kinship with the dumb creation is one of the points of contrast between the Hindu and the Semitic beliefs. This reverence seemed to him rather the growth of religious ideas than of Darwinian theories, which can hardly as yet have become general in their influence. He himself had been a Darwinian in theory before Darwin ever wrote, but he believed these Darwinian theories must be supplemented with something else; something, perhaps, corresponding to Swedenborg's doctrine of influx, — the breathing in of spiritual life. This influx must be in proportion to development; and it is only when man, in his upward progress, has reached a certain stage that he is capable of receiving it.

Mr. FROTHINGHAM thought that the movement for the protection of animals was hardly the offspring either of religion, so-called, or of Darwinism, but of philanthropy, — of a tenderness for suffering which has grown with our civilization. He spoke of Mr. Bergh, who he believed was an Orthodox believer, and not a Darwinian philosopher. "As to the belief in immortality," he said, "there is surely no reason to fear any war which science can wage against it: one cannot put an ethereal soul into a crucible, nor dissect it with a scalpel. At present either is not subject to science. What right have we to immortality if our mortality bears no fruit; if the years go on and leave us no better or wiser than they find us? Immortality means growth, and is to be seized upon with endeavor, justified by progress."

LUCRETIA MOTT said that she had been interested for the last fifty years in the developments of science, and she had learned to welcome it as a friend, not to fear it as a foe. She considered the conjunction of theology with religion lamentable, and would fain depose the usurper, theology. Religion is not a thing of dogma; its fruits are not to be found in creeds and forms, but in clean living, in doing right, in common honesty.

Mr. LONGFELLOW opposed Mrs. Mott's condemnation of theology, because all statements of religious truths are theology, and statements of great truths have not yet become unnecessary; but he believed religion should fashion theology, and satisfy reason as well as sentiment.

Mr. CHADWICK agreed with Professor Shaler that science tends not away from religion, but toward it; for to pursue science is to think God's thoughts after him, — and thought, as much as action, greatens the soul.

At a later meeting the Darwinian theory was again discussed, FRANCIS E. ABBOT reading an essay, which in substance was as follows: —

The importance of the theory itself is evident from the fact that it has created a literature in many languages. There have been two attempts to penetrate the mystery of the universe. Imagination developed and formed the great myths of the creation of the universe, and created the supernatural as a distinct being in the guise of matter, but vaster, because it looked upon matter as dead until breathed into by this supernatural Being. Reason finds that Nature is infinite in duration and space, and that natural causes produce the endless evolution of the universe. The God of the granite and the rose, the God whom reason discovers working in Nature, is infinitely superior to the God of the imagination. Science always has won when pitted against the imagination, and progress of science may be measured by the extent to which the natural dispossesses the supernatural, and supersedes it. The great point of Darwin is that he substitutes natural for supernatural causes. We cannot hesitate to accept the leading principles enunciated by him, for their great feature is not speculations, but facts. No one maintains that Darwin supplies a complete explanation of the origin of species, but we know the development theory is the only scientific one, and that it is in harmony with the records of history and consonant with the spirit of the age. Man, as never before, glories in his future. I would call this theory the Ascent of Man, it being the one hopeful and scientific, while the supernatural is imaginative and discouraging.

Dr. Bartol began the conversation. "I am a Darwinian so far as Darwin goes; but his theory of evolution is insufficient to account for the universe, and I would not call Nature a cause, but an effect, — the apparent effect of an unapparent cause, and a part of the psychological and supernatural. The universe was not made from a vesicle. If dust is the beginning of the ascent of man, may it not be the end of the descent of spirit? Certainly it is not the beginning of spirit. We must begin and end our scientific theory in dust, which is but the pathway of the spirit. Darwin cannot deny volition, nor can he account for it on the theory of evolution. There is one solemn fact of which we are cognizant, — we have known individuals and types to degenerate. We have the phrase 'primeval night': it is hateful. The primeval condition was glorious day, — Cosmos."

Rev. JOHN WEISS said: "I wish to say a word for Darwin. This question of will or no will is not the one he has undertaken to answer. His question is one of method, — how, not why. People think because he does not write the three letters of the word *God* into every sentence that he ignores will and spirit. If we did not believe in God, every page of his, read thoughtfully, would require us to invent God. The great naturalist is a man who has undertaken a special work, — the study and exposition of the natural development of species; he has kept to it with wonderful tenacity, concentration, and exclusiveness, and this characteristic, which can hardly be praised sufficiently, has given rise to a remarkable, strange, and absurd misunderstanding of him. Not only Darwin, but every scientific writer with whose works I am acquainted, — except a few German materialists, — makes a God necessary. Every page of a really scientific work is a door which opens into infinite will, infinite mind. Darwin's province is to classify and explain: what would he gain by pausing to say, 'In the beginning was spirit,' when spirit he could neither classify nor explain? The inference that Darwin denies the existence and supremacy of a Divine Being is utterly without reasonable warrant in anything in his scientific writings."

Rev. Mr. WASHBURN of Milton replied: "I understood that it had been said natural causes are the all, and that the theory of evolution leaves no room for the supernatural. In that case there is inevitably a controversy between those who believe in a Divine Cause, — a self-acting Volition, independent of and above Nature, — and those who believe Nature began and develops her own manifestations by her own involuntary laws."

Dr. BARTOL objected to the phrase "natural causes" as

applied to the evolution theory, if it is to be interpreted inclusively; for although these are causes in Nature, they are not all causes.

Mrs. CHENEY expressed the opinion that evolution accounts only for the method of the working of natural causes, and does not deny the permanence of God in Nature, and leaves unsolved the point concerning the permanence of species.

Col. HIGGINSON sympathized with Mr. Washburn, and added: "The most which can be said at present in favor of Mr. Darwin's theory is that it is a theory, and therefore entitled to candid consideration. It is true that most of the outspoken opposition in this country comes from the theologians; but there are two sides to the question even in the scientific world, and several men of acknowledged position in scientific circles abroad do not accept it. Professor Agassiz will tell you no scientific men accept it; but he, despite his eminent abilities and character, is one-sided and tenacious of his own theories. It is said Darwinism is the only scientific theory of the origin of species. Emerson says the world is yet too young by several thousand years to formulate a creed. For myself, I am disposed to believe Darwin is right, but that he is not yet proved. To claim more is unwise. It is a remarkable fact that, in spite of all the marvellous concentration of ingenuity and industry in investigation, not a single example has yet been discovered of the origin of a species in the way Darwin shows they might have originated.

"So far as personal feeling is concerned, the Darwinian theory is far nobler than any other ever formed. After the ignoble scheme of the theologians, it is like opening the windows to sunlight and heaven, and in its light the great march of humanity becomes superb. The theologian is defunct as a power in the world; but I fear the despotism of science more than the despotism of theology. Science monopolizes the thought and activity of man, drawing him away from religion, poetry, and art. If the God of theology were put out of the world, what would take the place of the sacred literature of all ages and all nations? Poets who patronize science assume faith and love and reverence, but science does not. We may hope and expect that Darwinism is correct, but cannot affirm it is; and much less may we construct the whole theory of the universe on it."

ROBERT DALE OWEN was invited to join in the conversation. "It is hard to deny Darwinism, and as hard to affirm it. May not the appearance of species at a certain time, man for instance, be owing to an inherent condition of the law of evolution? Babbage's calculating machine can be set to continue for a long time making computations by one process, and suddenly, without any warning, at a certain stage, to completely change the process. We see a similar condition of law operating in various fields of knowledge. Man lives one day very much as another, and is on Thursday very much the same man he was on Monday; but there comes a time, without any special interference of superhuman agency, when the law of his being suddenly changes, — and he changes, we do not know to what extent, but he certainly drops the body. Might not such a change, inherent in the law of existence, occur in the gradual evolution of species, the new one appearing suddenly when the time was ripe? I do not deny Darwinism, but I see no proof of it."

Rev. L. T. CHAMBERLAIN, being asked to speak, said he came only to listen, and had taken great pleasure in the development of the views of those present. He sympathized with the view that there is not in the scientific writings of Darwin, or of other much-feared scientists, any necessary antagonism with the conception of an infinite God, and felt it was a sad and unfortunate circumstance that Christian people had assumed that there is.   A Calvinist himself, he rejoiced in the work of these able, sincere, and devoted searchers for truth in the realm of Nature. He sometimes thought it a blessed thing that such men cast themselves loose from theological ties ; for, under this ban of an unjust prejudice, they showed more grandly the consecration of their lives.   He saw nothing in the theory of evolution inconsistent with the supremacy and glory of the infinite God, and doubted not that, when more fully understood and more accurately defined, it would appear an additional motive for reverence and love.   He anticipated that the theory would eventually have a wider application than Darwin had given it, and particularly that it would reconstruct the science of geology.   To him this Divine Being would continue to be the personal God to whom he prayed and whom he loved ; Nature would still remain the impress of the divine mind ; and the noble conception of the divine immanence, for which we have to thank the Pantheists, will fill and satisfy us as never before.

Mr. Potter thought Mr. Abbot's idea had been misapprehended, and that he included spirit in Nature.   He believed Darwinism, when confined to *physiology*, to be strong and apparently indubitable ; but he doubted the universality of the theory of evolution if stretched to envelop the all.

Mr. Abbot closed : " I believe Nature is the great word. I do not exclude spirit from the universe.   Nature includes the spiritual and the material realm, and science will include all soul and mind, as well as matter, and the science of the future will unify philosophy."

XXXVIII.

INDIAN ETHICS.

By J. W. POWELL.

MAJOR POWELL, who has been a twenty-years' traveller among the wild tribes of savage countries, gave an account of the theology and mythology of the North American Indians.

First giving the cosmology of the North American savage, he slid into a fine story-telling vein, depicting by graphic touches the myths and customs, the curious materialism of the Indian, which had within it at every turn a spiritual or mythical belief. "The arts and industries of savagery and civilization are not in greater contrast than their philosophy. To present to you fully the condition of savagery, as illustrated in their philosophy, three obstacles appear. After all the years I have spent among the Indians in their mountain villages, I am not certain that I have sufficiently divorced myself from the thoughts and ways of civilization to appreciate properly their childish beliefs. The second obstacle subsists in your own knowledge of the methods and powers of Nature, and the ways of civilized society; and when I attempt to tell you what an Indian thinks, I fear you will never fully forget what you know, and thus you will be led to give too deep a meaning to a savage explanation; or, on the other hand, contrasting an Indian concept with your own, the manifest absurdity will sound to you as an idle tale, too simple to deserve mention, or too false to deserve credence. The

third difficulty lies in the attempt to put savage thoughts
into civilized language, — our words are so full of meaning, carry with them so many great thoughts and civilized
ideas.   In English I say *wind*, and you think of atmosphere
in revolution with the earth, heated at the tropics and cooled
at the poles, and set into great currents which are diverted
from their courses in passing back and forth from tropical
to polar regions.   But I say *nein* to a savage, and he thinks
of a great monster, a breathing beast, beyond the mountains of the West.   In treating of savage philosophy I
shall speak of their cosmology, theology, religion, and
mythology.

   " Their cosmology is not always cosmogony.   Some of the
objects in the universe are supposed to have had an origin,
to have been created ; but many others to have had everlasting existence.   They are accepted as facts, or existences
without origin, — primary concepts, if you please.

   " A savage philosopher believes in a system of worlds,
not globes swinging in the heavens, but places of existence,
— the world of this life, the land on which we tread and the
water in which we swim, and the world or worlds of land
and water to which we go.   Among the different tribes of
North America, two methods in the arrangement of worlds
are observed.   The lower tribes have their worlds arranged
horizontally or topographically : the Nu-gun-tu-wip, the
Ghost Land, the Land of the Hereafter, is beyond some great
topographic feature.   The coast tribes say, ' beyond the
sea ;' the dweller on the river-banks, ' beyond the river ;'
tribes who dwell in valleys surrounded by crags and peaks
say, ' beyond the mountains ;' the tribes who dwell on
the brinks of the great cañons, ' beyond the chasm.'
Among those tribes having their worlds arranged topographically, a past world is not an item in their philosophy : with some the progenitors of the human race, with
all the animal races, came from the ground, where they

burrowed in miserable existence; with other tribes the progenitors of the human race, with the races of animals, came from the depths of the sea. There are always two future worlds, one for the good, one for the bad, — a land of joy and a land of sorrow.

"When the future world is 'beyond the chasm,' the way is by a magical bridge; when 'beyond the mountains,' by a dangerous pass among the rocks; when 'beyond the river,' or 'beyond the sea,' a ferry is provided.

"Among the higher tribes, we find the worlds arranged vertically or architecturally, — a world or worlds below a world or worlds above. In this higher stage of savagery there is also a past world: that is, humanity came to this existence from a former, another land. Sometimes the land from which he came is above, sometimes below; but the land to which the righteous goes is always in a direction opposite to that from which he came.

"Thus, among the Pueblo Indians there are seven worlds, one world below this and five above. We came from the world below by a magical ladder held by Ma-chi-to, one of their hero-gods, who had previously discovered a hole in the sky from that lower world, — the floor of this world, the sky of the lower. The souls of the newly born have escaped from below to be clothed with bodies here; and the souls of the righteous shall go on from world to world until the bliss of the seventh heaven is reached.

"I must content myself with this brief account of the worlds of savagery, though the theme is attractive by reason of the many wonderful myths told of these worlds.

"*The Heavenly Bodies.* — The sun and moon are always personages; with nomadic tribes primordial personages, uncreated personages, but slaves, compelled to travel in appointed ways. They have been subjugated. With the Pueblo tribes the sun and the moon are personages created for a purpose, to give light and warmth.

"The stars of the nomads are human beings or animals translated from earth to the firmament for various reasons; but the stars of the Pueblos were created from the fragments remaining when the moon was made.

"*Meteorologic Phenomena.* — Indian cosmology also deals with all the meteorologic phenomena. The aurora is the dancing of ghosts; the rainbow is made of the tears of the eagle-god; the thunder is the screaming of a great bird; the lightning is the arrow of Ta-vwots, the hare-god. Rain and snow are variously explained. Among the Pueblos the rain-god dips his brush, made from the feathers of the birds of heaven, into the lakes of the skies, and sprinkles the water therefrom over the face of this world; in winter time he breaks the ice of the lakes and scatters ice-dust over the earth.

"*Geographic Phenomena.* — Their cosmology explains the origin of mountains. Each mountain had a special creation; the shapes of all the storm-carved rocks were determined by the gods; the great bends of the rivers were fixed; the lakes were made, and the springs had a miraculous beginning.

"*Remarkable Facts in Nature.* — Their cosmology also deals with all the curious minutiæ of Nature. It explains the tawny patch of fur on the shoulder of the little rabbit, the cardinal head of the woodpecker, the top-knot of the crested jay, and the rattle of the serpent. So there is nothing seen which is not explained.

"*Important Facts of Human Society.* — In like manner all the more important facts observed by them in human society, all the institutions, and all the habits and customs have their origin, and were determined by the gods. Every tribe has its Babel myth, its explanation of the dispersion of the human family over the earth, and the diversity of tongues. They tell when birth and death began, and when marriage was instituted.

" The theology of the North American Indian is not fetichistic, though there are many survivals from fetichism.
All of the nomadic tribes are zoöloters; their gods are
animals. The savage, the sylvan man, as the word signi-
fies, is intimately associated with the animals with which
he is surrounded. From them he obtains the larger part
of his clothing and much of his food, and he carefully
studies their habits and finds many wonderful things.
Their knowledge and skill and power appear to him to be
superior to his own. In all animal nature he sees things
too wonderful for him; and from admiration he grows to
adoration, and the animals become his gods. Another
trait of character comes in to modify his theologic beliefs.
I mean ancientism, — veneration for the past and for the
people of the past. This is a very common trait in human
nature. Individuals of every species are supposed to have
descended from the more ancient animal, the progenitor
of the race, who was a wonderful being. The wolf of
to-day is a howling pest, but that wolf's grandfather was
a god. And so they have a grizzly-bear god, an eagle
god, a rattlesnake god, a trout god, and a spider god,
— a god for every race or species of animal. There is
another very curious and interesting fact in Indian philosophy. They do not separate man from the beast by
any broad line of demarcation. Mankind is supposed
simply to be one of the many races of animals, — in some
respects superior, in many others inferior, to those races.
So the Indian speaks of our race " as of the same rank
with " the bear race, the wolf race, or the rattlesnake race;
and, as he deifies ancient beasts, he deifies ancient men,
and thus he has a special class which we may denominate
hero-gods. I have said that the theology of the North
American Indians was not fetichistic, but among them we
find many survivals from fetichism, and one of these is a
survival by special development. I mean their *daimon*

gods. I use the word 'daimon' rather than 'demon,' for the latter has a Christian meaning of devil, while these daimons are simply the presiding spirits of places. It must be understood that these daimons have animal forms, but they have the power of transforming themselves and assuming any shape at will, anthropomorphic or zoö-morphic. This is true also of the beast-gods. The sun, moon, and stars are also gods, and do many wonderful things, though they are not usually held in very high esteem. So all their gods are animals, and the form in which they may appear at any time is a matter of momentary whim; a vicious human trait plays some strange freaks in Indian theology, and often their gods become monsters, beasts with seven heads and ten horns. The third-class monsters are those based on the discovered bones of extinct elephants and mastodons. Avarice plays a very important part in Indian theology. The Indian has but a small store of material things, and the religious element greatly prevails in his life, and his desire for possession, ownership, is very strong. Families also have tutelar gods and so do clans and tribes.

"Such are the gods of the nomads of North America, — firmament-gods, which are animals; hero-gods, animals also, as man is an animal; beast-gods, the progenitors or prototypes of the present races of animals; and daimon-gods, presiding spirits of places, also zoömorphic.

"In studying the myths of North American Indians many have sought to evade this conclusion; and one of our brilliant writers on the myths of the New World exclaims: 'Man, the paragon of animals, praying to the beast, is a spectacle so humiliating that, for the sake of our common humanity, we may seek the explanation of it least degrading to the dignity of our race.'

"There have been many curious ways of interpreting Indian myths. The latest and most attractive is that by which they are converted into wonderful symbols, so that whenever an Indian calls his god *wolf*, he does not mean wolf, he means wind, — for the wind howls, and the wolves howl; when he says *serpent*, he does not mean serpent, he means lightning, — for the serpent darts and the lightning darts. Now that such symbolism has existed among people whose grade of culture is higher cannot be denied. The fact of general Nature-worship by the ancient Indo-European people is fully established, and in many ways and by diverse methods a wonderful system of symbols grew up among these earlier Aryans. This Nature-worship was the personification and deification of the forces and phenomena of Nature. The later Greek and Roman philosophy was a personification and deification of human attributes, passions, and sentiments.

" The literature of North American ethnography is vast, and scattered through it is a great mass of facts pertaining to Indian theology, — a mass of nonsense, a mass of incoherent folly, whenever those facts are looked upon from that standpoint which assumes that Indian theology is a degeneracy from some higher type ; but when accepted as it is understood by the Indian himself, the great multitude of facts fall into place, and assume the form of a theological organism : ethically a hideous monster of lies, but ethnographically a system of great interest, — a system which beautifully reveals the mental condition of savagery.

" I have no time to dwell on the theology of the Pueblo Indians, but simply to say that a mixture of Nature and animal worship exists among them, so that they may be considered as in a transition state.

" In Indian philosophy the gods are not very far from us in intrinsic nature. They are poor brutes like ourselves, with like passions and like prejudices ; quick to anger, and of generous impulse ; revengeful to enemy, and faith-

ful to friend. In many respects they have no greater
power than ourselves, and none of them have greater
power than the ancients. The gods are the ancients. Our
inferiority is due to our late degeneracy.

"The lowest grade of priests I call witches. This craft
is carried on chiefly by women. There is a general belief
that old women, unless they die at a reasonable time, are
transformed into witches, and are finally carried away by
whirlwinds. So great is the dread of some of the Indian
women of the approaching witch-stage that they commit
suicide to avert the fate." The Major gave a graphic picture of a scene which he himself witnessed in a rocky defile
on one occasion. Riding along, he suddenly came upon
two "old hags," as he expressed it, who had probably
had too much of the unenviable witch reputation. They
were standing before a certain cleared space, where at
intervals they swayed and swung their bodies, while they
sung in mournful monotone, in the Indian dialect, something to this effect: —

> " ' Here we have stayed long enough ;
> Here we have worked long enough.
> It is time that we died,
> It is time that we died. ' "

The Indian dialect which Major Powell first gave was
exceedingly musical, reminding one of some of the soft
syllables in " Hiawatha."

" Among many of the religious ceremonies which prevail
is *amuletism*. This is probably a relic from fetichism.
The Shamans are very skilful in the decoction of sorcery
broth, — usually foul mixtures which are prepared prior to
engaging in any important enterprise. Religion also has
to do with admission to the Land of the Hereafter. Admission to the Land of Want is always free ; the terms of admission to the Land of Plenty are variously and vaguely

fixed. All the living righteous, who are few, will go to the former; all the living bad, who are many, to the latter. The dead, those who lived in the happy days of yore, are almost all good, and few have been denied entrance to the home of the blessed. But who are the wicked, and who are the good? The ethic standards of savagery and civilization are as widely contrasted as their ideas of meteors. The bad man is he who failed to sacrifice to his tutelar god the spleen of the last elk killed; or he slept on his back the night before the battle, when the gods have taught him to sleep on his belly. They have some very curious soulometers!

"Sometimes the good land is beyond the bad, and through the latter the ghostly traveller passes in great dismay, happily reaching the former if his savage sins have been duly propitiated and the angry gods appeased; but woe to him who dies with savage guilt resting on his ghost. Sometimes there are two ways: the angry gods lead here, the appeased gods lead there.

"In every Indian tribe there is a great body of story lore, — tales purporting to be the sayings and doings, the history, of the ancients, the gods. Every tribe has one or more persons skilled in the relation of these stories, — preachers. In all the Shoshoni tribes the preacher is called a Nar-i-gwi-nump, one who tells of the ancients. The long winter evenings are set apart for this purpose. Then the men and women, the boys and girls, gather about the camp-fire to listen to the history of the ancients, to a chapter in the unwritten Bible of savagery. Such a scene is of the deepest interest. A camp-fire of blazing pine or sage boughs illumines a group of dusky faces intent with expectation, and the old man begins his story, talking and acting, — the elders receiving his words with reverence, while the younger persons are played upon by the actor until they shiver with fear or dance with delight. An Indian is a great actor. The conditions of Indian life train them in natural sign-language. Among the two hundred and fifty or three hundred thousand Indians in the United States there are scores of languages, so that often a language is spoken by only a few hundred or a few score of people; and as a means of communication between tribes speaking different languages a sign-language has grown up, so that an Indian is able to talk all over with the features of his face, his hands and feet, the muscles of his body. And thus a skilful preacher talks and acts; and, inspired by a theme which treats of the gods, he sways his savage audience at will, and ever as he tells his story he points a moral. The mythology, theology, religion, history, and all human duties are taught. The whole body of myths current in a tribe is the sum total of their lore, — their philosophy, their miraculous history, their authority for their governmental constitutions, their social institutions, their habits and customs; it is their unwritten Bible. In a single lecture I cannot introduce many of these tales; one must suffice for illustration.

"ORIGIN OF THE ECHO.

" I-o-wi (the turtle-dove) was gathering seeds in the valley, and her little babe slept. Wearied with carrying it on her back, she laid it under the ti-hó-pi (sage-bush) in care of its sister O-hó-chu (the summer yellow-bird). Engaged in her labors, the mother wandered away to a distance, when a tsó-a-vwits (a witch) came, and said to the little girl, 'Is that your brother?' and O-hó-chu answered, 'This is my sister,' for she had heard that witches preferred to steal boys and did not care for girls. Then the tsó-a-vwits was angry and chided her, saying that it was very naughty for girls to lie; and she put on a strange and horrid appearance, so that O-hó-chu was stupefied with fright,

and then the tsó-a-vwits ran away with the boy, carrying
him to her home on a distant mountain. Then she laid
him down on the ground, and taking hold of his right foot
stretched the baby's leg until it was as long as that of a
man, and she did the same to the other leg; then his body
was elongated, and also his arms, and behold! the baby
was as large as a man, and the tsó-a-vwits married him
and had a husband. But though he had the body of a
man he had the heart of a babe, and knew no better than
to marry a witch.

"Now, when I-o-wi returned and found not her babe
under the ti-hó-pi, but learned from O-hó-chu that it had
been stolen by a tsó-a-vwits, she was very angry, and
punished her daughter very severely. Then she went in
search of the babe for a long time, mourning as she went,
and her friends joined her in the search. Chief among
her friends was her brother Kwi-na (the eagle), who travelled far and wide over all the land, until one day he heard
a strange noise, and, coming near, he saw the tsó-a-vwits
and U-ja her husband; but he did not know that this large
man was indeed the little boy who had been stolen. Yet he
returned and related to I-o-wi what he had seen, who said,
'If that is indeed my boy he will know my voice.' So the
mother came near to where the tsó-a-vwits and U-ja were
living, and climbed into a cedar-tree, and mourned and
cried continually. Kwi-na placed himself near by on another tree to observe what effect the voice of the mother
would have on U-ja, the tsó-a-vwits' husband. When he
heard the cry of his mother, U-ja knew the voice, and said
to the tsó-a-vwits: 'I hear my mother, I hear my mother,
I hear my mother!' But she laughed at him, and per-
suaded him to hide.

"Now, the tsó-a-vwits had taught U-ja to hunt; and, a
short time before, she had killed a mountain-sheep which
was lying in camp. The witch emptied the contents of

the stomach, and with her husband took refuge within; for she said to herself: 'Surely I-o-wi will never look in the paunch of a mountain-sheep for my husband.' In this retreat they were safe for a long time, so that they who were searching were sorely puzzled at the strange disappearance. At last Kwi-na said: 'They are hid somewhere in the ground, may be, or under the rocks. After a long time they will be very hungry and will search for food; I will put some in a tree so as to tempt them.' So he killed a rabbit and put it on the top of a tall pine, from which he trimmed the branches and peeled the bark, so that it would be very difficult to climb; and he said: 'When these hungry people come out they will try to climb that tree for food, and it will take much time; and while the tsó-a-vwits is thus engaged we will carry U-ja away.' So they watched some days, until the tsó-a-vwits was very hungry, and her baby-hearted husband cried for food; and she came out from their hiding-place and sought for something to eat. The odor of the meat placed on the tree came to her nostrils, and she saw where it was and tried to climb up, but fell back many times; and while so doing, Kwi-na, who had been sitting on a rock near by and had seen from where she came, ran to the paunch which had been their house, and taking the man carried him away and laid him down under the very same ti-hó-pi from which he had been stolen; and behold! he was the same beautiful little babe that I-o-wi had lost.

"And Kwi-na went off into the sky and brought back a storm, and caused the wind to blow, and the rain to beat upon the ground, so that his tracks were covered, and the tsó-a-vwits could not follow him; but she saw, lying upon the ground near by, some eagle-feathers, and knew well who it was that had deprived her of her husband, and she said to herself: 'Well I know Kwi-na is the brother of I-o-wi; he is a great warrior and a terrible man. I will go to To-gó-a (the rattlesnake), my grandfather, who will protect me and kill my enemies.'

"To-gó-a was enjoying his mid-day sleep on a rock, and as the tsó-a-vwits came near her grandfather awoke, and called out to her: 'Go back, go back! You are not wanted here, go back!' But she came on, begging his protection; and while they were still parleying they heard Kwi-na coming, and To-gó-a said, 'Hide, hide!' But she knew not where to hide, and he opened his mouth and the tsó-a-vwits crawled into his stomach. This made To-gó-a very sick, and he entreated her to crawl out, but she refused, for she was in great fear. Then he tried to throw her up, but could not, and he was sick nigh unto death. At last, in his terrible retchings, he crawled out of his own skin and left the tsó-a-vwits in it; and she, imprisoned there, rolled about and hid in the rocks. When Kwi-na came near he shouted, 'Where are you, old tsó-a-vwits? Where are you, old tsó-a-vwits?' She repeated his words in mockery.

"Ever since that day witches have lived in snake-skins, and hide among the rocks, and take great delight in repeating the words of passers-by. The white man, who has lost the history of these ancient people, call these mocking cries of witches domiciliated in snake-skins 'echoes,' but the Nu-mas know the voices of the old hags. This is the origin of the echo."

After giving various myths and fables which were points of the Indian theology, and which reminded one of nothing so much as Æsop's fables, Major Powell cunningly said that he would conclude with a wise Indian proverb, which he gave in Indian sing-song that by no means detracted from its pith: —

> "Let a man talk a very long time,
> Let a man talk a very long time,
> Let a man talk a very long time,
> A hole he will bore into a rock."

And, amidst general laughter and applause, the Major took his seat.

———

Mr. CLARKE asked if the Indian believed in the doctrine of purification by transmigration.

Major POWELL replied that such an idea was altogether too high for the Indian mind, and that the great mistake which the missionary had made was to learn the Indian language that he might teach the Indian the Christian religion; for they have no words for the ideas which must be conveyed to them. But he had no hesitation in declaring that the Indians must of necessity die out as a race. To the question, if the Indians had not been greatly changed and influenced by the teachings of the missionaries, he replied emphatically, "No; there has been very little impression made upon them." "But about the Great Spirit, — why had he said nothing of that?" asked one. Major Powell replied that the Indian knew of no such being until the white man came with his teaching of God. But in accepting the Great Spirit he had only taken another god, and given up none of his old ones.

As to the treatment of the Indians, Major Powell said that the missionaries made a great mistake in trying to teach them in the Indian language. The savages should learn through the English, which the children acquire easily. The right policy has at last been reached in setting them to work, and teaching them to supply their physical wants. After that they can have religion preached to them.

XXXIX.

THE PHYSICAL AND CHEMICAL HAR-
MONIES OF THE UNIVERSE.

By T. STERRY HUNT, LL.D., F.R.S.

MY DEAR MRS. SARGENT, — When a few weeks since you asked me for a copy of a communication made by me to the Chestnut Street Club one spring morning in 1877, I feared that I should be unable to comply with your request. The communication in question was not of the nature of a formal essay, and being delivered without notes I had no record of it whatever. Fortunately for myself, you had however two printed preserved abstracts, which, unknown to me, had been prepared by friendly hands. From these I was enabled to prepare a more detailed sketch of the lecture, which I now offer for your acceptance.

In my remarks on that occasion I aimed at a presentation, in a popular form, of some of the teachings of modern chemical and physical science as to the history of our earth and its relations to the macrocosm, supplemented, however, by certain speculations for which I alone am responsible. I shall feel gratified if these pages are found worthy of a place in the memoirs of the Club which for so many years has furnished a tribune where the newest and boldest thoughts of the time have found free expression and sympathetic listeners, and which will always hold an honored place in the intellectual history of our generation.

I remain, my dear Mrs. Sargent,

Always gratefully yours,

T. STERRY HUNT.

MONTREAL, Sept. 27, 1880.

THE essayist, after remarking that he should depart in a measure from the traditions of the Club, which have been to discuss questions of philosophy and theology,

gave in a conversational manner and without notes a
sketch of the physical and chemical history of the earth
and its relations to the visible universe. He spoke of the
conception of the unity of Nature which had inspired the
early hermetic philosophers and their successors, the alche-
mists of the Middle Ages, but had been too often lost sight
of by later students of science. The studies of modern
physicists, chemists, and naturalists have, however, now
given a higher and deeper significance to what were formerly little more than poetic imaginings. The speaker then
alluded to the well-known relations and interdependence
of the animal, vegetable, and mineral kingdoms, and to
the fact that, while plants are nourished by mineral elements, they in turn subserve the wants of the animal world,
which, by its decay, restores once more to the air and
waters the plastic elements of the vegetable kingdom. All
this complex order is, in the view of some philosophers, sub-
servient to man, while to other teleologists man has seemed
destined only to hold in check the carnivorous animals,
which in their turn keep down the herbivorous creatures,
the end of which seemed, to a botanist like Linnæus, to
keep in check a too abundant vegetation. The weakness and the inherent contradictions of all such modes of
reasoning were commented upon, and it was declared that
the only adequate conception of Nature was that of an organic
whole, which attains its end in its own perfect development.

The speaker, while thus briefly defining his position, disclaimed any intention to discuss the philosophical aspect
of the question. His object was to present a few thoughts
respecting the physical and chemical agencies which have
presided over the development of our planet, or rather of
the material universe of which it forms a part. It would
seem at the first glance as if there were no field for such
investigations outside of our own earth, and that having
exhausted this planet, the votary of science must, like

Alexander, weep for the lack of other worlds to conquer. But modern science has given us arms wherewith to reach and to conquer new worlds, and we are enabled by means of the spectroscope and the telescope to learn somewhat of their chemistry and their physics, and to discover that the same great laws which reign here on earth rule in the remotest spheres.

The history of the cosmos is unfolded in the study of the nebulæ, — those cloud-like masses of luminous matter which the telescope discovers far beyond the limits of the solar system. From these nebulæ, as we have reason to believe, suns, planets, and satellites are generated by internal forces, thus repeating the process by which our own system, with the sun for its centre, was itself formed from some nebula of an earlier time. The light which comes from these far-off suns is, through the medium of the spectroscope, made to reveal the secret of their chemical constitution and to telegraph us the fact that the chemical elements there present are the same with those of our own planet, and, furthermore, that the constituents of the luminous clouds themselves are identical with those of our atmosphere. More than this, we are led by various considerations to the conclusion that this very atmosphere, which surrounds our earth and becomes less and less dense as we rise from its surface, extends in an attenuated form throughout all space, and constitutes the so-called ether of the interstellar regions. Wherever, then, worlds exist, a portion of this medium will be found condensed around them, and they will have atmospheres in constitution like our own.

When we trace still further the history of these forming worlds, we learn the progress of the birth, growth, and subsequent changes of suns, and find the various stages marked by changes in their chemical constitution; while from the successive appearance of new chemical species during the development of these bodies, we are led to con-

clude that these new species are likewise the result of a
process of growth, — that they are not really elementary, as
formerly supposed, but compound. Suns which are white
in color exhibit fewer of the so-called chemical elements
than those which give a yellower light, and in the light of
the red stars we find a still larger number of these elements
identical with those found in our earth. In that process
by which glowing suns are condensed from nebulæ, combinations are effected by a cosmical chemistry of which our
laboratories have not yet learned the secret, and which probably depends on temperatures far higher than we have at
our command. Heat, as we know, breaks up or dissociates
chemical compounds, and those suns which present the
fewest chemical elements in their light are doubtless the
highest in temperature.

But whence come the nebulæ themselves, which have
hitherto been accepted as primordial parts in the history of
the cosmos? In the opinion of the speaker, the air and
watery vapor which make up our atmosphere are, as
already said, diffused in a highly rarefied condition throughout all space ; and, this conceded, the nebulæ may be conceived to be formed from it by a process of condensation.
This he illustrated by an analogy : we see in the trans-
parent blue of our atmosphere the formation of a haze,
which gathers into a cloud that later condenses into drops
of rain or into frozen hail. In like manner a nebula is
but a cosmic cloud produced by some cause in the far-off
ether, — this universal atmosphere, — of which its light reveals to us the elements. From this cloud we have already
traced the progress to suns and planets. This conception
of the origin of nebulæ seems to be necessary to the com-
pleteness of the so-called nebular hypothesis.

Our own earth, in accordance with the view here advanced, was once a glowing mass of vapor detached from
a still greater mass which became our sun ; and we have

next to follow its history as it slowly condensed into a molten liquid, and finally into a solid mass surrounded with ocean and atmosphere. Astronomy traces a similar history in our sister planets from still luminous globes like Jupiter, to Mars, in which the telescopic changes observed show summer and winter seasons, and the alternate accumulation and disappearance of snow in the circumpolar regions. The chemical and physical history of the various planets is doubtless similar to that of our own earth. We are not, indeed, wanting in messengers from other worlds, which help to support this *à priori* conclusion. Aërolites or uranolites, those rocky masses which come to us from beyond our atmosphere, are composed of the same mineral elements as our own earth, and even tell us, by signs unmistakable to the chemist, of the presence of water and of organic life in the far-off and unknown regions from which these falling stars have come down to us.

The history of the changes which took place in our own cooling globe belongs to geology. There was a time when it was a mass of intensely heated rock, solid at the surface, — and probably also solid to the core, — and surrounded by a heavy atmosphere, the condensation of which set up chemical action upon the half-cooled surface and began the series of processes which have resulted in the present mineralogical and chemical conditions of the earth's crust. In the earlier times of its history the conditions were unfavorable to the existence of life on the planet. The atmosphere was too highly charged with carbonic acid, and the ocean with noxious salts. The rocks which then formed the surface (which were not granite, but probably more nearly allied to basalt in composition) were slowly disintegrated by the action of the atmosphere, which separated from them their combined soda, lime, and magnesia in the form of carbonates soluble in water, and converted the rocks into clay. These soluble salts, carried by rains to the ocean, there gave rise to limestones, and changed its bitter waves into waters fitted to sustain the life of sea-weed, mollusk, and coral, for the growth of which the same process furnished abundance of carbonate of lime. Every mass of clay thus generated by the decay of the rocks corresponds to a definite portion of carbonic acid removed from the air, and to its equivalent of salt dissolved in the sea and of limestone deposited from its waters.

These processes were not accomplished in years or in centuries, but required the long process of ages, which probably intervened after the first appearance of. life in the sea before the land was prepared for vegetation. The records of unnumbered· dynasties of vegetable and animal life are written on tables of stone in the earth's crust, wherein we read of the successive appearance of higher and higher forms of life, till man at length appears upon the scene.

The climatic changes of the earth form a curious chapter in its geological history. In former ages a semi-tropical vegetation extended over islands and continents, even within the polar circle ; and there seems no evidence of the exist-ence of ice in those early periods, save on mountains or high plateaus, where it may be found to-day in tropical regions. Changes in the relations of sea and land, and in the distribution of the heated waters whose currents flow from the equatorial region towards either pole, are potent elements in modifying climate ; but the speaker believed that there is another still more potent and a cosmical cause of the greater mildness of climate in former geologi-cal ages, and of the slow progressive refrigeration which is shown in the successive arctic floras from the time of the cretaceous period to that of the middle tertiary.

It is demonstrated that the presence of small quantities of carbonic acid gas in the air exerts by its absorbent power a great influence on terrestrial radiation and consequently

on climate ; so that a slight increase in the proportion of this
gas in our atmosphere would suffice to produce everywhere
at the sea-level an almost tropical climate.   The effect of
such an atmosphere would be analogous to that of a vast
protecting dome of glass, which, while permitting the passage of solar heat to the surface of the earth, would prevent
its escape.   Such a condition of things, the speaker supposed to have existed throughout long ages ; nor was it until
a time, geologically very recent, that the slow condensation of the carbonic acid, by processes already explained,
brought about the present climatic conditions of our earth,
in which much of the polar area is now permanently covered with snow and ice.   A small proportion of this gas, however, still remains in the atmosphere and helps to protect
us from the cold of the interstellary spaces and to nourish
vegetation.   Vegetable life could not exist without carbonic
acid in the atmosphere, and its total removal would cause
the death of every plant, and consequently of all animal
life.   An interchange, though perhaps a very gradual one,
in the speaker's opinion, goes on between our atmosphere
and that of all other worlds, by which the changes at our
earth's surface are shared with the universe.   The minute
portions of mineral matter which, in the form of so-called
cosmic dust, are believed by many to come to us from the
regions of space are, he conceived, evidences of that free
commerce which is carried on throughout the cosmos ;
so that not only gravitation and light, but material inter-
changes, connect us with the remotest orbs in space.

   And here we may well inquire whether the present order
of the universe is permanent.   The suns, which are the centres and the sources of life to systems, may fade and grow
cold.   Although we may discern agencies which afford them
fresh supplies of heat, the very process of growth, which
we have watched from the nebula, implies their decay.
Change is written on all things.   The energy dormant in

each orb would, if called into action, suffice, as is mathe-
matically demonstrated, to reduce it to a condition of
vapor, a tenuous gas, which, in accordance with our previously exposed hypothesis, would soon be diffused and form
a part of the infinite azure, — an insignificant contribution
to that all-pervading universal ether of which our own life-
giving atmosphere is a part, and from which, as we believe,
new nebulæ, new suns, and new worlds are generated.

Thus in the words of our own Emerson, in his divine
song of "Nature," —

> "And thefts from satellites and rings
>   And broken stars I drew;
> And out of spent and aged things
>   I framed the worlds anew.
>
> .   .   .   .   .   .
>
> "No ray is dimmed, no atom worn,
>   My oldest force is good as new,
> And the fresh rose on yonder thorn
>   Gives back the bending heavens in dew."

With this view of the Cosmos and its divine harmonies,
which modern science permits me to set before you, we are
prepared to understand the words of Faust, as he contem-
plates the sign of the Macrocosm: —

> "Now each the Whole its substance gives,
> Each in the other works and lives !
> Like heavenly forces rising and descending,
> Their golden urns reciprocally lending.
> With wings that winnow blessing
> From heaven through earth I see them pressing,
> Filling the All with harmony increasing."

XL.

CLUB RECEPTION GIVEN TO MR. EMERSON IN 1873.

EMERSON.

Midway in summer, face to face, a king
I met. No king so gentle and so wise.
He calls no man a subject ; but his eyes,
In midst of benediction, questioning,
Each soul compel. A first-fruit's offering
Each soul must owe to him whose fair land lies
Wherever God has his. No white dove flies
Too white, no wine too rich and red, to bring.
With sudden penitence for all her waste,
My soul to yield her scanty hoards made haste,
When lo ! they shrank and failed me in that need, —
Like wizard's gold, by worthless dust replaced.
My speechless grief, the king, with tender heed,
Thus soothed : "These ashes sow. They are true seed."
O king, in other summer may I stand
Before thee yet, the full ear in my hand !

H. H.

IT may be said, that while the genius of Ralph Waldo Emerson belongs to the whole world he is essentially the property of Boston, in whose people he finds the warmest recognition of his gentle and noble qualities as a man.

Among those who assembled on the last day of the year to show their respect and admiration for Mr. Emerson, were John G. Whittier, Henry W. Longfellow, Dr. Hedge,

Wendell Phillips, Henry Wilson, and Henry James; and the half lights of bright wood-fires and gathering twilight revealed many familiar faces, including some of the choicest spirits in New England and guests from other continents. Mr. Emerson doubtless understood the welcome greeting him on every hand, though, as the principal actor, he probably did not realize the impression the scene inspired.

There could have been a no more fitting day for the reception, or one more lovely in clear winter beauty; and as the poet and philosopher sat in the fading light, reading to these friends his rhythmic story of the Boston Tea Party, one hundred years ago, the picture passed into history, — its very simplicity and dignity being in harmony with all that is known of the wise and gentle Emerson.

BOSTON.

The rocky nook with hill-tops three
   Looked eastward from the farms,
And twice each day the flowing sea
   Took Boston in its arms;
The men of yore were stout and poor,
And sailed for bread to every shore.

And where they went on trade intent
   They did what freemen can,
Their dauntless ways did all men praise, —
   The merchant was a man.
The world was made for honest trade, —
To plant and eat be none afraid.

The waves that rocked them on the deep
   To them their secret told:
Said the winds that sung the lads to sleep,
   " Like us be free and bold!"
The honest waves refuse to slaves
The empire of the ocean caves.

Old Europe groans with palaces,
  Has lords enough and more :
We plant and build by foaming seas
  A city of the poor ; —
For day by day could Boston Bay
Their honest labor overpay.

We grant no dukedom to the few,
  We hold like rights and shall, —
Equal on Sunday in the pew,
  On Monday in the mall.
For what avail the plough or sail,
Or land or life, if freedom fail ?

The noble craftsman we promote,
  Disown the knave and fool ;
Each honest man shall have his vote,
  Each child shall have his school. —
A union then of honest men,
Or union nevermore again.

Mr. Emerson reads with beautiful simplicity, as if the words were just whispered to him out of his best experience, — as if translating to our comprehension some dream and unintelligible harmony of the upper sphere.

Mr. BRADLAUGH, at the close of the reading of the poem, said : " I ascribe to Mr. Emerson's essay on Self-reliance my first step in the career I have adopted. Twenty-six years ago, when too poor to buy a book, I copied parts of that famous lecture ; and I now stand for the first time in the presence of the great preacher, an example at least of a self-reliant man."

Many were present who had little sympathy with Mr. Bradlaugh's peculiar teachings, but none could fail to be touched by the deep feeling with which he spoke.

A question whether the Boston of to-day would always act with the same spirit as it did a century ago drew out divers opinions as to the causes of that uprising, and touching the minorities of great men who had always won against the majorities of public opinion.

WENDELL PHILLIPS opened the discussion : " I believe the pictures of that Boston, a hundred years ago, are very highly colored. That the word ' caucus ' has been even guessed to have taken its origin from the *Calkers* betrays the popular notion and estimate of the rising Rebellion. John Hancock's scarlet coat becomes historic as being the only one which covered a rebel. That ' brace of Adamses,' whom Hutchinson has immortalized, were then men of no repute, vulgar fanatics heading a crowd of workingmen, scoffed at and scorned by the respectables of the day. The marvel is that the middle, well-to-do, and commercial classes headed a rebellion which had no religion in it. That is explained by the fact that every successful merchant in Boston was obliged to be a smuggler. England crippled our trade to save her own, as she has been doing with Ireland for the last century. So the traders, angered by self-interest, *calculated* it would pay to join the mob and rise. But Toryism had the fashion, the old wealth, and the prestige, as it has always had.

" As to our day rising as high even as that, I doubt. Not much if a reform city is one which puts a rope round Garrison to hang him, which even yet hates Sumner; one whose Unitarian pulpit deserted and betrayed Pierpont for his temperance fidelity, and where there never has been, even to this day, a fashionable Orthodox church opened for an abolition meeting. Would any young enthusiast, on fire with a new reform idea, be crazy enough to go to State Street, Beacon Street, the Old South, or Harvard College for countenance? If so, he must be *very* young, and will soon learn better. The young patriots who when Sumter called leaped to arms, ten years ago, were exceptions, not average specimens by any means."

HENRY WILSON replied, mentioning many men who in the last thirty years had been the brain and sinew of New England, and whose work proved that the age of action had not passed into empty words.

It would be injustice to the speakers to attempt to reproduce fully the eloquent impromptu discussion thus briefly sketched.

XLI.

JOHN TYNDALL.

PROFESSOR TYNDALL, of London, delivered a course of lectures on Chemistry, in the winter of 1873, under the auspices of the Lowell Institute.

His mastery of the whole subject, the clearness with which he opened its abstruse mysteries, the witchery of a manner which made the dryest details interesting, and the generous self-forgetfulness with which, in closing his lectures, he gave the merit of any success he had achieved to the two assistants, whose accuracy and adroitness had made every experiment wonderfully perfect, charmed an audience which night after night crowded the old Marlboro Chapel, and which included Professors Agassiz and Peirce and Dr. Holmes.

In closing, he thanked his hearers, and added : " I have now seen America. I wish every Englishman could see it, and that every American could see England ; for I am sure mutual misunderstanding is the root of nine tenths of the wars between nations. Every lover of peace should wish, first of all, that nations should *understand* each other ; and I go home to do all I can to make England *know* America."

Half an hour after he was seated, with a few friends, — the late Rev. John Weiss, Mr. Goddard of the " Daily Advertiser," Mr. Wendell Phillips, and a few others, — at a small supper-table under Mrs. Sargent's roof. Tyndall was in excellent spirits, relieved of the responsibility of his lectures, and poured out reminiscence and anecdote without ceasing.

He spoke of the Lowell Institute, under whose auspices he had delivered the course of lectures just closed, and was full of praise of the benefits resulting from such institutions; "though," he added, "they tell me Emerson has never been asked by the managers to lecture in all these forty years."

"No, and will not be," said some one, "if he lives another forty years. You, sir, never would have been asked had you proposed in *Boston* to test prayer by statistics. London is at a safe distance, and *English* radicalism grows less frightful to Boston conservatism four thousand miles off. A running stream, you know, breaks the fairy charm; so distance opens doors tightly closed against home heretics."

"But you don't really mean that anybody in Boston ignores Emerson?"

"Yes, all that clusters round the Lowell Institute. Such a class disowns Emerson and Parker. Parker, during all the years when he drew crowds, was never invited to lecture by the Institute. Neither Oriental Societies nor Historical Societies dared to ask the first scholar Boston had in both their fields to join them."

"Surprising! I don't think even London could beat that," was Tyndall's comment.

Some one repeated the well-known sarcasm of Thackeray when in Boston. The first places he had sought were Theodore Parker's church and study. Talking, towards the close of his visit, with George Ticknor, Thackeray burst out: "Ticknor, I have not got into the best Boston circle after all, — no, not the best."

Mr. Ticknor assured him that he certainly had; and counted up the known Boston men and women he had met.

" True," answered Thackeray, " but still I can't have seen the best. No, no! Why, Prescott tells me he does not visit Parker," — and the portrayer of snobs smiled archly, not to Ticknor, but to a friend sitting on the other side.

" Well," said Tyndall musingly, and half to himself, "the first time I ever knew Waldo Emerson was when, years ago, a young man, I picked up on a stall a copy of his ' Nature.' I read it with such delight, and I have never ceased to read it; and if any one can be said to have given *the* impulse to my mind, it is Emerson. Whatever I have done, the world owes to him."

We involuntarily clapped our hands at this cordial testimony to the serene genius at Concord.

Mr. GODDARD said : " That reminds me of an incident told me a short time ago by Mr. E. H. Derby, who had then just returned from the International Statistical Congress at St. Petersburg. At a banquet given in the imperial palace to the members of the congress and ladies with them, the Grand Duchess Marie, aunt of the present emperor, a lady of seventy years, who speaks English perfectly, said to Mr. Derby that she was familiar with the books of one of his countrymen, Mr. Emerson. She had read his essay on ' Nature ' many times, and never travelled without it as a companion."

It was now Tyndall's turn to clap his hands. " You see what august indorsement I have."

Mr. WEISS proposed three cheers for the grand-duchess, which Tyndall's cousin timed.

It is said that Professor Tyndall generously devoted the profits of this American lecture tour to the aid of poor students.

XLII.

DOM PEDRO.

IN the month of June, 1876, His Imperial Majesty Dom Pedro II. of Brazil visited Boston. While here he showed the keenest interest in scientific, practical, and educational matters, visiting public works and private manufactories, in the evident desire to take back with him a knowledge of the best methods of the world's work. He evinced a quiet determination not to be lionized, it being soon understood that he declined invitations of a social nature, making exceptions only in favor of Mrs. Louis Agassiz and Professor Longfellow.

The Emperor had for years, however, been a warm admirer of John G. Whittier, with whom he had corresponded both in regard to poetry and the emancipation of slaves. He had translated into his own tongue Whittier's beautiful poem entitled "The Cry of a Lost Soul," beginning,

"In that black forest, where, when day is done,
  With a snake's stillness glides the Amazon,"

and had sent to the poet several beautiful specimens of the bird from which the lyric takes its name. The Emperor expressed to Mrs. Agassiz a wish to meet Whittier, and accordingly arrangements were made for their coming together in the Chestnut Street parlors. Being asked to fix the time, Dom Pedro named three o'clock of the following day, Wednesday, June 14, and a few distinguished gentlemen were invited to be present.

When the Emperor arrived, the other guests had already assembled. Sending up his card, His Majesty followed it with the quickness of an enthusiastic school-boy; and his first question, after somewhat hastily paying his greetings, was for Mr. Whittier. The poet stepped forward to meet his imperial admirer, who would fain have caught him in his arms and embraced him warmly, with all the enthusiasm of the Latin race. The diffident Friend seemed somewhat abashed at so demonstrative a greeting, but with a cordial grasp of the hand drew Dom Pedro to the sofa, where the two chatted easily and with the familiarity of old friends.

The rest of the company allowed them to enjoy their *tête-à-tête* for some half hour, when they ventured to interrupt it, and the Emperor joined very heartily in a general conversation. "I went," said he, "to see the Frog Pond, — no frogs!" He told of his driving over to see the Bunker Hill Monument at six o'clock in the morning; found the keeper a-bed, and when he was at last roused, His Majesty was obliged to borrow half a dollar of his hackman to pay the entrance fee. He did not know what the rest of the company had heard, that, two hours later, Mr. Richard Frothingham coming in and seeing the signature in the book, asked the keeper how the Emperor looked. Putting on his glasses to examine the handwriting, the fretful guardian muttered: "Emperor! that's a dodge; that fellow was only a scapegrace without a cent in his pocket."

He described with a boy's glee his visit to Wellesley College and the girls rowing on the lake; indignantly exclaiming, in answer to a query whether such a bevy of ladies did not awe him, "No, indeed; I am not afraid of girls." With more seriousness he entered somewhat into the details of his examination of the Medical College; spoke of its perfect arrangements, etc., adding, "You know I'm a Doctor of State diseases." He spoke warmly, too, of Channing, whose grave at Mt. Auburn he had visited, copying carefully into his note-book the inscription on the tomb-stone. As he sipped his coffee, he noted the hour. "It is five o'clock, Mrs. Sargent; not my fault, only my misfortune," and, rising, he placed his arm round his brother poet's waist and gently drew him downstairs.

Speaking of the distinguished Brazilian's courtesy, a young lady friend, who had served the guests with ices, said, "The other gentleman thanked me, but the Emperor rose." As Dom Pedro and Whittier passed downstairs one of the company began to repeat an incident which occurred on the occasion of His Majesty's visit to the famous Wartburg. The commandant was conducting the Emperor over his beloved castle, and when they reached the *Kemnate*, the room which had served Luther as a chapel, the Reformer's noble hymn — *Eine feste Burg ist unser Gott* — was played on the long-silent organ, in honor of the royal visitor. As the first notes of the hymn broke the summer stillness, startling into song the birds which fill the tree-tops about that ancient tower, the Emperor fell on his knees, and remained devoutly kneeling until the solemn strains died away. His wife, more Roman and less catholic, crossed herself devoutly, shocked to see the chapel of the arch-heretic so honored. While this tale was told, the parting of poet from poet took place unseen by any curious observer. Some did suspect that, in the privacy of that farewell, Dom Pedro asserted the continental manners; and, as Blücher kissed Wellington the evening of Waterloo, in the same way Dom Pedro celebrated his achievement in securing an interview with the poet of the Merrimac. What the company actually saw was the delighted Brazilian potentate standing erect in his open barouche, waving his hat with a seeming hurrah at the house which held his venerable friend.

· XLIII.

CHARLES SUMNER.

" But the final greatness of a fortunate man is rarely made by any violent effort of his own. He has sown the seed in the time foregone, and the ripe time brings up the harvest. His fate seems taken out of his own control ; greatness seems thrust upon him. He has made himself, as it were, a *want* to the nation, a thing necessary to it ; he has identified himself with his age, and in the wreath or the crown on his brow the age itself seems to put forth its flowers." — BULWER.

THE gathering in honor of Senator Sumner was one of the most brilliant ever witnessed here. The parlors were full of flowers and fragrance ; of men honored, gifted, and famous. On a stand was Milmore's grand bust of Sumner, — a stately and noble presentment, by which Mr. Sumner expressed his desire to be known to posterity. In front of this, at a little distance, sat Carl Schurz, with his graceful wife by his side. Not far off was the poet Longfellow, with his countenance as serene and refined and full of gracious charm as one of his own poems. Whittier was near at hand, a man whose very look is a benediction. Clergymen and men of letters, politicians and artists and solid Boston merchants, — take it all in all, such a company is seldom gathered together ! The poet Stedman told an "interviewer" the next day that the literary centre was being removed from Boston to New York ; but one felt to-day as if the Hub had not yet been shorn of its glory.

Rev. J. T. Sargent paid an eloquent tribute to the moral worth of Mr. Sumner, — a man of deeds rather than of professions.

Rev. John Weiss followed him. He began by speaking of the necessity for utterance and action which the possession of lofty qualities imposes upon their possessor, compelling him to speak when he would rather be silent, and said that the life of Sumner might teach us not to condemn all things in these later days. He then dwelt briefly upon the great senator's habit of devoting himself to literary study, and finding solace therein for the social condemnation which he had brought upon himself by his uncompromising adherence to ideas which were unpopular; and afterwards proceeded to consider Mr. Sumner's religion. "We incline," said the speaker, "to call him the most religious person of this or any other age, because his life was devoted to the ideal method of the Deity. Such divine work as his only a religious soul would set itself to do. If to aspire towards the higher life be a religious gesture, he was perfectly religious, for he climbed strongly and incessantly upwards." Mr. Weiss drew strongly contrasting portraits of Mr. Sumner and the so-called "religious" slaveholders whom he opposed, and said that if at the Judgment he should ask, "Lord, when saw I thee in prison and visited thee?" the answer would be, "Four million times you saw me in prison; beneath four million dusky skins you recognized me." Mr. Weiss then spoke of Mr. Sumner's eloquence, and, after warning young men to remember that he who wore the breast-plate of truth, and cut down all wrong with the sword of the spirit, belonged to no sect, spoke of the duty of imitating his noble example, following in his footsteps, and "taking care of his civil rights bill."

Rev. W. J. Potter then spoke of Mr. Sumner's conduct after the battle of Bull Run, when he, seeing that this

20

temporary defeat would be productive of final good results, rejoiced while others were despondent; and said that this did not show heartlessness but prophetic clearness of sight.

He was followed by John G. Whittier, — the first time I ever knew him to speak in any assembly.

Mr. WHITTIER said: " Had Sumner supposed while in life that I should attempt to talk of him in a memorial gathering, he would have exclaimed with the Scotch poet, when told that a certain militia company would fire a salute over his grave, ' Don't let that awkward squad fire over me! ' " Mr. Whittier then spoke a few words, expressing his gratification that the vote of censure passed by the Massachusetts Legislature had been repealed before Sumner's death. Only a few words did Mr. Whittier give to his friend, but they were eloquent in their brevity and simplicity.

Senator SCHURZ said: " In regard to my feeling for Sumner there is little more that I can say. We fought side by side, or rather back to back, during the three bitterest years of Sumner's life. I feel like a man who, seeing his comrade fall by his side, holds his body in one hand and waves his sword with the other. I, perhaps, more than any other know how Sumner's work must be carried on, and I shall defend him and his memory to the end."

WENDELL PHILLIPS felt that nothing could be added, indeed nothing need be added, to what had been already said so heartily. He quoted Gerard Hamilton's words when Johnson died: " He has made a chasm which not only nothing can fill up, but which nothing has any tendency to fill up. Johnson is dead. Let us go to the next best: nobody can be said to put you in mind of Johnson." So, in civil life, we may say, Sumner is dead. Let us go to the next best: there is no other Sumner.

Mrs. E. D. CHENEY alluded to the national sorrow at

the death of Mr. Sumner, saying that it amounted almost
to a feeling of orphanage ; and then spoke of the feeling at
the time of the Trent affair, when the popular sentiment
was so easily changed by Mr. Sumner's decision that the
prisoners must be returned, and said that precisely such
a spirit of uncompromising fidelity was that which was
needed to carry the nation forward.

The poet and painter, C. P. CRANCH, was the concluding speaker ; and his brief speech contained so perfect a
picture that I give it to you in full : —

"It may be superfluous for me, who had so slight an
acquaintance with Mr. Sumner personally, and who saw
his public career chiefly from across the Atlantic, to add
my humble testimony to the well-deserved eulogies which
have been spoken by so many eloquent lips. Of his commanding position in our political history ; of his uncompromising steadfastness and unshrinking courage ; of his
persistent assertion of absolute justice in behalf of an
oppressed race, and against the overbearing assumptions
and brutal assaults of the defenders of Slavery ; of his
large and far-sighted vision, which made him the prophet
of a new era in America, and of his untiring labors that
the nation should recover its lost ideals, — there has been
and can be but one opinion, as there has been but one
voice of praise, among the friends of truth, freedom, and
humanity.

"But allow me to recall one little circumstance, — a trifle
in itself, yet symbolizing to me the man and his career.
Many years ago, long ere the land was convulsed by the
earthquake whose premonitory tremors should have proved
on what a volcanic soil we stood, I was staying at Nahant
with my friend William W. Story, where I afterward met
Mr. Sumner, then in his sunny and elastic youth, before
he was elected to the Senate.

"On one of those summer afternoons I was seated on the shore, busily engaged in painting the picturesque rocks and views in front of Mr. Story's cottage, stretching out towards the sea. All that the picture needed was a figure on the rocks. Just then, at the farthest end of the long ledge, the tall form of Sumner appeared, and was at once, in landscape-painter's fashion, jotted down into the picture. He stood in the right place. But he was quite unconscious of his position, or that any one was observing him. Nor did he stand there as a lounger. He was waiting impatiently for the evening steamboat to bring him the papers from Boston. He had his eye on the State and the nation, while I had mine only on that little ledge of picturesque rock and that stretching sea, and the tall figure which happened to stand there just at the right moment.

"As I recall that little study from Nature, it seems to fix and symbolize the future senator. As he stands there in the picture, on the end of the long gray ledge, looking seaward, so did he stand through his life upon the firm rock of political principle, facing the great uncertain sea of the future destinies of America. There he stands, — always in the right place, though on the extreme point of the time. There he stands, eagerly waiting for the news, — the latest news which year after year might bring, — of the slow gains of justice upon force and fraud and compromise. There he stands, looking into the misty distance of the coming twilight, — the mist which afterward gathered into storm and hurricane, — while I and my friends were thinking chiefly of Nature and art and literature, and the poetry of life.

"This is only a picture, hardly an incident; but it may, perhaps, serve to add a small vignette or bit of scroll-work to the earnest pages of his biography."

With these words the exercises fitly concluded. They left in our minds the picture of a great soul in a great body, opposing with his kingly presence and with the majesty born of pure intentions and a pure life all shams and all wrong-doing.

XLIV.

JOHN T. SARGENT.

(The first meeting of the Club after his death.)

DR. BARTOL spoke in terms of the utmost feeling of respect and affection of Mr. Sargent, the one in whose place he had been called to preside, whose mind he felt was upon them, — "the eye of the mind, more piercing than the eye of the body," — and whose presence he welcomed. The Club has now reached its second decade. Its reputation abroad is that it is the jumping-off place of all belief into negation. On the contrary, it has *never* been an anti-Christian company. It has stood for freedom of thought and freedom of speech, not "negative," but valuing the elements of freedom and truth beyond all price, as also its fidelity to its precepts and premises. It has held to no atheism or flouting of belief, neither has it made of Jesus a fetich; but it has wished for larger faith and freedom, fuller and freer investigation of religious belief. Let it be judged on the just principle that the cause is equal to the effect.

The host, moderator, president, has risen in his seat. Farewell, let his peers and comrades say, with greeting, to the man who saluted his human sisters with intellectual respect, in whom the old love for his clerical brothers survived all degrees of sectarian heat, having in his soul a glow beyond the warmth of his own ardent temperament, and whose last effort on earth was a smile, which on dying lips is, beyond all knowledge or tongues or prophecies, the clearest announcement of heaven.

Mr. W. H. Channing addressed the company, and in a few brief remarks paid a just and fitting tribute to the late Rev. J. T. Sargent, " whose spirit he felt was with us ; " and, from the earnestness and pathos of his face, words, and manner, one could almost imagine that he saw the one of whom he spoke, and felt as if each might recognize him through the mute appeal from all the surroundings and their influences, with which he was so closely identified. Mr. Channing gave but an outline of Mr. Sargent's life, — his boyhood, college days, and the later years, with their varied experiences; dwelt on his generous, high-toned nature, his quick wit and always ready badinage, his unswerving integrity and great moral courage, which never failed him under the severest tests, — one of which was exchanging with Theodore Parker, which cost him his ministry. " Keep him close with Theodore Parker, with dear Charles Sumner, with Edmund Quincy. We will not think of them as gone, but *near* in spirit."

The following words of tribute were spoken on another occasion.

Rev. John Weiss said : " Let me anticipate the spring which will soon blossom over his resting-place, and add my offering to these fragrant flowers. It will be at least fragrant with the recollection of one of the truest men who ever lived. His opening manhood met an epoch in American history which the present generation cannot appreciate. Hardly, by any effort of imagination, can the young men and women of to-day understand what was involved in being faithful to private conviction in 1840, and from that time downward through the dark period. As Jesus said, ' Come unto me, all ye who labor and are heavy laden,' so said our friend : and his life opened with that practice. When every politic and aristocratic privilege might have claimed him, when the influences of society and of his own rearing would have attracted him into an easier career, he quietly put away all these associations, and began to collect around him the poor and neglected classes of this city of his birth; going from tenement to tenement at the South End, inspired with the feeling to make a chapel for these unchurched people, which he did at length, in Suffolk Street, and preferred his post there to any other."

Mr. HIGGINSON said: "In recalling him it is impossible not to place him in imagination by his own ample fireside, fit emblem of the old-time hospitality of the house. That which gave the peculiar charm to the meetings of the 'Radical Club'—the combination of the most modern thoughts with those stately colonial parlors—was expressed also in the manner of Mr. Sargent in his own home. It linked us with other days,—with the mother as she was portrayed in the old portrait above his head : there she sat at her harp, in perpetual youth,—the harp itself stood, now unstrung and tuneless, in the corner; and the serene and courteous manners, which the son had learned from her, still kept their youthful strain and were never out of tune. High or low, rich or poor, it made no difference; you might meet an emperor there, or a city pauper, but so far as the host's manners went there was no visible variation. Even advancing age and declining health left untouched this innate courtesy. The habit of hospitality remained.

"The practice of the house, in these respects, dated from the period of the Antislavery reform, when there existed among New England reformers an activity of fellowship such as the milder antagonisms of to-day can hardly create. There must be a sense of common danger, a mob, in the air, to bring out that full identity of life and purpose. At least, there must be some social isolation or ostracism to give the complete charm to the warm meeting of reformers, — the excitement of ' Convention Day,' the storms of the platform, the rebellion of the galleries, the final reunion in the hospitable home, fighting the battles over again. There is to this day a great closet in the Sargent house, where all the remaining copies of all the Antislavery tracts are arranged on shelves, neatly sorted and ticketed by the careful hand of Mr. Sargent. I never went into that room without drawing a long breath, to think of the accumulated thunders that lay asleep there. Slavery dead! and there were the spare weapons of the conflict! Those solemn halls in the Tower of London, where the effigies of knights and sovereigns sit silent, each in his gleaming armor, are not more impressive to the imagination. I cannot bear to think that this closet is ever to be disturbed; it should be kept sacred, like the Old South."

WENDELL PHILLIPS said there never was a better illustration of Wordsworth's line, "The child is father of the man," than the life which had just ended. Those who were old enough to remember his boyhood could not fail to recall the simplicity and honor and purity of those childish years. Inheriting almost everything that men work for, it was beautiful to see the way with which he put aside all those openings and facilities for ambition, and gave himself to the work of the ministry of the poor, — the service of those whom many men forgot. It was no lack of spirit; it was from no poverty of gifts. Dowered with the wit and taste and graces which seem to go with his blood, the exquisite instinct of beauty in word, in art, in action, which gave a certain fitness and beauty to his whole life, they graced but they did not weaken. Life with him was no plaything. It was a great career, to be entered upon with courage and ended in self-sacrifice.

It was only another illustration of his serious mood, which made one able to say with truth that the seventy years of that life were a prayer. The earnest mood, which never trifled with an hour, justified this. There are very few lips which God touches with fitness to utter for us our prayers. Only a life of peculiar simplicity and seriousness can give this grace. Those who knelt at the altar with him cannot fail to remember the simplicity and tenderness, the deep feeling and trembling pathos of his prayers, which seemed to lift us into the very presence of God; and one was sure that he who uttered them must stand with familiar love at the very feet of the Father.

XLV.

HEREDITY.

DEAR MADAM, — My recollections of the first time I was invited to your house are dimmer than I should have suspected, if you had not asked me to write them out. I can only recall a few things of a personal nature. It was an informal gathering, of about fifty persons in all, and among these were Moncure D. Conway, Mr. Richard Proctor, Mr. Wasson, and Mr. Weiss. I had the honor of being called upon to speak, and tried to explain, as well as was possible without the aid of diagrams or blackboard, the laws of heredity, etc., which were subsequently given in full before the Club.

Rev. M. D. Conway expressed his satisfaction that the hypothesis of evolution was being adopted in this country, and astonished me a little in a subsequent conversation by saying that "in London they thought Professor Agassiz' influence had given a wrong turn to the minds of young American naturalists in this part of the country." I took the opportunity of showing him that Professor Agassiz' influence in this respect was wholly good. He had prevented us from becoming speculative before we knew enough to think effectually, and had kept nearly all of his students from being swept away by the fascinations of Darwinism, or any other single theory of evolution.

Mr. Proctor also took a lively interest in the communication, and asked several questions, as also did Mr. Wasson and Mr. Weiss.

One of the most curious results of this and the subsequent lecture was the impression which some very good people seemed to get, that my facts were aimed with deadly intent at the doctrine of the immortality of the soul. One stout gentleman asserted privately "that he had that within him which he felt could not die, in spite of what I had said," — an undeniable proposition, if I had said anything against his claims, or if quantity alone could have settled them!

Why will many people persistently skip all that is reliable in what you say, and present you with some remote inference? You observe that it looks like rain to-day, and they infer that you mean that the rains will increase to a flood involving the world in a deluge within a certain limited period.

My impressions of the Club, derived from my first and subsequent visits, were that it embraced a number of unusually active people, very much in earnest, and disposed to respect the same quality in others. I have learned much from the various more or less eminent and well-informed persons with whom I have come in contact, and have had more appreciative audiences in the parlors of your house than anywhere else. I judge of this from the lively interest which has been manifested on several occasions, and the incisive, impartial, and instructive criticism of the "after-talks," as they have been appropriately called.

Hoping you will not cease from your efforts in our behalf,

        I remain very sincerely yours,

                 ALPHEUS HYATT.

THE lecture was directed to the exposition of the peculiar views of the lecturer, with regard to the laws of heredity and the relations of the life of the individual to the phenomena presented by the history of the rise and decline of the group of which it formed a part.

Beginning, then, the subject proper of the lecture, the professor showed a specimen of the nautilus as now existing, and explained the internal structure of the Nautiloids, accompanying the talk with blackboard sketches. Next he passed around a fossil Nautilus, belonging to one of the middle geological periods; then another one of a still older period, and in this the coil of the Nautilus was more unwound. It, with the other forms given, also showed the fact that the young of the present species is represented in the adult forms of ancient times, — a fact which was gener-

alized into a law by Professor Louis Agassiz. Other more
ancient forms were shown, where the uncoiling progressed
to absolute straightness of form, but the continuity of
the species was more or less demonstrable throughout.
These changes were the result of perhaps millions of years
of progress.

Having reached the bottom of the series in the simple,
straight form of the Orthoceras, the course of the lecture
was again turned upward to trace the branching off of the
Ammonoids from the Nautiloids. The first simple form met
is that of the Goniatites. The difference between Ammonoids and Nautiloids is very slight, consisting in a bag,
the egg-shell being attached to the shell in the Ammonoids, and containing part of the animal, while in the other
a scar marks the spot where the bag was attached.

Professor Hyatt then showed drawings of the young of
Goniatites in which the form of the shell was straight, as
among the earlier Nautiloids, the straight Orthoceratites, and
others, in which the coiling and many of the characteristics
of the septa between the air chambers and the structure of
the siphon at early periods were similar to the characteristics of the same parts in the more ancient but full-grown
adult forms of the lower Nautiloids.

According to the well-known laws of heredity, that like
produces like, this repetition of the older Nautiloid forms
and characteristics in the young of the later-occurring
Ammonoids can only be explained on the supposition that
the Ammonoids are the direct descendants from the same
stock as the Nautiloids, — branches, at least, from the same
common trunk.

From this point, having established the probable identical origin of the two, the lecture treated of the Ammonoids. The Clymenia, one of the lowest, simplest forms,
intermediate between Nautiloids and Ammonoids, is identified with the Ammonoids by the egg-bag, though it has

been confounded with the Nautiloids. Following the development and change of the Ammonoid forms, illustration after illustration was given, till nine had been shown, coming down to comparatively recent time through long geologic periods, all showing a gradual uncoiling of the form, till one was reached which was almost perfectly straight, with the exception of the young spiral shell on the pointed end. The later straight forms resembled the earlier straight ones, just as in old age any animal resembles its youthful condition. This gradual straightening of the form of the Ammonoid is due to the introduction of diseased forms, and the inheritance of their disabilities by the race in the same manner that other characteristics are inherited.

In order to make these statements clear the lecturer traced again the history of the Ammonoids. The straight, cone-like Orthoceras type and its coiling up as it was evolved into the modern Nautilus — a closely-coiled shell — was shown. The loose coiling of the oldest of the Ammonoids and of their young in the Silurian, and the prevalence of both closely-coiled young and closely-coiled adults in the later times of the Carboniferous, Trias, and Jura were described. The appearance of diseased individuals in some species of Jurassic Ammonoids, and the gradual increase of these more or less uncoiled shells until they supplanted the whole of the closely-coiled forms in the Upper Cretaceous, and the young closely-coiled, and resembling the healthy closely-coiled adult forms of the older formations of the Jura, were shown. Thus the deformities, the uncoiling, etc. of a few species in the Jura, which had been transmitted, had been inherited at earlier and earlier periods in the different species of Cretaceous Ammonoids; but though in this way the whole form had become straightened out, the process had not gone far enough to destroy the form of the young, which even in the almost straight Toxoceras was still closely coiled.

The young of these newer uncoiled forms thus resemble the adults of the Devonian and Silurian Ammonoids, just as the young of the latter resemble the adults of their still more remote uncoiled ancestors. Thus, whatever the process by which a character becomes fixed in the organization, it is inherited at earlier and earlier periods in successive generations, until it finally enters the earliest periods. This law is what has been called by the discoverers — Professor Cope and the lecturer — the law of acceleration, or accelerated heredity.

When a characteristic comes within the reach of this law there is no exception, no interference possible; neither natural selection nor physical influences can affect the result, except, of course, to the same degree that they can interfere with or affect the action of the laws of growth and heredity.

The lecturer then proceeded to show the resemblances which exist between the old and young forms of the same individual, and traced out the way in which these occurred. The loss of the ornaments and shape of the adult shell is easily followed out in large specimens which are very aged, and when the extremely old whorl has become smooth and round and slightly uncoiled, it is very similar to its own young. The process of retrograde development by which it has lost the adult characteristics reduces it again to a resemblance to its own young. This produces a close parallelism between the life history of the individual and the life history of its race.

Thus the individual has a smooth, cylindrical, more or less straight, uncoiled or loosely-coiled shell in the young; and, though it becomes highly ornamented, extremely closely coiled, and of a different form perhaps in the adult, it returns at last to a similar, smooth, cylindrical, more or less uncoiled, and sometimes straightened-out shell in extreme old age.

In the same manner the race springs from cylindrical, straight, or loosely-coiled forms, and becomes in course of time distinguished for its numerous species of various forms, ornamented with spines, etc.; and then, disease creeping in, the malformed species with which it terminates return to the straight, cylindrical, or loosely-coiled type of form with which the race began.

Professor Hyatt did not attempt to trace the causes of this remarkable parallelism further than might be done by referring them both to laws of accelerated heredity, and ended by pointing out the fact that these phenomena indicated that there was a law of death as well as of life, which probably limited the evolution of the life of the race, as we know it does that of the individual; that, in fact, if a race were not cut off by physical change, and lived out a full term, it would not fail to show signs of decay, and these would be malformed species resembling the old age of individuals among their immediate ancestors. Old age was a pathological condition, due to the fact that the organs failed to perform the function of assimilation. The waste of the body could no longer be supplied by new structures derived from food. This failure was evidently due to the unfavorable character of the physical surroundings, which called for perpetual exertion on the part of the function, and it was evident that a wearing-out took place in the self-acting machinery of the body which could not be supplied.

Wounds, etc. cause uncoiling in recent shells, and other unfavorable surroundings produce diseased forms similar to the cretaceous forms of uncoiled Ammonoids.

Thus it may be said that the race and the individual live in the presence of forces which are tending perpetually to destroy, and which always do eventually destroy them; and that both alike have limited lives and limited capacities for progress, dependent upon their original organization, inherited strength, and so on.

The lecture was rather a talk. It was delivered without reference to notes, and it was illustrated by blackboard diagrams. These eluded reproduction in a printed account, but were easily seen and understood in the bright gaslight of the parlors.

In answer to questions by Dr. Bartol as to whether any of the higher qualities of the adult age seemed to disappear in the older ages of races, Professor HYATT remarked that, while this was a matter of some doubt, it seemed to be so indicated. The life of races seems to be epitomized in that of individuals. If you know the individual, you know the whole race. Evolution does not seem to indicate perpetuity. This he had tried to illustrate in the groups of Ammonites and Nautiloids. Races develop as individuals; groups branch off, grow old, and finally the race becomes worn out; the power of heredity to reproduce the type diminishes, as in individuals, and the race dies.

Dr. BARTOL asked if the essayist had noticed, when extraordinary powers were inherited by individuals in the human race, whether they had appeared earlier than in the parents, and that vitality had become sooner exhausted in their descendants. While ignorant on this subject, he had the impression that this tendency is indicated in history and biography.

Professor HYATT could not answer this question, having only investigated animals; but its discussion was extremely interesting to him. If the facts were as Dr. Bartol supposed, it was a very strong point. Darwin had only accounted for the inheritance of favorable qualities, not of unfavorable ones.

Dr. BARTOL. — Then are the so-called "missing links" a necessary consequence of the facts of the case in the disappearance mentioned by you?

Professor HYATT.— There is no possibility of ever trac-ing all the links; for the distinction of species really means nothing. No two persons would decide alike in marking out species; it is only an idea. Mediterranean and West Indian sponges are examples. Even dealers could see great differences; yet when you try to draw the lines defining the differences, you find it very difficult. Species run together as you get more facts. Darwin's hypothesis does not explain all the facts, as for instance those of old age. He does not treat of growth or the laws of heredity, at least in his published writings.

Dr. WARREN. — At what point in the history of races do new races originate? Do they always spring from the younger growth of races and never from their old age?

Professor HYATT. — This is a very important question. The investigations so far made point decidedly in this direc-tion. Some races also are much longer-lived than others. In fact, the hypothesis I have stated seems to agree with the fact almost too well. It seems as if there should be some exceptions to prove the rule.

In reply to questions by Mr. Wasson, Professor HYATT said that the whole discussion lies in the fact that succes-sive small variations may be traced, showing that wide differences, like those between man and animals, are only differences of degree, not of kind.

Mr. SAVAGE. — If the evolution and Darwinian theories be discarded, is there anything else which can take their place?

Professor HYATT. — I will not go so far as to say that there is no other possible hypothesis. Agassiz believed in special creations.

Mr. SAVAGE. — Is the Creator, then, a performer of miracles?

Professor HYATT. — Not to me. We cannot take ac-count of miracles in scientific investigations.

Mr. Abbot was glad that discussions like this were introduced into the Club, and was confident that in the future the scientific method would be introduced with great advantage in the investigations of religious questions. He believed that no solutions arrived at by other methods would ever again command general credence.

Here Professor Hyatt had a sketch upon the board, showing a trunk-line with many branches, but all originating in a single point at the bottom. Mr. Wasson, stepping to the board, and pointing to this origin, asked: "Have you any theory of the production of this point?" Professor Hyatt replied that he had no explanation to offer.

Dr. Hunt. — It seems to be the question in the minds of the people here, What is the nature of life itself? We are shown how animals differ from each other, — how they change from lower to higher. If man has sprung from a lower type of animal, what is the *vis* or force within which is creating these new forms?

Professor Hyatt. — I do not believe we can go beyond what we can show. Science can at present take no note of any force exclusive of physical force. Forms can be explained by inherent physical powers, and science tends to establish Huxley's opinion that there is no principle *vitality* any more than water has the principle *aquosity*. But a different conclusion may be reached when the solution really comes to the world; it is not safe or scientific to prophesy so far in advance of what we really know.

On another and later occasion Professor Hyatt again addressed the Club on topics complementary to the subject of Heredity. In opening, the Professor alluded to his paper before the Club some months ago, showing the gradual development of forms in the Ammonoids, and their dying out, and the correlations he had traced between these phenomena and those of the rise and decline of life in the individual. He then exhibited diagrams illustrating the acquisition by a species of new characteristics, and the equally rapid development in the young of traits which had originated in the adult period of life among its ancestors. The stage of youth, in which are so many traits formerly adult, is a protected stage; hence the young are able to maintain the ancient characteristics of the type and transmit them to future generations.

In the order of thought there follow the consideration of the relationship of animals to their surroundings, and the facts which support the theory that physical forces alone produce organic changes. Animals leading very simple lives, such as those which float in water or are attached to rocks under water (corals, barnacles, and the like), have little protection from the action of the surroundings, and show corresponding modifications in their forms and many of their characteristics.

Parasites usually give the strongest argument for this theory. The barnacles are parasites in one sense, being sedentary upon the rocks, and having an organization modified so curiously for this purpose that no explanation is possible except the one which attributes their characteristics to the direct action of the sedentary habitat. They are true swimming crustacea in the young, but in the adult are cemented to the rock, head downwards, surrounded by a calcareous shell, and otherwise greatly changed, so that if it were not for the young we should never suspect they were really the remote allies of the crabs and lobsters. They have also true parasites, also barnacles, living on them, which show still greater changes to correspond with their surroundings. One of these has no stomach, and is otherwise greatly modified. The males in several cases live on the female, and being true parasites have in some lost nearly every vestige of the true barnacle. There is

but one explanation, — that change of habitat and surroundings has produced change in organization; then that
these organic changes have been inherited at earlier and
earlier periods in successive generations, until finally the
barnacle characteristics have almost all given place to the
new parasitic characteristics, except in the earliest stages,
which have been protected from the effects of the parasitic
surroundings. The experiments of Schmankewitch in
changing Artemia into Branchippus with an additional
joint in the tail, and other strong proofs of the theory of
the origin of characteristics solely through the action of
physical agencies, were next presented.

Coming back to the other side, the truth remains that
certain animals go on growing larger and larger, becoming
more and more complicated in their relations with others,
as well as in their individual structure, through many generations. It is done by the acquisition of new characteristics. These originate in ancestral forms during the adult
period, and are then inherited in succeeding generations
at earlier and earlier stages of life, perhaps even before
birth; so they are protected more and more as they near
the embryonic stage, and the surroundings are more uniform. Now the animals in which this concentration of
characteristics is greatest are the highest in the scale of
existence. The young of man resembles many different
forms of animals in different respects. It concentrates in
the early stage a larger number of traits than the young
of any other class of vertebrates. Thus we get an immense
protection in our young days; we combine the results
of the development of large numbers of ancestral forms,
and have the chance of growing higher and becoming
more complicated.

Professor Hyatt next considered the protection which is
given to the young by a storing up of food in the egg. In
the lower animals the egg all goes to form the individual.

As we reach more complicated forms, more food in proportion is stored up for the young. The egg is divided into two parts, — the food part and the generative part. In fishes the food portion of the egg is very large, especially in the sharks and skates. When we reach mammalia, the law is universal that protection is given to the animal. Not only is the egg in two portions, but the young is connected with the mother so that she nourishes the young with the blood which circulates in her own body. Another element of protection comes in nursing. By this the young are kept under control of the mother. An extension of the idea would be that protection is also seen in the education given to children, though Professor Hyatt would not yet state that as a part of a scientific system at this stage of investigation. It is not wholly the physical theory of the origin of characteristics which must govern us in this matter. We must introduce another element. Physical influences explain well enough the origin of different characteristics, but not their perpetuation. Animals protect themselves against their surroundings. Man is everywhere man, the same creature, though the physical surroundings are different. The inner force which he derives from growth and heredity makes the embryo develop in a certain way. This position cannot be overthrown. If physical surroundings are different, they cannot produce similarities, but must produce differences; they cannot preserve the type and change it at the same moment.

Dr. BARTOL, opening the after-talk, said that the thought of education as a form of protection to the human young had come to his mind before Professor Hyatt stated it. It ought to be the means of making a bigger man, of getting a new ring or wrinkle into him. It seemed that a powerful argument had been brought for the old doctrine of a new birth or regeneration. There is hope that man may acquire new characteristics ; there is hope for a bigger man, a bigger State and a bigger Church, a better South than the old or solid one, a bigger and better North than a solid one, a bigger and better country and human race.

In reply to a question by Mr. Savage, Professor HYATT stated the position of the advocates of the physical theory to be that all characteristics are produced by the surroundings.

Mr. WASSON expressed immense satisfaction with the facts advanced. He regards the forces of Nature without and of the animal within as working together to produce given characteristics. There is a concurrence or correlation of forces. So it is impossible for him to be a monist. There are always two forces concerned. There is a response of the animal to its surroundings. Changes are not simply mechanical.

A remark by Mr. Wasson led Professor Hyatt to observe that there is now absolutely no proof of spontaneous generation, and till it is a proved fact scientific men ought to have nothing to say. The conversation was then mostly sustained by Professor Benjamin Peirce and Mr. Hyatt. Professor Hyatt told of his studying the changes of a score of different species of fossil shells in a lake-bed in Wurtemburg, and thought they could all have been developed from one form in several hundred years. He would not be positive ; five hundred would probably be the outside limit. From the analogy of his studies he should think there was a very rapid acceleration in the development of man in early times. Darwin's periods seem extravagant. Professor Peirce asked if fifteen million years was long enough time in which to bring the earth to its present condition, but Professor Hyatt was not ready to give an opinion. Geologists want a hundred million years, but he would doubt the necessity of so many. Calculation of time by the erosion of rocks is a method which is just now in a state of chaos.

Professor PEIRCE then went on to speak of the time required by the cooling of the earth to reach its present condition, and stated that about a hundred million years would be required. The heat from the sun at the present rate, with the supply of meteors considered, shows also that about the same time has elapsed since it began its radiation. At present the heat we get from the direct meteors is about the same in amount as that which we get from the sun. They fall into the sun (whose heat is maintained by them), and their heat is radiated back to us. More accurately, the direct heat from meteors is about ninety per cent of that from the sun. A large amount of the heat of the sun is due to the contraction of its mass. If meteors did not fall into the sun, the temperature of the earth would fall to 200 or 300 degrees below zero. The heat of space and of the earth (in part as is shown by night temperature) is caused one half by meteors. The mass of the sun is enlarging by them, and the orbits of the planets becoming less eccentric. By independent modes of calculation upon these facts, the time necessary for the development of the solar system to its present state is computed at a hundred million years, though a few years, a million or two, would be of little account; and for this reason Professor Peirce was much interested in Professor Hyatt's opinion that there was not need of so much time for the development of the animals on the earth.

XLVI.

EVOLUTION.

By PROFESSOR ALPHEUS HYATT.

PROFESSOR HYATT'S essay was somewhat didactic, and especially directed against the hasty and sensational inferences made by many evolutionists in advance of what was really known. He considered this to be an abuse of the authority at present given to scientific utterances by the confidence of the public.

Professor Hyatt illustrated his paper by blackboard diagrams, and confined himself closely to the subject in hand. A brief sketch of the development of the theory of evolution occupied the beginning of the reading, and the date of rising interest in the idea was fixed in the latter part of the seventeenth century. The theory is a revolt against the theocracy of the Middle Ages, has been strongly opposed by religious teachers, and has never won general approval in France. After deprecating the unwise excesses of rash converts of evolution, Professor Hyatt paid a deserved compliment to the modesty and caution of some of the leading men of the school to-day, especially Virchow, from whose address before the Society of German Naturalists he repeatedly quoted.

The opposition which the Darwinian theory has met would have crushed it had it not been for the state of preparation in which it found naturalists and educated classes. The rightful claims of Darwin's " Origin of

Species" are that it led to a revolution in the methods of thought on the question of evolution; that it turned the attention of investigators to more exact methods of research; that it presented a most perfect type of scientific morality; and that it proved a new and true view of evolution. The first three points show that the " Origin of Species" is the book of the day, and its author the leading mind of this century. The last point, though important in the view of most men, is least in Professor Hyatt's opinion; for the Darwinian laws, he affirms, have only a limited application. He thinks Mr. Darwin unwittingly prefixed a misleading title to his book, and that the theory fails to explain the origin of a single characteristic or modification. The title should have been, " The Laws of the Survival and Perpetuation of Differences between Species." Darwin based his theory upon a now admitted axiom in biology, that species have a constant tendency to vary. Huxley, the exponent of radical Darwinism, says the world now needs a good law of the origin of variations; and this statement is undoubtedly true. Darwin's theory rests upon variations already existing, and tries to account by the law of natural selection for their success, or their survival and perpetuation, as compared with other competing variations, which fail or die out.

The larger divisions did not originate by this process; they arose from the increasing number of those possessing ancestral differences which belong as much to them as to the original forms. It is begging the question, after the most approved form of the teleological school, to make a cut between the ancestors and the successive groups of descendants, saying the species originated here or there.

In every large species two classes of differences seem to be perpetuated, and others are transitory. These are those which distinguish the species from other closely allied species, and those which correspond to the local physical surroundings. The former have more or less independence and distinguish the species everywhere, whereas the latter change with the habitat.

At this point the lecturer read from a memoir on sponges, of which he was the author, and gave the details of several noted experiments showing the effects of light, heat, food, etc. upon the specific and even generic characteristics of animals.

The Darwinist replies that those animals only survive in the tanks of the experimenter which are peculiarly fitted to live under the new conditions in which they are placed; but the answer is equally reassuring and convincing. No selection of certain varieties takes place. All the animals experimented upon change without the intervention of such causes. They are protected from a struggle for existence. Single varieties which may be supposed to have been better fitted than others to survive are not selected. And here we strike out the very keystone of the arch which supports the universal application of Darwin's theory.

If Darwin's theory does not explain the origin of variations, yet we have no right to say that physical causes would produce all variations; for many variations are transient, and many more are derived from inheritance, and may be traced often to remote ancestors.

————

Professor PEIRCE spoke first, as belonging more to the scientific school than any other present. He is a man of marked and venerable aspect, — his head and shoulders of rather a leonine appearance; and when he rose to his feet, his dark eyes glowing beneath his wide brow, snow-capped with thick white hair, I thought, as Charlotte Brontë thought of Thackeray when she first saw him:

" And there arose a lion out of Judah." It was a little
odd to hear this mathematical lion take up for the ideal as
he did, and declare that the great danger in the scientific
researches of the present day lay in the fact that it seemed
to strike at the ideal. But it was only in seeming. The
ideal was indestructible ; it would ever elude the positive
approach. And the professor made a most happy illustration of his meaning by stating that two magnetic forces
of entirely opposite poles would never destroy each other.
Professor Peirce condensed Professor Hyatt's paper into
the statement that the events and phenomena in the
world have followed certain immutable laws ; that, given
anywhere in the universe the conditions existing in our
planet, the subsequent history would be exactly the same ;
that if any characteristic disappears from the system, it
will never reappear. Yet the gist of Professor Peirce's
comments was directly against the adequacy of the mate-
rialistic philosophy to explain the *idea*, — that which is
above the physical.

Mr. WEISS expressed the general opinion of the audience
when he warmly commended the simplicity and modesty
of scientific men like Professor Hyatt. He said that he
was profoundly grateful for the facts which had been given
him ; but that, when a scientific man led him down to the
physical basis of all things, he always wanted to know
who made this basis. Then, following Professor Peirce,
only a good deal more so, Mr. Weiss declared for the
ideal. The best results of materialism, he said, were from
the ideal, — the inspiration of the imagination.

Mr. WASSON politely and kindly attacked the paper on
the same grounds, and said that the scientists could never
explain the mental and spiritual phenomena.

Colonel HIGGINSON gave his opinion that, considering
the state of science at the time when Darwin's book on
evolution was published, its title was not a misnomer. He

also said that it was possible that Darwin's law may hold good in higher orders of animals, while it seems to fail in the lower, and stated that Agassiz had admitted privately that he had some doubts of the absolute permanence of species in all cases, though he was a strong opponent of the theory of variation.

XLVII.

INDIVIDUALITY.

By THOMAS DAVIDSON.

MR. DAVIDSON traced the progress of philosophical thought from its beginning with the Greek philosophers, and concluded with a statement of his own views on the doctrine of individuality, and the necessity of contradiction in our ideas of unity and multiplicity. " Individual," in its radical meaning, is much like " atom " as it is used by modern physicists. The fundamental question of all, which embraces the whole subject of philosophy, is, " What is the nature of individuality ? " All early attempts at philosophy were to find a rational explanation of the external universe. Thought first rested upon the conception of a universal physical element; then Pythagoras introduced the idea of abstract form or number. First there was the idea of unity ; Pythagoras introduced that of multiplicity, though he really assumed it in his very argument. Thus we get the primitive forms of the antithetic identity and multiplicity which runs through all philosophy. Heraclitus developed the Ionic school, and the Eleatics the Pythagorean. Among the followers of the former are the Stoics and the whole school of Hegel. Neither Heraclitus nor the Eleatics arrived at permanent individuality. The one assumed absolute matter and denied absolute form ; the other assumed absolute form and denied absolute matter ; but both matter and form are predicates of individuals, though neither is alone.

Mr. Davidson traced the progress of philosophy in its quest for a tenable individuality through Anaxagoras, Socrates, the Sophists, Plato, and Aristotle, showing that each had a logical place in the development of thought, — the succession being, first, a positing of formless matter; second, of matterless form, or number; third, conditioned matter; fourth, conditioned ideas. But none of these accounts for things as they are. A *deus ex machina* is always needed, and, being the ground of all real existence, is, of course, all real existence, — a pantheism with which no human mind was ever satisfied. After Plato had brought philosophy to the conditioned idea, came Aristotle, and tried to account for all being. His great service to philosophy was, that he saw the law that the true individual is always subject, and never can be predicate; but he failed to find a permanent real individuality. In the Middle Ages the contest between Platonism and Aristotelianism came into the Church with success to the latter; and to this day the Roman Catholic Church holds the doctrines of Aristotle.

In the later part of his paper Mr. Davidson elaborated his theory of individuality. Individualism implies unity and multiplicity and the absolute identity of the two. If God's creating man in his own image means anything, it is that he gave as his substantial essence something which should at once be one and many, and one in the very same sense in which it is many. In consciousness we have the only thing which corresponds to the conception of unity with multiplicity. The unity is in the subject or *ego*, and the multiplicity is in the objective world which is necessary to our thought of personal identity, and the two are identified in thought. The entire unity of consciousness is in every thought, and every separate thought presupposes the entire unity of consciousness. This identification of individuality with triune consciousness makes both atheism and pantheism impossible.

In the Middle Ages, freedom — that is, individuality — was nearly quenched by the doctrine of the omnipotence of God and the nothingness of the human creature. Since the Reformation the case has been nearly reversed. The present cry for freedom, which takes the form of atheism, license, and universal suffrage, is just as one-sided and leads to results as little desirable as the theory of entire subjection which prevailed in mediæval Europe. Only with freedom in subjection and subjection in freedom is perfect individuality possible.

Professor PEIRCE followed. "We would like to know more of the connection between the old Greek and the Chaldaic philosophers," he said. "From the tablets lately discovered in Nineveh it seems that the final result of their philosophy was, that there were two beings, — the idea and chaos. Power and motion then came in, and the universe was developed. Moses probably got his accounts from the Chaldees, and added the idea of a deity." Professor Peirce doubted if the human mind could reason with regard to the Infinite. From our observations of the stars we find that the universe is finite. If we go back to chaos and have nothing but that, there would be a stable equilibrium. If it was disturbed by force, it would come to rest again. In the beginning there must have been a force in which all change was differentiated. Chaos must have had a plan of the universe put upon it from without. The tendency of modern science is to come to a point where there shall be no final action. Then the force in the universe must be a finite force. But the power in the universe could not have had a beginning, and it must have been in the world at its beginning. If anything is true in physics this is; and this power is infinite. Man cannot reason about it: we may call that power bad, or anything else, — you have God in every part of the universe.

Professor FELIX ADLER stated that the mind demands a first cause ; but immediately, finding that everything which conditions is conditioned, it demands the cause of the first cause, and so we have no first cause at all. Both these demands of the mind — for first cause and its cause — should be recognized. If God was the cause of the world and was eternal, then the world was eternal, — a contradiction. The doctrine of the trinity is only a fair, alluring fantasy. It covers the abyss of the infinite, and is simply a bridge of flowers, which does not bear substantial footsteps.

Mr. WASSON followed with an earnest protest against individualism, and the sophistry that there is no universal truth. In that doctrine there is nothing which has power to say "Thou shalt." We have ten thousand million "I wills," and out of them comes our democracy. Until we get a ". Thou shalt" into politics, we have no commonwealth.

Mr. HIGGINSON was not in favor of insisting upon the importance of authority at the present time. He shrinks from communism and the principle of absolute obedience to an absolute authority. It points directly to the time when the people will rise, and take all the railroads and trains, perhaps, and work them in the interest of that absolute power. The only ways in which we can get that absolute power are through a hereditary monarchy, through the Roman Catholic Church, or through the commune. He believes the only safe way is not to rebel against universal suffrage or individualism. He believes it best to have as little government as possible ; and the laws here are respected because we make them ourselves.

Mr. WASSON again urged the necessity of a "Thou shalt," saying that behind this lies the "ought;" and Mr. HIGGINSON replied that the representative teacher of that doctrine, Carlyle, had always stopped short of telling how

22

far the "ought" went. For a practical way of learning what it is, — apart from the three arbitrary ways above mentioned, — we are left to the clumsy method of educating the race. That is the best way of finding the "ought."

Professor HYATT doubted the conclusion that may be reached regarding the nature of thought. At present he thinks we can predicate nothing beyond the statement that matter is infinite. Nothing is proved about form or thought, and the world is disputing whether they exist at all.

At the close Mr. DAVIDSON spoke briefly. The purpose of his essay had been to show that all existence implies an absolute balance of contraries; that Being itself, as Being, as thinkable, is necessarily triune, — an object implying a subject and a relation of entire real unity and ideal difference between the two. He expressed satisfaction at finding that those who understood him agreed with him.

XLVIII.

IDEALITY.

BY BENJAMIN PEIRCE.

"IDEALITY in Physical Science" was the subject of Professor Peirce's essay, as will be seen by the sketch of the discussion that followed. The paper was regarded as one of remarkable importance, and was decidedly anti-materialistic in tone.

There were a few changes made in Professor Peirce's essay since it was first given, but these were in the direction of greater explicitness, and did not alter its character. Professor Peirce closed as follows: "Men of science, be not false to your childish faith in your bedside prayer. Your logic of induction may be as pellucid as ice, but beware lest you be bound in its frigid and rigid bonds as were the traitors seen by the divine comedian in the lowest depths of Tartarus. Retrace your steps upward through the narrow avenue of Ideality, and you will drift from this threatened darkness to see the stars again, will again perceive the central light to be the unfailing fountain of knowledge, and in it and through it will join in the praise and worship of the almighty, omniscient, and all-loving God."

Dr. BARTOL said that the authority of fact had been spoken of, and he rejoiced in the presence of a man in our midst whom the weight of this fact did not prevent from being an idealist. Professor Peirce had been weighing the sun and the stars, but they had not weighed him down. With the soul in the other scale of the balance, all this aggregation of matter was outweighed. All study presupposed a spiritual faith in the student. Atheism might be construed as a demand for a truer theism. The God of the old theology was one we could neither have nor worship ; the true God might even be a God utterly unconscious of himself in the self-forgetfulness of his universal love and wisdom. He was willing that atheism, in its proper place, might speak its own word as a provocation for the enlargement of our spiritual vision.

Mr. WASSON said there was a human world of which man himself was the author, and this for him was the real world. The physical philosophers themselves called this an ideal element, and regarded it as superior to that which they regard as fact. It was refreshing to know that we were not standing in a world without thought, but that ideality was something indispensable to the physical universe. It has seemed obvious that the one-sided philosophy of evolution could not stand all by itself, and now it has been upset. We could take no one step in the entire process without finding there a thought, the evidence of spiritual power. For instance, it had been said by disciples of that school that the existence of light called the eye into being ; that the eye was a consequence of light. But until there was an eye there was no susceptibility to light. There was a motion of fine ether, but no light until the creation of an eye to see it. The doctrine of evolution was lame in proceeding from one side only. There was that Something which designed the eye and proceeded to the making of it ; and in that Something thought was manifest.

Dr. BOWDITCH was delighted to find a man like Professor Peirce coming forward with such views as had been expressed in his essay. He felt that the idea of the function of a part was brought out in it before the organ was formed. His own observation of the growth of living organisms had confirmed him in this view. In studying the growth of the snail from the egg to the adult creature, he had noticed what had seemed to be an impulse toward a growth in a particular direction or manner. Before the heart was formed the tendency seemed to be towards the formation of that organ in a certain place, and it was formed there. In this the speaker saw evidence of thought and intention.

Professor HYATT remarked that efforts to reconcile science and revelation had failed. Now Professor Peirce gave us a declaration of faith unsurpassed in the literature of physical science. Such a declaration could only come after scientific investigation. It was necessary that the facts must have accumulated to make such a declaration of value. Hæckel he regarded as the foremost biological scientist of Germany, and was probably the nearest approach to a materialist. Hæckel's hypothesis would derive life from the mineral, and carry it along through the successive steps of development; and he goes so far as to place a soul in the lowest form of living matter. Professor Hyatt did not think scientists were disposed to sacrifice belief, but he felt that they had no right to anticipate discovery with belief any more than to pass false coin.

The Rev. Mr. CARPENTER felt that the poet and scientist had been shown to have the same great work to fulfil, — to seek and perceive the law within the law.

Mrs. LIVERMORE touched upon what might be called the insolence of certain men of science; and this impelled Dr. BOWDITCH to say that he considered it insolent in Hæckel to have attacked Agassiz for his belief in something higher.

To this Professor HYATT replied, — while acknowledging that Hæckel had been extremely ready to quarrel with every one, — that Hæckel had criticised Agassiz for pre-conceiving a teleological plan of the creation ; and in that, so far as it was purely scientific, he agreed with Hæckel.

In conclusion Professor PEIRCE explained that he had meant to impress upon scientists to beware lest they forget the first words of their childhood's prayer, — " Our Father who art in heaven."

XLIX.

DON QUIXOTE.

By CHARLES CARROLL EVERETT.

LONG ago, the members of the Club learned that the days on which they listened to Dr. C. C. Everett must be marked with a white stone, and the paper on "Don Quixote" only confirmed them in their opinion.

Dr. Everett began with a sketch of the life of Cervantes, and a brief analysis of the peculiar mental endowments which caused him — in a period when a man of narrow nature might have hated his age and time, and when a religious man might have abandoned himself to devotional fervor — to see the ridiculous side of affairs, consider them as a perfect and irresistible joke, and fall into a laughter in which all the world was forced to join him. "It is true," said Dr. Everett, "that some blame him while the world applauds, and some weep while the world laughs. Cervantes is accused of having destroyed the dignity and chivalrous feeling of his nation : like the philosopher who saw his ass eat figs and perished in a fit of merriment, Spain fell to laughing and so died. It is certain that with the 'Don Quixote' the Spanish zeal for chivalry ended, and the romances of chivalry came to a sudden stop. It was once thought that the woodpecker killed trees, because men noticed that the trees that he tapped soon after died ; but we know now that he attacks the trees because they are rotten." The essayist then alluded to the scene

in which Don Quixote mistakes the recognition which he
owes to the label fastened to his back for the result of his
wide reputation ; and pointed out the fact that to-day the
good knight's dream had become reality, and his portrait,
as he looked arrayed in battered armor, helmeted with a
barber's basin, mounted on Rosinante, and yet bearing
himself with an air of lofty enthusiasm, would be known
anywhere. "This," said Dr. Everett, "is the prerogative
of genius ; it is crowned king of the world. Coin from its
mint, bearing its stamp, circulates everywhere, and we,
seeing its image and reading its superscription, know that
it is issued by Cæsar." He declared that, in showing the
ludicrous side of the controversy between old chivalry and
the modern world, Cervantes often made the best things
seem most ridiculous, and caused the essence of chivalry
to seem as ludicrous as he strove to make its forms.

The object of the essay was to show, first, that the institution of chivalry was not ridiculous, but worthy of honor,
if not of reverence ; second, much that passes for Quixotism is worthy of reverence ; and third, what is real Quixotism? "It was inconvenient," said the essayist, "to
have illustrations for this lecture ; but if any of you wish
to see companion portraits of Don Quixote and his Squire,
look at your own faces as they appear in the bowl of a
spoon, when looked at longitudinally and latitudinally, and
you will have a fair idea of their appearance ; " and he
then pointed out several of the more obvious antitheses
between the two characters. Then, entering upon a consideration of the age in which the scene of the romance is
laid, he protested against "ascribing the errors of feudal-
ism to chivalry," and slyly insinuated that perhaps, after
all, an age which carefully removes the element of intelligence from a jury-trial has not much to say concerning
another which believed in the trial by combat. He then
showed that in time the forms of chivalry overlaid and bore

down its principles until they were crushed beneath it, as
the knights were weighed down by the cumbrous armor
made necessary by the yearly improvements of weapons,
until at last the first boom of the cannon sounded the knell
of the system.

"With the new civilization," he said, "comes the absorption of the individual into the State, and by the abstraction
of his individualizing qualities society gains, but man loses."
Going on to show that much which passes for Quixotism
is worthy of reverence, Dr. Everett included under this
name all love, — since lovers always exaggerate, — and
the youthful anticipations of a life of success unmarred by
failure. "Still," he said, "although we laugh at love, there
is no creature on earth that might not look noble to us had
we love's insight; and though we laugh at youth, we must
reverence its dreams, because they are the truth. We
sometimes speak as if those who were not men of one idea
were men of all ideas, whereas they are often men of no
ideas; but he who is intoxicated with one glowing thought
is no longer an individual, but has entered into immortality. We live in and through all things; we cannot live
apart. Man, if not a drop in the main current, is a drop
in an eddy. The age lives in and through us all, and is
sure not to speak to us alone."

L.

LANGUAGE.

By JOHN FISKE.

JOHN FISKE began his paper with notice of the great difference wrought by modern thought in the treatment of the question whether human languages had a common origin. The old theories have been superseded, without being refuted. The antiquity of the human race comes in to alter entirely the point of view of the facts. From this point of the essay an abstract is given below. Considering how multifariously language has varied from age to age, and that mankind has doubtless possessed the power of articulate speech for some thousands of centuries, it no longer seems worth while to seek immediate conclusions about primitive speech from linguistic records which do not carry us back more than four or five thousand years. From the vantage-ground which we now occupy it is not difficult to see that the hypothesis of a single primeval language, from which all existing languages have descended, involves an absurd assumption. After fifty years of comparative study of languages, in a cautious and prudent way, we have succeeded in making out some few cases of demonstrable genetic kinship among groups of languages. Beside the Aryan family, we have clearly made out the existence of the Dravidian family in southern India, and of the Altaic family (to which the Finnish, Hungarian, and Turkish belong), to say nothing of the long-established Semitic family. Other families of speech no doubt exist, and will by-and-by have their relationships definitely marked out. But the moment we try to compare these families with each other, in order to detect some definable link of relationship between them, we are instantly baffled. Any true family of languages will show a community of structure as conspicuous as that which is seen among vertebrate animals. The next family you study will be as distinctly marked in its characteristics as is the group of articulated insects, spiders, and crustaceans. But to compare the two families with each other will prove as futile as to compare a reindeer with a lobster. The only conclusion to which you can logically come is that, while certain languages here and there have become variously modified so as to give rise to well-defined families of speech, the like process has not taken place universally. A language which gives rise to several mutually-resembling descendants must be spoken for a long time by large bodies of men spread over a wide territorial area, and a good illustration is afforded by the ancient Latin, from which have come several languages of modern Europe. But when literary men gave up writing in classic Latin and began to write in their own languages derived from it, then a movement toward unity set in. Parisian is asserting its sway over the other dialects of France, and Tuscan is becoming the universal tongue of Italy. Railroads and telegraphs, newspapers and novels, have already sealed the death-warrant of all *patois*, and the execution is only a question of time. It is not at all likely that there will ever spring up in this country such dialectic variations as those of France and Italy, or that any essential divergence will ever arise between the English language as spoken in England and in America. For the language of the thriving people to whom the ocean has become a common pathway, who have taught mankind

how to drive ships with steam and how to send electric
flashes of intelligence through the watery abyss, — for
this language a future of unprecedented glory is in store.
By the end of the twentieth century, English will no doubt
be spoken by something like four hundred millions of people, crowding all over North America and Australia, as
well as over a good part of Africa and India, with island
colonies in every sea and naval stations on every cape.
By that time so large a proportion of the business of the
world will be transacted by people of English descent
that, as a mere matter of convenience, the whole world
will have to learn English. Whatever other languages
any one may have learned in childhood, he will find it
necessary to speak English also. In this way our language will become more cosmopolitan, while all others
become more and more provincial; until after a great
length of time they will probably one after another assume
the character and incur the fate of local *patois*. One by
one they will become extinct, leaving English as the universal language of mankind. But, however the actual
result may be, the considerations brought forward seem
to indicate that complete community of speech belongs
rather to the later than to the earlier stages of human
progress. Mere practical business convenience is the
factor which will settle the question.

Taking up the languages of Asia, Professor Fiske recognized three distinct families, — the Finno-Tartaric (or
Turkish), the Mongolian, and the Samoyed of Siberia.
Speaking of the peculiarities of their structure, he said
that the inference from the Mongolian tongues is that
there never was a primitive speech corresponding to the
Aryan in its relations to modern languages. Then he
pictured the rapid changes in savage dialects, and the
utter lack of a conservative element in them, and ended
as follows: "We shall conclude, I think, after a survey of

the whole matter, that in speech, as in other aspects of social life, the progress of mankind is from fragmentariness to solidarity. At the beginning, a multitude of feeble, mutually hostile tribes, incapable of much combined action, with hundreds of half-formed dialects, each intelligible to a few score of people : at the end, an organized system of mighty nations, pacific in disposition, with unlimited reciprocity of intercourse, with very few languages, rich and precise in structure and vocabulary, and understood by all men."

Among the guests of the day was the late OLE BULL, the distinguished violinist, and one of the happiest features of the discussion which followed the reading of the paper was the Norwegian's conception and graphic description of the difference between the Spanish and English tongues. He subscribed to the opinion of Professor Fiske as to the Finnish and Hungarian languages. Though he agreed that commercial business would be done in English, yet he thought it impossible for any language to get the coloring of another language. The Spanish language is beautiful. The English is stiff, like the Englishman himself. The Englishman says, " A nail is a nail," — not a big nail or a little nail; but the Spaniard puts on his words a beautiful twist (and here Ole Bull illustrated by a gesture to express his meaning better). The English are military and quick. In Spanish you must spin out to make it grandiose and flexible. The Spanish cannot depict a situation in a few words. Everything will be unfinished to him ; he will have to jump, jump the whole time. It must be spun out so that his system and nerves will feel good.

LI.

THE COMIC.

By CHARLES CARROLL EVERETT.

AFTER the opening sentences of his paper, Dr. Everett spoke of the habit of philosophizing upon everything, and showed how in this way the comic takes on a serious aspect. The essayist then came to the distinctions between the comic and the tragic, and the peculiar qualities of the comic. He recognized the incongruous as the chief element of the comic, and regarded it as a difficult matter to tell *a priori* whether a given fact would strike the observer as comic or tragic. There is in the tragic as much incongruity as in the comic; it depends upon the person interested whether the incongruity brings laughter or pain. The distinction between the comic and tragic has no existence, said Dr. Everett. The greatest suffering in any incongruity cannot take away its comic aspect to many minds. Very much of the comic, also, has its tragic side. Even in Falstaff and Dogberry there are qualities which would by no means appear comic to relatives or associates of those well-known, fun-making characters. Taking up Schopenhauer's analysis of the comic, Dr. Everett said that the German erred in making two classes of the comic. The ludicrous is defined as the incongruity in different forms, which we bring together in a single organization. The comic is like a lambent flame, which may play over the surface of things without scorching

them. There is absolutely no comic in Nature. It is purely
subjective; objectively considered, it does not exist. In
this respect there is a difference between the comic and the
tragic. Objectively, the tragic does exist. In the great
struggle for existence there is the very essence of tragedy.
The competition for life is a tragic struggle. The tragedy
may exist without any one seeing it, but the comedy must
be seen in order to exist. There is nothing comic without the mind, which sees the incongruous relations of
things. In this respect the world is what we make it. In
regard to the real nature of the comic, the problem is not
yet solved. Both the comic and the tragic are composed
of incongruities, and the difference between them lies in
the fact that the comic is found in the incongruous relation considered merely as to its form, whereas the tragic
is found in the incongruous relation considered as to its
content. The comic is on the surface; the tragic is the
real content of things. Thus the comic is the froth and
foam of life. Wit sees the distinction between the form
and the content, but has no regard for the humanity in
the content. Humor, on the contrary, throws a deep sympathy over the content. It sees the distinction between
the form and content, but behind the latter sees the individual, and sympathizes with him. Seeing this characteristic of humor, we can understand why friends jest about
each other, and why smiles and tears contend with each
other. By this quality of the mind to see incongruity of
form we are relieved from the tragic of the contest, and
enjoy what is on the surface. Shakspeare takes us into
the realm of the form or of the comic, and, when we return
to the real, it seems more real and endurable. Perception of
the comic implies a separation of form from substance. He
who sees only the ludicrous in things, sees only the surface;
he sees mere vacancy. He sees most wisely who can see a
serious thing seriously, but in little matters, where little is

involved, recognizes the comic relations which lie on the surface.

At the close of his essay Dr. Everett, after referring to certain theories in regard to the origin of laughter, urged that natural selection would sufficiently account for its existence. He presented, in defence of this position, a humorous imaginative sketch of the evolution of man, — according to which, while others sank beneath the burdens of the new humanity, the first man who laughed alone survived to become the parent of the race of man that laughs.

LII.

PHILOSOPHY.

By GEORGE HOWISON.

BEGINNING with a quotation from Goethe's "Prometheus," in which the Titan defies Zeus, Professor Howison stated that in the conception we have the principle of progress in man in deadly feud with the principle of conservation and reverence, the spirit of the present and future rending itself utterly from the past, the human reason quite at fault about the divine, and come to open revolt against it and to repudiation of it. The chief question for philosophy to answer is, How shall the human principle of freedom and progress be brought into harmony with the permanence of man, the validity of his past, the possibility of his future, and the voice of that moral law in conscience which declares the nation valid as against the subject man, our neighbor valid as against our selfishness, and God valid as against our mere propensities? This question has been the problem of Christendom since the beginning of Protestantism, and is the key to every crisis in human history. It is probably no exaggeration to say that, at present, a larger and more influential mass of men are bewildered by it and give evidence of not holding any key to its solution than at any previous time in the history of the world. As Christianity is a higher and profounder ideal of life than any that preceded it; as Christendom is the most com-

23

plex, most brilliant, and most comprehensive form society
has assumed; as recent science has laid tributary a wide
realm of natural resources, — so the problem to-day assumes a reality and difficulty never known before. The
free individualism of to-day is engaged in that very conflict with the traditional ideal of the conscience which
appears in the "Prometheus." That free thinking, which
we may well assume to be itself an eternal factor in
man's eternal aim, is apparently on the eve of bidding
farewell to the three propositions of God, free-will, and
immortality, — that triune theistic ideal which may be said
truly to be the other eternal factor in that aim. These
questions are to be solved by thought alone, and the position of nescient scepticism, or even of materialism, is
unquestionably of legitimate place in philosophy; for philosophy proceeds by stages, and materialism and scepticism are unavoidable stadia on the way to conviction of
truth.

Coming to the question of the value of philosophy, Professor Howison said he regarded it of absolute worth,
because he sees in it the conditions without which we cannot fulfil our human vocation, as distinguished from our
avocations. Our avocations are means to an end, —
man; philosophy has the right to stand as an indestructible factor in that end. Human life can be an end only
in virtue of holding in itself the conditions of an eternal
aim, — an aim that, fulfilling the utmost desire of thought,
stands to thought as necessary and immovable. Hence
we see that the possession of a reasoned thought is essential to man's being an end. It is the absolute *worth* of
philosophy, its existence as a *good*, which is to be shown.
Any valid end is one forever in the process of getting
actualized: the real conception of end is dynamic, not
static; not rest, but perpetual movement; not excludent
of means, but containing means within it. The real end,

in which philosophy is a vital part, is a life always actualized, yet being perpetually more and more actualized. The value of philosophy lies in its conditioning the solution of individual human freedom as against the supremacy of God and the nation, or of the realized man in mankind, who is the sole depositary of that end in which philosophy is a conditioning factor. Freedom may be nothing higher than caprice, and thus often antagonizes the complete idea of a spiritual or human being, which finds its realization only in the family, the community, the nation, the church, — institutions of ever-ascending self-sacrifice. In and through these must the self-will or abstract freedom of the individual be transformed into the concrete, realized, or rational freedom of the universal man; or, lacking this transformation, not only does the universal or real humanity fail of existence, but the single man, naked and unsheltered, must perish miserably too. The fulfilment and aim, then, even of the mere freedom of the individual, is that rational freedom which is wrought by the sacrificial discipline of the practical world alone. We see now that of a surety "he alone is the freeman whom the truth makes free."

The question of the scope of philosophy involves the two sub-questions: What is it in the complete process of human life that it has to do? — And in what scale, over how great a field, can it perform its task? What philosophy has to do is simply to realize and bring to completion one of the three primitive factors in human reason, — the factor called intelligence or reason, — and thereby complete and realize that very nature itself. For the being of man is a strict trinity, a mystical union in one's self of three hypostatic powers called impulse, will, and reason, or the intellect, susceptibility, and will of psychology. Each impersonation would be null without the other two. If by "perception" we signify the note we take of an object actually present before the senses, and by "reflection" the mental idea which is present in absence of the real object, then we may say the intellect is summed up in perception and reflection. In the transcendental powers of intellect we have not only that element which we call "reason," — a being with the beyond,— but we have also the key to the reality as well as to the conception of our moral freedom. Man has his beyond with him, and by his own conscious thoughts, imagination, and will participates in generating it from his own being. Nature's beyond is without it, and hence it is ruled forever by a necessity which is fate. If we add the fact of our continually transforming the unreal objects of reflection into the real objects of perception, do we not reach in this power, not merely the fact of will, but the nature and actual existence of its freedom? In the human will, as in dumb nature, there is a phase of necessity; but it is a necessity which annuls fate because it works by motive, not by force. What the reason does in the realization of human freedom is to render it possible by grounding it in God and immortality. But while philosophy in its native order simply *creates* the moral world of freedom, in its ideal order it *recreates* man's moral world, to rear on the ruins of the merely natural caprice of his heart the far more majestic proportions of the temple of revealed religion, — the religion of his intellect, the religion not merely *felt*, but *seen;* a building where the heart glows not in faith only, nor in hope, but in *love*. Such is the function of philosophy as ideally conceived, and as actually realized for many a mind that has adorned our world.

The latter part of the lecture, that relating to the compass within which philosophy can perform its work, dealt with modern philosophy to some extent. The question here is, "What can I know?" Professor Howison maintained that human knowledge is limited in degree only, not in kind, and condemned the doctrine of "thing-in-itself," and upheld the permanence and immanence of the "idea" as a controlling influence in human history.

The discussion which followed was sympathetic with Professor Howison's views.

⁏ LIII.

COLOR–BLINDNESS.

By B. JOY JEFFRIES.

DR. JEFFRIES gave a lecture on the color sense and color-blindness. He illustrated the natural or normal color perception not touched on particularly in his recent work on "Color-blindness: Its Dangers and its Detection." As with the perception of form, the eye has the best power directly at the centre, objects are only distinctly seen when we turn the eye so that the image falls on this portion of the retina, and thus colors fade in intensity from here outwards. A red wafer seen quite eccentrically will appear black, etc. There is a central zone by which we see all of the three colors now regarded as primary, — namely, red, green, and violet. In the zone outside of this we perceive green and violet, and beyond only violet or blue. This is a general expression, and seems related to the three forms of color-blindness, — namely, *red*, *green*, and *violet*, — as also to the Young-Helmholtz theory of color perception, which assumes that one set of retinal fibres receives red, another green, and another blue or violet light.

Complementary after-images were experimentally illustrated. Gazing at the *red* setting sun and turning to the east we see a *green* rising sun. This is an instance of the phenomenon. Its practical application on railroads and the sea was dwelt on. This and other defects of the normal color sense having been explained, the speaker described color-blindness as a condition where the person sees gray or grayish, where we see red or green or violet, according to his special form of trouble. Red and green blindness include each other; violet blindness includes yellow. Red blindness is most common, then green, violet blindness occurring very rarely. The defect is congenital, largely hereditary, but may come from alcohol or tobacco poisoning, or brain disease, etc. When congenital, it is incurable. It may appear in but one eye. It can be produced by hypnotism or the cataleptic condition. A color-blind person when rendered hypnotic may see colors normally. It may be palliated by a colored glass, artificial light, or looking through certain solutions, as fuchsine, but is never altered thereby or the person cured of the defect. From the more than thirty thousand examinations the speaker has made, and the reports from all over the world of similar tests, the proportion is deduced of four per cent of males and perhaps one quarter of one per cent of females being color-blind in greater or less degree.

The speaker especially explained how the color-blind escaped detection heretofore, and were only discovered after we had the recently devised practical and scientific method of testing, since all means calling for the naming of colors were long ago, by Goethe and by Helmholtz, shown to be valueless. As age, education, race, condition of civilization, or special study of color do not affect color-blindness, the value of Professor Holmgren's method of testing — which with the many others both for qualitative and quantitative perception the speaker showed and described — is as readily seen as appreciated. By it we can scientifically test the color-perception of a deaf-mute, an uncivilized man whose language we cannot speak, and a child of three years. Hence its value in quickly detecting color-blindness among railroad employés and sailors, where it is naturally so dangerous, since the very colors red and green are and must be used as signals by night on land and sea.   The necessity for and the difficulty of establishing legal control of this curious defect, the speaker particularly explained and dwelt on.

While color-blindness cannot at present be cured and but little palliated, we can educate and develop the normal sense of color, as the ear, the voice, the touch, the taste, etc.   The necessity for teaching color-names and colors themselves, and the education of the color sense in our schools as a part of school-life, the speaker illustrated from his own and others' experience of the ignorance of color-names on the part of males, referring to his work in the public schools of Boston and his report to the school committee (School Document, No. 13, 1880).   The value of this teaching to the mercantile interest was shown, and as well how it would probably detect and forewarn color-blind school-boys.   Dr. Magnus's color chart, which the speaker will introduce into this country, was exhibited and its use explained.   It obtained a diploma of honor from the International Medical Society at Amsterdam, September, 1879.

The speaker was enabled to illustrate the rarest form of color-blindness, — namely, violet blindness, — by a full-length portrait, hanging on the walls of the parlor, painted by Mr. Henry Sargent.   A long mantle hangs from the shoulders of the sitting lady, now of a dark color, but originally painted *yellow* by Mr. Sargent, under the perfect conviction he was making it a bright blue.   There are numerous instances, on record and otherwise, of red or green blind portrait or landscape painters ; here, however, is positive proof of a violet-blind one.

A curious coincidence is that the speaker, living in the adjacent house, subsequently found in his grandfather's (Dr. John Jeffries) diary, the following : —

"1793, June 15. — Received a billet from Mrs. Powell requesting an introductory letter for Mr. H. Sargent to Mr. Copley, London. Wrote one accordingly and gave to Mrs. Powell."

The original " billet " was also found, and reads thus :

"Mrs. Powell will esteem it a particular favor if Dr. Jeffries will be so obliging as to give a letter of introduction to her cousin Henry Sargent to Mr. Copley in London. Mr. Sargent is thought by Mr. Trumble, under whose patronage he goes home, to possess an uncommon genius for painting, and is in every respect a most amiable young man. He will be in England some time before Mr. Trumble arrives there, and therefore is under a necessity of making this request, as he will sail in the 'Galen' Saturday morning."

Dr. John Jeffries, while residing in England, was a great friend of Mr. Copley, and the two families very intimate. The "Galen" was one of the regular sailing packets of those days.

LIV.

JONATHAN EDWARDS.

By OLIVER WENDELL HOLMES.

IT has always been well understood by the friends of Dr. Holmes that his many and varied duties made most unwelcome to him any invitation to read before literary societies. The Radical Club had therefore refrained from laying claim to time already too fully occupied, and until the spring of 1880 the genial poet had never read before them. His own kindliness prompted him at that time to volunteer an essay in the following pleasant note : —

296 BEACON ST., March 31, 1880.

MY DEAR MRS. SARGENT, — I once spoke to you about the possibility of my reading a paper before your Club. I have been getting ready to write on a somewhat interesting subject, and might tack my thoughts together, — *baste* them is what you ladies would say, — and try them on in the course of a couple of weeks, if I were admissible to the conclave, desirable, and not inopportune.

A word from you would settle all these doubtful points, and set me basting the pieces I have not yet put together for my essay.

Yours very truly,

O. W. HOLMES.

It is needless to say that the proposition was received with delight, to which was added the piquancy of a lively curiosity when the subject of the paper became known. The appointed morning was a beautiful one, and the parlors were early crowded with the members of the Club, whose expectations were amply rewarded by the reading of the following brilliant essay : —

" Of all the scholars and philosophers that America had produced before the beginning of the present century, two only had established a considerable and permanent reputation in the world of European thought, — Benjamin Franklin and Jonathan Edwards. No two individuals could well differ more in temperament, character, beliefs, and mode of life than did these two men, representing respectively intellect, practical and abstract. Edwards would have called Franklin an infidel, and turned him over to the uncovenanted mercies, if, indeed, such were admitted in his programme of the Divine administration. Franklin would have called Edwards a fanatic, and tried the effect of Poor Richard's common-sense on the major premises of his remorseless syllogisms.

" The feeling which naturally arises in contemplating the character of Jonathan Edwards is that of deep reverence for a man who seems to have been anointed from his birth ; who lived a life pure, laborious, self-denying, occupied with the highest themes, and busy in the highest kind of labor, — such a life as in another church might have given him a place in the ' Acta Sanctorum.' We can in part account for what he was when we remember his natural inherited instincts, his training, his faith, and the conditions by which he was surrounded. His ancestors had fed on sermons so long that he must have been born with Scriptural texts lying latent in his embryonic thinking-marrow, like the undeveloped picture in a film of collodion. He was bred in the family of a Connecticut minister in a town where revivals of religion were of remarkable frequency. His mother, it may be suspected, found him in brains, for she was called the brighter of the old couple ; and the fact that she did not join the church until Jonathan was twelve years old implies that she was a woman who was not to be hurried into becoming a professor of religion simply because she was the wife of the Reverend Timothy Edwards. His faith in the literal inspiration of the Old and New Testament was implicit; it was built on texts, as Venice and Amsterdam are built on piles. The 'parable of Eden,' as our noble Boston preacher calls it, was to him a simple narrative of exact occurrences. The fruit, to taste which conferred an education, the talking ophidian, the many-centuried patriarchs, the floating menagerie with the fauna of the drowning earth represented on its decks, the modelling of the first woman about a bone of the first man, — all these things were to him, as to those about him, as real historical facts as the building of the Pyramids. He was surrounded with believers like himself, who held the doctrines of Calvinism in all their rigor. But, on the other hand, he saw the strongholds of his position threatened by the gradual approach or the actual invasion of laxer teachings and practices, so that he found himself, as he thought, forced into active hostilities, and soon learned his strength as a combatant, and felt the stern delight of the warrior as champion of the church militant. This may have given extravagance to some of his expressions, and at times have blinded him to the real meaning as well as to the practical effect of the doctrines he taught to the good people of Northampton, and gave to the world in pages over which many a reader has turned pale and trembled.

" The more we study the will in the way of analysis, the more strictly does it appear to be determined by the infinitely varied conditions of the individual. At the bottom of all these lies the moral 'personal equation' of each human being. Suppose sin were always literally red, — as it is in the figurative expressions, 'though your sins be as scarlet,' 'though they be red like crimson,' — in that case, it is very certain that many persons would be unable to distinguish sin from virtue, if we suppose virtue to have a color also, and that color to be green. There is good reason to believe that certain persons are born more or less completely blind to moral distinctions, as others are born color-blind. Many examples of this kind may be found in the 'Psychologic Naturelle' of M. Prosper Despine, and our own criminal records would furnish notable instances of such imperfect natures. We are getting to be predestinarians as much as Edwards or Calvin was, only instead of universal corruption of nature derived from Adam, we recognize inherited congenital tendencies, — some good, some bad, — for which the subject of them is in no sense responsible. Edwards maintains that, in spite of his doctrine, 'man is entirely, perfectly, and unspeakably different from a machine, in that he has reason and understanding, with a faculty of will, and so is capable of volition and choice; in that his will is guided by the dictates or views of his understanding; and in that his external actions and behavior, and in many respects also his thoughts and the exercises of his mind, are subject to his will.' But all this only mystified his people, and the practical rural comment was in the well-known satirical saying, ' You can and you can't, you shall and you sha'n't,' and so forth, — the epigram that stung to death a hundred sermons based on the attempt to reconcile slavery to a depraved nature, on the one hand, with freedom to sin and responsibility for what could not be helped, on the other.

" It is as hard to leave this subject without attempting to help in clearing it up as it is to pass a cairn without the desire of throwing a stone upon it. This impulse must excuse the following brief excursion.

" In spite of the strongest-motive necessitarian doctrine, we do certainly have a feeling, amounting to a working belief, that we are free to choose before we have made our choice.

"We have a sense of difficulty overcome by effort in many acts of choice.

"We have a feeling in retrospect, amounting to a practical belief, that we could have left undone the things that we have done, and that we could have done the things we ought to have done and did not do, and we accuse or else excuse ourselves accordingly.

"Suppose this belief to be a self-deception, as we have seen that Hobbes and Leibnitz suggest it may be, 'a deceiving of mankind by God himself,' as Edwards accuses Lord Kaimes of maintaining, still this instinctive *belief* in the power of moral choice in itself constitutes a powerful motive.   Our thinking ourselves free is the key to our whole moral nature.   'Possumus quia posse videmur.' We can make a different choice because we think we can. Happily, no reasoning can persuade us out of this belief; happily, indeed, for virtue rests upon it, education assumes and develops it, law pronounces its verdict, and the ministers of the law execute its mandates on the strength of it. Make us out automata if you will, but we are automata which cannot help believing that they do their work well or ill as they choose, that they wind themselves up or let themselves run down by a power not in the weights or springs.

"On the whole, we can afford to leave the question of liberty and necessity where Edwards leaves that of our belief in the existence of the material universe : —

"'Though we suppose that the Material Universe is absolutely dependent on Idea, yet we may speak in the old way and as properly and truly as ever.

"'It is just all one as to any benefit or advantage, any end that we can suppose was proposed by the Creator, as if the Material Universe were existent in the same manner as is vulgarly thought.'

" And so we can say that, after all the arguments of the metaphysicians, all the experiments of the physiologists, all the uniform averages of statisticians, it is just all one as to any benefit or advantage as if a real self-determining power, and real responsibility for our acts of moral choice, were existent in the same manner as is vulgarly thought.

"The true source of Edwards's Dante-like descriptions of his Inferno is but too obvious. Whatever claim to the character of a poet is founded on the lurid brilliancy of these passages may as well be reconsidered in the red light of Thomas Boston's rhetorical *autos-da-fé*. But wherever such pictures are found, at first or second hand, they are sure causes of unbelief, and liable to produce hatred not only of those who teach them, but of their whole system of doctrines. ' Who are these cruel old clerical Torquemadas,' ask the ungodly, ' who are rolling the tortures of ourselves, our wives and children, under their tongues like a sweet morsel?' The denunciations of the pulpit came so near the execrations of the street in their language, and sometimes, it almost seemed, in their spirit, that many a ' natural man' must have left his pew with the feeling in his heart embodied in a verse which the writer of this article found many years ago in a psalm-book in a Glasgow meeting-house where he was attending service, and has remembered ever since : —

> " 'As cursing he like clothes put on,
>   Into his bowels so
>   Like water, and into his bones
>   Like oil down let it go.'

" God forgive them ! Doubtless many of them were as sincere and conscientious as the most zealous officers of the Holy Inquisition.

" It is impossible that people of ordinary sensibilities should have listened to his torturing discourses without becoming at last sick of hearing of infinite horrors and endless agonies. It came very hard to kind-hearted persons to believe that the least sin exposed a creature God had made to such exorbitant penalties. Edwards's whole system had too much of the character of the savage people by whom the wilderness had so recently been tenanted. There was revenge — 'revenging *justice*' was what he called it — insatiable, exhausting its ingenuity in contriving the most exquisite torments ; there was the hereditary hatred glaring on the babe in its cradle ; there were the suffering wretch and the pleased and shouting lookers-on. Every natural grace of disposition ; all that had once charmed in the sweet ingenuousness of youth, in the laughing gayety of childhood, in the winning helplessness of infancy ; every virtue that Plato had dreamed of, every character that Plutarch had drawn, — all were branded with the hot iron which left the blackened inscription upon them, signifying that they were accursed of God, — the damning word *nature*.

" With all his powers, his virtues, his eloquence, it must have been more than people could do to stand being called ' vile insects,' ' filthy worms,' ' firebrands of hell,' and other such hard names. But what must have been the feeling of Northampton mothers when they read what Edwards said about their darlings ! It seems that there had been complaints against some preachers for frightening poor innocent children, as he says, with talk of hell-fire and eternal damnation. But if those who complain really believe what they profess to, they show, he thinks, a great deal of weakness and inconsideration. Then follow the words which the writer once quoted on a public occasion, which use of them brought him a letter from a much respected orthodox clergyman, asking where they could be found. It is not strange that he asked, for he might have looked in vain for them in the the ten-volume edition of Edwards's works, published under the editorship of his

own predecessor, grandson of Edwards, the Rev. Sereno
E. Dwight, or the English reprint of that edition. But
the editor of the edition of the work on Revivals, published
in New York in 1832, did not think it necessary, perhaps
honest, to omit the passage, and this is the way it reads :

" ' As innocent as children seem to be to us, yet, if they are out
of Christ, they are not so in God's sight, but are young vipers, and
are infinitely more hateful than vipers, and are in a most miserable
condition, as well as grown persons ; and they are naturally very
senseless and stupid, being *born as the wild ass's colt*, and need much
to awaken them.'

" Is it possible that Edwards read the text mothers love
so well, ' Suffer little *vipers* to come unto me, and forbid
them not, for of such is the Kingdom of God ' ?

" There is reason to fear that Edwards has not been fairly
dealt with in all respects. We have seen that in one instance expressions, which it was probably thought would
give offence, were omitted by his editor. A far more important matter remains to be cleared up. The writer is
informed on unquestionable authority that there is or was
in existence a manuscript of Edwards in which his views
appear to have undergone a great change in the direction
of Arianism, or of Sabellianism, which is an old-fashioned
Unitarianism, or at any rate show a defection from his
former standard of Orthodoxy, and which its custodians,
thinking it best to be wise as serpents in order that they
might continue harmless as doves, have considered it their
duty to withhold from the public. If any of our friends
at Andover can inform us what are the facts about this
manuscript, such information would be gratefully received
by many inquirers, who would be rejoiced to know that so
able and so good a man lived to be emancipated from the
worse than heathen conceptions which had so long en-
chained his powerful but crippled understanding."

Dr. BARTOL began the discussion, and declared his sympathy with the views expressed by Dr. Holmes. In allusion to Edwards's argument upon the will, he said: "We are told that free-will is impossible, or unprovable. So it is, — like God, heaven, virtue, beauty, life, and the other great things which prove all the rest and give them their worth!"

Professor BENJAMIN PEIRCE said it was surprising that from a gospel whose corner-stone is love there has grown a belief in such a horrible doctrine as this of infant damnation and eternal punishment. It seems as if the Devil must have been at Edwards's ear.

Dr. BOWDITCH affirmed that clergymen must take a different position from that they now hold if they want to preserve anything of the present beliefs in Christianity. Christ was one of the most holy men who ever lived. He propounded noble principles, and died a horrible death because he was true to those principles. Christ is not divine, and in that sense could not have died to save men. Of Jonathan Edwards's doctrine of punishment, Dr. Bowditch said it was a damnable thing, and he wondered that men ever lived under such teachings.

Next came Mr. D. A. WASSON, who was the most emphatic of all the opponents of the Edwards theology. At the very outset he asserted that he did not believe any good ever came out of Edwards's philosophy. The idea of making a church of the community in all its civil and economic order was being abandoned, and religion became the concern of each individual. In his diary Edwards said that he desired so to live as to secure for himself the greatest amount of future happiness. "I don't believe he was a good man," asserted Mr. Wasson. "In that is the key to his character. Edwards, as some one said of Luther, had a realizing mind, which understood fully the terrible import of eternal punishment and total depravity. Now the man who realizes those things and rolls them as a sweet morsel under his tongue and then becomes a father — that man is a scoundrel." Mr. Wasson thought most men did not thoroughly realize the full terrible truth of these doctrines, but Edwards did. He was a cold-hearted, hard man.

Dr. Bartol called on WENDELL PHILLIPS, who said: " The picture drawn by Dr. Holmes, though truthful and accurate so far as it goes, cannot be full or complete. As a whole, it cannot be just to Edwards ; there must be other sides which would soften and redeem it; other doctrines that explain and fill out the full religious life and charac-ter, and justify the profound and loving respect our fathers had for him. Else how can we account for the great fact of New England, which is the outcome of his and similar pulpits?

" No one doubts that a large majority of the New Eng-land pulpits, one hundred years ago, sympathized with and sustained Edwards. These horrible doctrines, which Dr. Holmes shocked us with, were not Edwards's individual and singular views, but the common faith of New England. Now, religion and theological doctrines are great factors in forming character. If the pulpit of New England taught only, or mainly, these hateful, narrow, inhuman, and de-grading doctrines, — if such was the *character* of its teach-ing, whence came this generous, public-spirited, energetic, hopeful, broad, humane, self-respectful, independent, and free-thoughted New England, ready for every good work and willing for every necessary sacrifice?

" We must have a theory broad enough to cover all the facts. It used to be said that ' he who makes religion *twelve* and the world *thirteen*, is no true New Englander.' His religion was three quarters of a Yankee. What you gentlemen here call ' free religion ' and ' liberal Christian-ity ' is of very recent growth, and of still very narrow in-

fluence. But character is of slow growth. Any theory
which narrows and degrades the New England pulpit of
the eighteenth century fails to account for the community
which grew up under it."

To one who suggested as an explanation that our fathers
never really believed such doctrines Mr. PHILLIPS replied:
" It will hardly do to maintain that the hard-headed and
practical Yankee, so keen and ready-witted in affairs, so
free and bold in civil life, the world's intellectual pioneer,
did not know or understand what he believed, in — to him
— the most important matter of all, his religion. Four
generations passed over the stage, and left us this commonwealth, their creation, — sober, painstaking, serious,
earnest men. We cannot accept the theory which represents their religion as carelessly taken up, loosely held, and
only half understood. Great jurists, practical statesmen,
profound scholars, liberal founders of academy, college,
and hospital, boldly searching the world over for means to
perfect institutions on which the world now models itself, —
were these minds crippled by absurd dogmas, worldlings
without faith, or hypocrites afraid to avow their real belief?
True philosophy never accepts such theories to explain history. It is more natural and philosophical to suppose that
the sketch we have listened to, admirable as it is, has not
given all the sides of the picture."

Dr. BARTOL suggested that Edwards's parish repudiated
him : after twenty years listening to him they voted against
him ten to one.

Mr. PHILLIPS replied : " That argument proves too much.
We have just exhausted language in praising the eminent
Christian spirit and untold influence of Dr. W. E. Channing. But we all know that after Channing had preached
twenty years to men who idolized him, they mobbed him
for his Antislavery ideas, and refused him the use of his
own church for the funeral services of the Abolitionist

Follen, — Channing's most intimate and valued friend.
Channing failed as thoroughly, forty years ago, in teaching his church justice and humanity as Edwards did, a
hundred years ago, in bringing his hearers to relish the
idea of infant damnation. It will not do for Unitarians in
Boston to throw that Northampton vote in Edwards's face.
Northampton never mobbed Edwards for his infant damnation as Boston did Channing for his Antislavery in Faneuil Hall."

JAMES FREEMAN CLARKE, after expressing his satisfaction with the acute and clear treatment of the subject by
the essayist, said that "Jonathan Edwards has achieved
celebrity in three directions, — first, as a logician and
metaphysician; secondly, as a theologian; and, thirdly,
as a Protestant saint or religious mystic."

Remarking on each of these characteristics, he said:
"As a logician Edwards is unsurpassed in keenness and
subtlety of argument. No stronger argument against the
self-determining power in man was ever constructed. But
all such arguments beat themselves to pieces against the
rock of consciousness. In fact logic, like mathematics,
is only an instrument. The greatest logicians and the
greatest mathematicians are only remembered when they
have discovered and proved some important truth or fact.
Sir Isaac Newton, Pascal, Leibnitz, and Leverrier are remembered, not for their mathematics, but for what they
discovered by mathematics. Locke, Kant, and Anselm are
remembered, not for their logic, but for the systems which
their logic built. Edwards was a logician of unsurpassed
subtlety; but his logic was for the sake of his metaphysics,
and his metaphysics was for the sake of his theology. He
wished to prove the will bound, in order to show that natural
depravity did not consist in a corruption of the natural instincts, but in a wrong direction of the will, — a confirmed
and habitually selfish choice. This was the root of his

theology, — belief in a will habitually directed the wrong way.

"As a theologian, Edwards has been more influential than as a metaphysician, though not so famous. Edwards was the founder and father of New England Calvinism, which has greatly influenced all theology. What is called 'The New-School Theology' derives from him.

"The essential feature and tap-root of this New England Calvinism consists in making original sin consist in a wrong choice, and not in a corrupt nature. The supposed advantages of this view are twofold, — first, as a theodicy, in vindicating God from the charge of being the author of sin, in which, however, it signally fails, as Dr. Holmes has shown. But there is also a supposed practical advantage in showing men that no radical change of nature is needed for conversion, but only a change of purpose. To be sure, this change cannot be effected without God's influence, but then that influence comes as soon as one really exerts himself. Thus we reach this paradoxical result, — that a theology which declares that man has the power to change the whole purpose and direction of his will is founded on a metaphysic which declares the will fatally bound, and having no freedom at all.

"This theology, however, is not only inconsequential but also superficial. It is not true that a man can change his character by an act of the will. Character consists of habits of thought, of feeling, and action, which no single determination can alter. Therefore, the revival system which has followed the New England theology has always produced hosts of backsliders. The one important truth in the system is this, — that the most important step in our moral career is when we have decided to go in the right direction. The one essential error in the system is to suppose that when we have begun the journey we have reached its end.

" Edwards was not only metaphysician and theologian, but also a Calvinistic saint. He was a man much absorbed in mystic contemplation and communion with God. But this type of piety has not been continued among the Orthodox of New England. It would, perhaps, be well if it were. New Orthodoxy has been too coldly intellectual a system ; and even New England Radicalism, which has so bitterly opposed it, suffers from the same defect. Both are too severely logical to be deeply religious. The defining power of this New England telescope is greater than its space-penetrating power. A little healthy Concord mysticism is not a bad ingredient in this New England banquet.

" I cannot see that Jonathan Edwards is likely to exercise a permanent influence, either as a metaphysician, theologian, or mystic. His metaphysics have long since been outgrown ; his theology is too superficial to endure ; and his mysticism is not in accordance with the atmosphere of New England thought. He will be chiefly remembered as a powerful thinker, whose thoughts produced no lasting results."

Whether it was because of the popularity and brilliancy of the essay, or of the nearness with which the doctrines cited came home to every listener, or of the moulding influence of the old theology upon New England life, or of the keenness of the discussion, that the meeting was one of unusual note, it may not be possible to decide, for all of these elements entered into the success of the day.

·LV.

THE IMPOSSIBLE IN MATHEMATICS.

By PROFESSOR PEIRCE.

PROFESSOR PEIRCE spoke almost entirely without notes, taking as his general subject the advance beyond the limitations of number into a new sphere of mathematical knowledge which seems to be at hand from the development of the science of quaternions. The mathematical student, he said, meets problems which cannot at the time be solved, but which afterward are found to have in them more ideality than was suspected; they have their place in science, which is often important, though not known at the time they were discovered. Two classes of mathematical operations may be noted, — the direct and the indirect. Addition and multiplication were given as instances of the former, and subtraction and division of the latter. Professor Peirce mentioned the advance which has been made in the conception of negative quantities from the time when each case of a subtrahend larger than a minuend was made a distinct statement by itself, to the time when they were all covered by the statement of a general principle. Incidentally, to show how quickly the human mind reaches its limit in conception of number, Professor Peirce mentioned the African tribe to whom everything above five is infinity; and remarked upon the characteristic lack of superlatives in the language of great thinkers, and the frequent use of extravagant expressions by those who have no standard of thought. In one part of his lecture the professor said that he did not regard the introduction of the decimal system of so much moment as is commonly thought. No scientific instrument has been constructed based on that system; the natural way of thinking in fractions is by halves, quarters, and so on. It is doubtful whether the American system of reckoning money is any more convenient than the English.

The latter part of the lecture was upon the advance in mathematical knowledge made possible by the discovery of the science of quaternions. The algebra of quaternions is only an algebra which meets all the phenomena of space and solves them all. Most of the older definitions of mathematics are too narrow to include quality, which is covered by quaternions as well as quantity. A new definition of mathematics was given by Professor Peirce as follows : " Mathematics is the science which draws necessary conclusions," — a definition, he said, wider than the ordinary definitions. It is subjective ; they are objective. This will include knowledge in all lines of research. Under this definition mathematics applies to every mode of inquiry.

————

Dr. HOLMES said that he had once tried to compute the relative advantages on either side of the old problem of destiny. Suppose a period of time so long that it would be measured by the time it would take for the whole earth, if it was made up of grains of sand, to be wholly removed by carrying off one grain in a thousand years, to be compared with the time which comes after it without limit, would a man gain most happiness by choosing to enjoy himself in the first period and be miserable in the second, or by selecting to be miserable in the first and happy in the second? The doctor found by count under a microscope that about a hundred sands made a linear inch, or that there were a million in a cubic inch, but he did not remember the exact number of years in the first period.

Professor HOWISON found a parallel between the ideality in mathematical truths and the deeper meaning in religious truths. Professor Howison asked Professor Peirce whether his linear associative algebra afforded a means for deducing qualitative as well as quantitative results by means of formulæ.

Professor PEIRCE replied that it formed only a very small step in that direction.

Dr. BARTOL suggested that it could not be possible to invent a symbolism which should represent a thing in all its properties, as there are doubtless properties which we are unable to conceive; hence, that no symbolism can take the place of the thing itself.

In this connection a long metaphysical discussion ensued, in which Dr. Holmes and Professor Howison were the principal participants, Professor Peirce and Dr. Bartol also taking part. The conversation eventually drifted on to the questions whether there might be a class of beings for whom two and two would be five, and whether we should sometime live in space of four dimensions. Professor Peirce took the ground that he did not believe the first to be possible, but he did believe that the second would be realized.

In this connection Professor LANZA said that what is conveniently called space of n dimensions where n is different from three, has received this name on account of the analogies of its mathematics to that of ordinary space, or space of three dimensions. That we shall sometime find an interpretation consistent with the mathematics of this subject which will enable us by its means to compute something real and practical is scarcely to be doubted, as we have already found in so many cases of what Professor Peirce has well called the Impossible in Mathematics, — a hidden but an eminently practical ideality. Nevertheless, since this ideality must be different from our present conception of space, we can for the present, it seems to me, only regard the term " space of n dimensions," where n is different from three, as a convenient name, which does not necessarily imply that it is space under our present meaning of the word. We have an analogy to this in the imaginary in algebra, for which a practical use has been found in denoting by it perpendicularity; and yet we cannot say that when this interpretation was discovered we had found a number which, multiplied by itself, would produce minus one, as the interpretation is not number in the ordinary meaning of that word. Moreover, Professor Peirce had well said that " art precedes science ; " and although this fact is well known to mathematicians, a great many others are often seriously misled, because they fail to realize that pure mathematics is, after all, only a means of drawing " necessary conclusions " from the assumptions made at the beginning or in the course of the computations, and that it is only by an appeal to Nature herself that we can assure ourselves of the correctness of these assumptions.

Rev. Mr. SAVAGE asked Professor Peirce if he could tell him in a word what was space of four dimensions ; to which Professor Peirce replied that he could not.

At the conclusion of the discussion, Professor PEIRCE, in reference to his mathematical pursuits, observed that his son Charles was now engaged in carrying on his investigations in the same line to which he had specially applied himself; and it was a great gratification to him to know that his son would prosecute the work to which he had devoted the latter part of his own life. As this was the last occasion on which Professor Peirce appeared in

Boston, in view of his subsequent illness which soon followed, this statement is remembered by his friends as a sad premonition of what was so soon to happen to him, — an event which at any time would have been untimely.

REMINISCENCES.

REMINISCENCES.

I.

IT may not be out of place to give some idea of the way in which the newspapers have commented upon the Chestnut Street Club; and from a large number of clippings are culled the following extracts: —

"THE Boston Radical Club is an unique. Its organism is original, and has not been successfully counterfeited. It has survived three years without a kitchen. Its members attend the meetings with remarkable regularity, albeit they expect neither cakes nor ale. Thoughtful men meet to consider grave themes, but women are not excluded. It has neither constitution nor by-laws, yet it is one of the recognized institutions of Boston, and the fame of it has gone into other lands. It has never had a meeting outside the house of a private citizen, yet the conversations there have been reported to the country by the metropolitan press, and men of culture, in Germany and France, have thought them worthy of translation for the instruction and delight of the wise in their own lands.

"It was in the autumn, I believe, of the year 1867, when the Club was founded. The purpose in view was to bring together at intervals a few men and women of culture, most of whom were known to be daring thinkers on subjects of the highest import, and furnish them an opportunity for uttering their thought to an audience capable of appreciating its scope, of criticising its worth, and of developing its relations."

"THIS Club has defied all criticism, and swept into its train almost every bright name in the liberal ranks. How is it, why is it, that years cannot kill this Club? What is the secret? The same men who failed elsewhere make up this Club; the same public that sneered other clubs out of existence watched for this to fail; the same age and ideas which keep the interest in it at white-heat failed to supply oxygen enough to keep the others alive. Where is the magic, the charm? We have heard it urged that this gathering lives because its salt is always some new, start-ling idea, — what the public waits for, as wide eyes open for an eclipse, an earthquake, or conflagration. It does not seem to us that the times, or the men, or the ideas, or the place of meeting, quite explain this singular success. There is a great deal in the gracious welcome of the host, his ready repartee, his democratic recognition of all classes, races, and minds."

————————

"BUT what has contributed more than anything, I think, to the popularity of the Radical Club has been the real zest given to the conversation by the presence of both sexes. I remember that on one occasion after the meeting of the Club I went to a gathering of very similar nature, composed of men only. These men were to a considerable extent the same, and, as it chanced, the essayist was the same as in the morning; but it seemed to me that the conversation, good as it was, was lacking in a certain piquant and varied flavor, such as the presence of clever women gives to the Radical Club. I am sure that men themselves talk better, on the whole, where women take part in the conversation; and when it comes to arranging the plan and machinery of such gatherings, the tact and energy of women afford an immense lever; and the Rad-ical Club has always had in this respect some of the characteristics of a French *salon*.

"The Club has often done real good by eliciting those flashes of thought that come from the contact of mind with mind. The most meditative flintstone cannot develop out of its own con-sciousness in a hundred years as many sparks as another flintstone can extract from it in five seconds. Then the criticism, always frankly given by the members on any paper read before them, is a great blessing to the writer, albeit sometimes mingled with shame and humiliation. So complimentary is always the opening of these comments, and so keen the subsequent criticism, that Mrs. Howe once compared it to the ancient punishment whereby an offender was first smeared with honey and then hung up to be stung to death by wasps. Yet the wasps, at any rate, take an innocent pleasure in it, and I can answer for one case, at least, where the victim has found it a very useful form of martyrdom."

"WHAT a group the great parlors showed! Henry W. Longfellow, with his white head and patriarchal beard ; Oliver Wendell Holmes, looking as he always does, and as, I fancy, he will to the last of his days, — a boy in the midst of his white-headed contemporaries ; George William Curtis, with his refined face, whereon the work and wear of his faithful, busy life are beginning to tell visibly in the lines here and there; Frothingham, of New York, with his tranquil equipoise of manner, his cultivated face, and quiet humor ; and Lydia Maria Child, with scores of others, — clergymen, literary men, and journalists."

"ON one occasion some reference was accidentally made to the subject with which the name of Mr. Darwin is so intimately associated. . . . There followed a period of unusual restraint. The reputation of the Club for rapid and brilliant conversation was certainly in danger, when one of the members asked why it is that Mr. Darwin says nothing at all about a personal God, and what are his probable conceptions of the Deity. Restraint was gone in a moment. Here was a subject about which no one present knew anything whatever. There was not a single embarrassing fact on record. The talkers plumed their pinions and soared serenely aloft at once. The reputation of the Club was saved.

"It was extremely enjoyable to sit for an hour or two and watch these literary champions. When Higginson, Weiss, and Wasson were at their best, the frosting, as at the confectioner's, was apt to be much better than the cake. Much of the talk was excellent. It was bright, inspiring, hopeful. There was never a mean sentiment or offensive word."

THERE has been from time to time some impatience manifested to have the Club dead and buried. Several times elaborate obituary notices have appeared, declaring that the Radical Club had at last and forever departed this life, and betraying that the conviction had been born of the wish; but the rejoicing has in the event proved somewhat premature. In regard to such notices, the correspondent of a Chicago paper remarked : —

" A sensitive person might, after reading his own obituary, consider it a duty he owed the fitness of things to die forthwith. Not so the Boston Radical Club. Over this body the last sad rites have been performed, and the public has been informed that ' The harp that once through Sargent's halls the soul of Hegel shed,' to quote an enterprising weekly journal, had sounded its last note. But it was only a case of suspended animation (why should n't the Radical Club take a summer vacation, with the rest of the world ?), and the first meeting of the season, yesterday morning, showed no loss of vitality in point of numbers or interest."

II.

ROOM is made here for a few of the many letters which have been received from members of the Club; and to them are added extracts from the correspondence of Charlotte Cushman, which, although not directly connected with the meetings, related often to members, and share the interest which attaches to any memento of this noble woman.

From John Weiss.

DEAR MRS. SARGENT, — I feel like Audrey when Touchstone said to her, "I would the gods had made thee poetical." I am rather better off than Audrey in respect to knowing whether poetry be honest or not. But I should be dishonest in trying to participate in your poetical picnic, unless the verb "to participate" means to have nothing to do with anything. In that case I can attend. Otherwise, as verse must be the contribution to your picnic, Nature has debarred me, — for my versifying cannot train in Whittier's numbers.

I might come prepared with something choice out of Whittier himself, if I did not fear the possibility that he might recognize it. Once or twice Goethe, hearing some verses of his own, thought them very nice, but had forgotten their paternity. Old Gobbo was "high gravel-blind," and did not know his son; but Whittier has grit, and that's a different article to have in the eyes. . . .

Hardly room to say,

Ever yours,

J. WEISS.

From Mrs. Lydia Maria Child.

WAYLAND, April 30, 1871.

DEAR MRS. SARGENT, — I am extremely obliged to Mr. Sargent for the card he sent me, and to you for the kind invitation sent in a letter by Miss F. I should like much to attend the meetings of the Radical Club occasionally ; but circumstances . . . chain me very closely at home.

I am glad you are so situated as to be able to do larger work than I can do, and that you have souls large enough to make diligent use of your opportunities.

Blessings on those who strive in any way to strike off the shackles from human thought!

Yours cordially,

L. MARIA CHILD.

From Rev. O. B. Frothingham.

DEAR SARGENT, — It appears from your kind note of invitation that the New York "Tribune" of last week was in error, — that the Radical Club is not dead. I am glad of it ; for, though I am never present now at its meetings, I like to know that the meetings grow, and to believe that they are as interesting and profitable as ever. Even if the rooms of 13 Chestnut Street should resound with the voices of strangers, the Club, spiritualized and translated, would, like Kaulbach's Huns, fight the eternal battle with the Romans in the air. . . .

With kindest regards, I am

Faithfully yours,

O. B. FROTHINGHAM.

NEW YORK, Oct. 14, 1874.

From John G. Whittier.

AMESBURY, Wednesday Eve.

MY DEAR MRS. SARGENT, — Few stronger inducements could be held out to me than that in thy invitation to meet Lucretia

Mott and Mary Carpenter. But I do not see that I can possibly go to Boston this week. None the less do I thank thee, my dear friend, for thinking of me in connection with their visit.

My love to Lucretia Mott, and tell her I have never forgotten the kind welcome and generous sympathy she gave the young abolitionist at a time when he found small favor with his "orthodox" brethren. What a change she and I have lived to see! I hope to meet Miss Carpenter before she leaves us. For this and for all thy kindness in times past, believe me gratefully

Thy friend,

JOHN G. WHITTIER.

<hr>

From the same.

BOSTON, 27th Mo., 1875.

MY DEAR FRIEND,—I have been reading over the revised copy, which our friend Phillips was so kind as to send me through thee, of his well-timed speech at the Faneuil Hall meeting. It forcibly reminded me of his reply to James T. Austin,—the splendid prelude to his thirty years of oratorical triumphs. It was well he was there to speak once more in his best manner.

While I am sorry General Sheridan did not wait for some more direct act of violence and lawlessness, where his interference could not have been questioned, I am glad to see him vindicated so well, and the cause of the oppressed colored men so forcibly presented. May God give him and all the old advocates of freedom strength to do what none others can so well do in the struggle which is before us for the civil rights of the freedmen!

I am writing on the desk of our beloved Sumner. Let us hope and believe that, like John Brown's, his soul is "marching on" in forefront of the battle for the perfect freedom of the class for whom he labored and suffered. In a late letter from the Duchess of Argyle, his old and true friend says, "Dear Sumner! One does not get accustomed to his absence."

Always and truly thy friend,

JOHN G. WHITTIER.

From Edmund C. Stedman.

NEW YORK, May 26, 1876.

MY DEAR MRS. SARGENT,— How much I regret that your kind
and tempting invitation reaches me so late that I shall be unable
to provide for an absence from New York at the appointed time.
Still, your proviso— that I should contribute my proper entrance
dues (in the form of a poem) to your festival of Parnassus—
might of itself keep me back. For this year, so far as poetry is
concerned, I am paving Hades only, being merely able to go
through with the grosser duties of each day; and I would not
enter quite empty-handed, where our kings of song come with
their plenteous wealth.

You know that things always come too late, and 't is the unexpected only that happens. For years I have been meditating a
pilgrimage to Amesbury and Concord, that I might press the hand
of our saintly, beloved Whittier, and that I might listen with
mine own ears to the words of Emerson, — some knowledge of
whose empyreal song and thought has been my "liberal education." You now proffer me a chance to meet them both, but I
cannot accept it. On recovery from my two years' prodigalities
of sickness, I've been compelled to plunge into bread-winning;
am without an associate, and really can't leave my post for a
single day: but don't forget me another year, and let me know in
time. I shall have all these pleasures soon or late. *Ça ira!* . . .

Begging leave to proffer my respects to Mr. Sargent,

I am very faithfully yours,

EDMUND C. STEDMAN.

Extract from a letter.

WE had in Boston a small yacht which could be used for Antislavery purposes. On one occasion word was brought to us that
a brig was at anchor in the harbor, just arrived from New Orleans,
consigned to the late John K. Pearson, and on board of her a slave
was imprisoned, in order to be returned. The poor fellow had
secreted himself on board at New Orleans with the hope of escap-
ing when he got to Boston. After the brig got to sea he was dis-

covered. But being too far out to return to New Orleans, the captain was obliged to bring him to Boston, and was now watching for opportunity to place him on board some vessel that would return him to slavery.

Captain Bearse started on board our yacht with a few persons to rescue this slave. He knew the name of the brig, and also that the captain was said to be up in the city at the U. S. Marshal's office. As we sailed down the harbor I asked Bearse what plan he had. He replied that he had none, but should trust to the inspiration of the moment. This seemed to me rather a poor reliance; but as none of us had any plan or suggestion to offer, we left the management of the matter entirely to him. Before we got near the brig our colored men went below out of sight, and there were only a few white men visible on our deck when Bearse laid us alongside the brig, and shouted to the man on deck, "Is the captain aboard ?" "No, sir," was the reply. Bearse then said, "I want to see the first mate." "I am the mate," was the reply. Whereupon, instantly (he thinks by inspiration) and without a moment's hesitation, Bearse jumped on board the brig and said, "I want that nigger quicker than lightning!" whereupon the mate rushed below and Bearse after him. Directly above the keel the black man was found confined. He was set free and was on the deck of our yacht in less than a minute, and we immediately set sail for South Boston Point. The whole thing was done so neatly and expeditiously that we could hardly refrain from laughing out aloud ; and long before we got under full headway we could not restrain ourselves, and the mate saw that he had been mistaken and was entrapped. Apparently, he imagined we had been sent by his captain to take the black man down into the lower bay, where he could be kept in safety, cruising back and forth, until he could be placed on board a vessel to be returned to New Orleans. We also understood that John K. Pearson had seen us start, and watched our whole operation through his glass, but was wholly unable to prevent us, though he afterwards threatened dire vengeance.

We threw overboard the rags with which the man was covered, and when he appeared on our deck he was, in clothes at least, a staid, venerable Quaker named Joseph Southwick. We landed at the Point, and drove in a carriage to my house in Linden Place, Brookline, and after dinner I took him to William Jackson's house at Newton. The slave had been a field-hand, with no special points of interest about his history except his desire for freedom.

There was another case which had a very comical side. A slave in Boston said his master was after him (I think he had actually come upon him in the street), and was afraid to stay or even appear on the streets. He was dressed up as a woman, and one afternoon we drove down Cambridge Street in a covered wagon, and at a corner of one of the side streets we took up this woman and started over Cambridge Bridge and through West Cambridge, etc., to Concord. Arrived there, the man took off his bonnet, gown, etc., in the wagon, leaving them there ; after which we gave him in charge of one of the Concord friends. I have frequently laughed to think what an excitement might have been caused if any one had accidentally discovered this womanly gear in our carriage. We might all have been arrested for abducting a woman, as it was certainly true that we came into town apparently with one, and as certainly returned to Boston without one, but with the clothing of one.

I told also Richard H. Dana's story of his defence before the U. S. Court of a man who had run off a fugitive slave. The man was known to be guilty, but Mr. Dana made as strong a defence as possible. The jury retired ; and, instead of bringing his client in guilty as Mr. Dana expected, they remained out a long time, and finally came in and told the Court that they could not possibly agree, and were accordingly discharged. The prisoner was released on bail and molested no further. Some years afterward a man approached Mr. Dana, and said, " Good morning, Squire ! " Mr. Dana replied that he remembered his face, but could not recall the circumstances under which they had previously met. " Why, Squire," said the man, " don't you remember the trial of " so and so, mentioning the name of this particular client. Dana remembered the circumstance, and asked him to explain what had always been a great puzzle to him, why the jury did not convict his client. " Well, Squire," said the man, " all the rest of the jury were ready to convict, but I could not bring my mind to that conclusion, because I had myself driven that very slave across the State line from Worcester County."

How far away seems the time when these things happened ! And yet the same U. S. judge is still living who, in his charge to the Grand Jury, expressed the opinion that not even our con-

sciences should be enlightened beyond the law, and if we diso-
beyed the fugitive slave-law, even on conscientious grounds, we
were simply fanatics.

Respectfully yours,

WILLIAM I. BOWDITCH.

Mrs. JOHN T. SARGENT.

From Charlotte Cushman.

SWAMPSCOTT, Sept. 18, 1868.

DEAR FRIEND, — Do you hope to catch any poetry from me in
reply to your "jingling bidding"? (No offence *intended* by "jingling," only the word sounded fitting to anything so cheerful as
your dinner on Tuesday 23, at four P.M.) I can't write poetry,
or even doggerel. The circumstances of my position relative to
that same person, who shall be nameless, — but his individual initials are as like W. I. B. as it would be possible to find initials to
be, — are too sad to allow any rhyme or even reason to hold possession of this "distracted globe." But one must eat. I know it
is the way I get my living; and small as my appetite may be in
his presence, still, about the hour you mention, I am generally
materially minded, and therefore — in plain prose — I accept with
pleasure, and will try to be punctual. Only the Lord does n't
make the days half long enough for me, while I am in this beloved
land, and I am obliged to squeeze a quart into a gill; and even
then the measure is too full. Joking apart, I shall come. It
would have been wiser just to have said that and no more, but, as
I said before, "the circumstances of my position," etc. . . .

With kindest regards, ever, dear friend,

Yours truly,

CHARLOTTE CUSHMAN.

From the same.

LENOX, MASS., Oct. 1, 1868.

DEAR FRIEND, — Arrived here quite safely yesterday afternoon. Had a lovely journey, until I came under the shadow of
the Hill, when the sky began to show gray of blue, and on arrival we learned that it has rained here for three weeks; and
really the road seemed to justify the assertion, for I was nearly

dislocated between the station and the house, — if you know what part of one's anatomy that is! The wind has kept up a dismal howl all night, and this morning I cannot get out. My cold is all along between a sneeze and a bark; I am hoarse, and have a deafness in my ears and a rumbling in my head. But still I am hopeful when I go to bed at night that "something will turn up" to make me better the next morning. . . .

Oh! I am homesick for Boston already, and wish I had not left it to come up here! Then I should have had another chance of seeing you, and perhaps a talk with Charles Sumner, which I much wished. Perhaps I shall see him in Washington; if not, I shall confide what I want to you, and leave it in your hand to be carried out for me with him. Give my kind love to all your house, . . . and believe me,

Ever affectionately yours,

CHARLOTTE CUSHMAN.

From the same.

HYDE PARK, N. Y., Oct. 30, 1868.

DEAREST FRIEND, — . . . I left St. Louis on the 21st for Chicago; passed a day there, then (by night again) started on the way East, where I arrived on Saturday, 24th, and there I remained until the 28th. Most of the time I spent in a dentist's chair, where I was scrouged and gouged and rammed and jammed and crammed until all humanity was destroyed; and I failed to recognize in the tumbled, rumpled creature that came out of said chair the lovely old lady that *I* thought sat down in it. However, as I came out of it richer in some respects, though poorer in others, I did not dare to complain, for fear the man would insist on taking it all back. . . . Since then I have been in much whirl and hurry to get away from New York, which I did on Wednesday evening. Yesterday I wandered, drinking in the October brand of XX air, and have been slightly intoxicated ever since; so whatever you read in this letter which ought not to be written, you had better believe has not been written, but pass it on with a pitying sigh. . . . I wish I could have found time and backbone to go to dear old Boston again, I have left so much undone there, so many friends unseen, so much unsaid; but what can I do? There are friends to be seen, things to be done, and words to be

spoken elsewhere; and having given work to Boston and vicinity
which is nearly double what I have done anywhere else, I must
deny myself the going again. But my heart is there, and it is only
a machine which is now going about saying "Good-by." . . .

I go to Washington to stay with the Sewards for a week,
and then return to New York, whence I sail on the 25th of
November. . . .

And now good-by, and God bless you. . . . Believe me ever
faithfully and affectionately yours,

CHARLOTTE CUSHMAN.

From the same:

NEW YORK, NOV. 20, 1868.

DEAR FRIEND,— One single word to thank you for your note of
the 5th, with its enclosures. I have been so absorbingly busy since
I received it that I have not been able to reply to or to acknowledge
it; and now send only a hasty rude note. The account of the "Brain
Party" was most interesting, as was also that of Mr. Emerson's
Brook-Farm lecture. How I wish I could have heard him! but I
have been in other directions. First, among the flesh-pots of Philadelphia (society in Philadelphia is a committee on good eating),
and then having all sorts of business, — mortgages, instruments,
deeds, powers, receipts, drafts, — until I felt as though the next best
thing I could do would be at once to go into business as conveyancer
or banker or land agent, or some other occupation which should free
me from the social duties which men escape by being any one of
these; so that men are able to keep their minds to one thing, while
we poor women have to keep house and bake and brew and mend
and make for our servants, and dress and call and do our social duties
for ourselves. Then, with harassed brains and weak backs and trembling knees, we are obliged to sit at the head of the table opposite
our dear other halves, and smile and smile ("and be a villain,"
Shakspeare says) as though everything went on without trouble,
for fear of "worrying them, while they have so many worries, more
important!" As if anything could be so important as one's own
individual worries.

Why, how I am going on, as if I were at Sharon instead of in
New York, with more things to do than I have time to count! . . .

I am off on Wednesday. Give me your prayers! If you come
to New York you will find me here. I saw an account of the

Woman's Suffrage meeting. When *I* have got the suffrage, I don't believe I shall value it *because* I have got it ; and then I shall begin to cry for the moon or a monarchy.

God bless you ! Believe me ever faithfully your

Attached

CHARLOTTE CUSHMAN.

IN January, 1872, a letter was received, addressed to the Chestnut Street Club. It is interesting at least as showing how far-reaching was the unconscious influence of the society. It began as follows : —

No. 13 CHESTNUT STREET : —

Who lives here ? I do not know; but this I know, on Dec. 16, 1871, the members of the Radical Club of Boston met here ; and it is to them I want to speak.

Who am I ? An orphan; an obscure little creature that knows of your existence only through the friendly columns of the New York *Tribune*.

What can I have to say ? This only : that for months I have read what the great men and women who compose this body have said ; and I have learned to love them all. They are an entire family, — one in mind, one in heart, one in soul. As a unit I love them, and I wish to thank them for their kindness in publishing the proceedings of their meetings. . . .

Why do I sympathize with the great Republican Club of Boston ? It is the tiny tear crying to the mighty ocean, " We are water, and we are akin." For I too have read and written, — written all the year, and at its close have lighted my Christmas fire with my crude, unscholarly thoughts; and I would be a mouse in the wall, that I might sit and listen. . . .

If my waif reaches you, be lenient with its errors. . . And in conclusion, say to John Weiss that he " performed an *act of faith* without knowing it," when he wrote his last essay. That each act of the kind done in that Christ-like spirit of charity may set a new jewel in his crown of life immortal is the prayer of

Your lowly friend,

GEORGIA.   N. W.

III.

FROM time to time there have been held meetings at which original poems were read by members of the Chestnut Street Club. These gatherings were generally called "Poetical Picnics." Many of the pieces were afterward published; but the following, so far as is known, have never been in print : —

> THE world's poor hiss and poor applause
>   Let the wind bear away!
> To thine own soul be *true*, and scorn
>   The echoes of a day.
>
> FRANCIS E. ABBOT.

MAY, 1870.

> EXPRESSION is but feeling's ebb ;
> Why make of our thoughts a web ?
> To love, that flows from door to door,
> What words can add one drop the more ?
>
> C. A. BARTOL.

FEBRUARY 14, 1870.

> To thine eye, friend, the text was plainly written, —
>   Take in the stranger, give the wanderer food.
> In outcast Truth, in lonely Faith and smitten,
>   Thou didst discern and welcome Angelhood.
>
> O. B. FROTHINGHAM.

REST in no triumph won ;
    The best is yet to be ;
Not yet from half its woe
    Is this great world set free.

Thy part was nobly done, —
    To make the slave a man.
Let every cause of truth and love
    Still find thee in the van !

                              JOHN W. CHADWICK.

FEBRUARY 18, 1870.

IN the Greece that was, philosophers
    Walked in the gardens sunny,
And searched for truth with a loving ruth,
    As the Hyblan bees sought honey.

The old Greek days are dead and gone, —
    The truth blooms fresh as ever ;
As young and old and manifold,
    And open to endeavor.

                              ROBERT COLLYER.

THE birds are all singing, the blades are all springing,
    The sunlight is laughing o'er forest and lea.
O heart of my bosom, art thou in the blossom ?
    Is 't thou that art warbling, my heart, from the tree ?

For the singing and chiming might seem a divining
    Of that which is deeper than thought in my breast,
And lo ! as I ponder and question and wonder,
    These words to my ear — or I dream — are addressed.

                              D. A. WASSON.

1870.

THE beggar begs by God's command,
    And gifts awake when givers sleep.
Swords cannot cut the giving hand,
    Nor stab the love that orphans keep.

                              R. W. EMERSON.

THE UNDISCOVERED COUNTRY.

WERE we quite sure
To find the peerless friend who left us lonely,
    Or there, by some celestial stream as pure,
To gaze in eyes that here were lovelit only,
    This weary mortal coil — were we *quite* sure —
        Who would endure?

                    EDMUND C. STEDMAN.

TO——

FRIEND of the weary-hearted and the sad,
Whose joy has been in making others glad,
    We will not *write* thy praise.
In grateful hearts, which hold lip-homage cheap,
We choose, with long, sweet tenderness, to keep
    The record of thy ways ;
And pray for thee that highest suns may shine
    Through all thy peaceful days.

                    LOUISE CHANDLER MOULTON.

FEBRUARY 3, 1870.

MAY love be thine by sun or moon,
May peace be thine by stormy way,
Through all the darling days of May,
Through all the genial days of June,
To golden days, that die in smiles
Of sunset on the " Blessed Isles ! "

                    JOAQUIN MILLER.

1872.

SOMETHING that I live and feel
Be the text that I reveal, —
Whatsoever maketh young,
Bids the harp be newly strung,
And with latest rapture tunes
To re-sing the oldest runes.

Civil jar or challenge made,
But tears off the fancy's hood,
And shows its quarry in the sky,
And bids it from the wrist be cast,
Its jesses cut, its chafing past,
Its flight renewed, — this be the spell
For me, and neither book nor bell.

J. WEISS.

SOMETIMES a menagerie comes to this door,
With birds that can sing and lions that roar.
Through all the long morning they bellow and sing
Till the Queen of the caravan enters the ring ;
Her smile she distributes, her rations she shares
'Mid the lambs and the lions, the bores and the bears.
To make them as docile as doves she is able,
With a glance of her eye, or a glimpse of her table ;
Each anxious logician grows gay as a ballad
When she offers a morsel of soothing or salad.
He forgets in a moment his creeds and his causes
When she feeds him with apples or cheers with applauses.
Mr. A——— reverts to the Banquet of Plato ;
The tea-urn plays censer to P———'s Cato ;
W——— brings with him salt that the Attic surpasses,
And W——— disdains not to lunch with the masses.
Each favorite idol is laid on the shelf,
Mrs. H——— forgets Hegel, and everyone, self.

THOMAS WENTWORTH HIGGINSON.

PRE-EXISTENCE.

DREAMS that steal o'er me in my waking hours
    Tell of another life than that of earth.
For ante-natal memories sometimes come
    O'er the dark flood my spirit crossed at birth.

Visions of other scenes in other lands,
    Strange glimpses of a life, now mine no more ;
Thoughts, too, that tell me that what is has been,
    Forms I have known on some forgotten shore.

Friends that were mine before I crossed the flood
　Which darkly hides that vanished life from view,
Wakening my love as only brothers could,
　Tell me that all these memories are true.

This world is but one scene on life's great stage.
　My soul, to whom these visions now are given,
Passing beyond the dark'ning flood of death,
　Shall wake to fuller vision in high heaven.

T. STERRY HUNT.

THE DEAF BEETHOVEN.

HE sits like Memnon, turned to stone,
　Yet breathing notes of glory,
Strong as old Vulcan's hammer-strokes,
　Sweet as the swan's last story.

He cannot feel the mighty thrill
　That sways us at his gifting,
The thunder-echoes of his will
　The world to rapture lifting ;

He cannot taste the glowing cup
　His hand for us is pouring,
He cannot with those wings rise up
　On which he sends us soaring.

Strange Providence ! to crown us all,
　And leave the king bareheaded,
To rouse us at a deaf man's call, —
　And he to Silence wedded !

Yet it is thus and ever thus.
　The glory is in giving :
Those monarchs taste a deathless joy
　That agonized while living.

Great Tantalus ! go quench thy thirst
　At fountains sempiternal,
Where broken hearts need never burst,
　And all the year is vernal ;

26

A temple fair, not made with hands, —
　　Such was on earth thy building,
A house not set on garish sands,
　　Nor marred with foolish gilding.

Its walls colossal marches are,
　　Its steps sonatas golden,
Its vaults the boundless symphonies
　　Whereby the stars are holden !

Can Phidias o'ermatch thy feat ?
　　Amphion cannot reach it,
Nor Orpheus, with all his love,
　　Nor blazing Sappho teach it.

Gigantic architect of Sound,
　　Sublime though stricken mortal !
Heaven closed thine ears to all around,
　　And oped to thee its portal.

The tones seraphic streaming thence
　　Are ours for now and ever.
Then let us praise thy glorious gift
　　Till all our heartstrings sever !

JULIA R. ANAGNOS.

THE OLD HARP'S REVELATION.

ONE summer eve (on parlor couch reclining,
The room half-lighted by the rising moon)
I had a dream. — With symphonies repining,
Our old Harp in the corner hymned a tune.
No hand was seen to move its stricken wires,
No form sat near it, as in days of old ;
The strings seemed lighted by electric fires,
It sighed as if it would a tale unfold.
And thus it murmured : "Ah ! the good old time
When, at my thrill, these rooms would oft resound,
While grace and beauty touched me with a chime,
And patriots and sages gathered round!

I well remember all the good and great
Who listened to me then ; and grander yet,
As if to make my honors culminate,
George Washington and dear good Lafayette.
Then there was Winthrop, Bowdoin, Barlow, General Knox,
Adams, and Franklin, all now passed away, —
Men of integrity, who stood like rocks
Amid the storms which gathered round their day !
Ah ! those were times, indeed, when all of rank
Was in a loyal purpose, staunch and true ;
When men were men, with principle so frank
That what they promised they were sure to do ;
When patriot purpose meant a breadth of aim,
And 'love of country' (more than a pretence)
Rebuked self-seeking, while it put to shame
All low ambitions by plain common-sense ;
When love of right outweighed the love of place,
And public good was more than private thrift ;
When men in office had the gift and grace
To plead for justice and its claims uplift, —
Would it were always so ! By Heaven's behest
The hand that swept these chords is quiet now
Within the grave, or finds still better zest
On heaven's harpsichords ; while on the brow
Of her who once inspired me is a wreath
More noble, roseate, fragrant than all other,
With this inscription circling underneath, —
'A loving, faithful, and devoted MOTHER.' "

JOHN T. SARGENT.

ROYALTY.

THAT regal soul I reverence, in whose eyes
Suffices not all worth the city knows
To pay that debt which his own heart he owes.
For less than level to his bosom rise
The low crowd's heaven and stars ; above their skies
Runneth the road his daily feet have pressed ;
A higher heaven he beareth in his breast,
And o'er the summits of achieving hies

With never a thought of merit or of meed, —
Choosing heroic labors through a pride
Of soul, that holdeth appetite to feed
Ever on angel-herbage — nought beside ;
Nor praises more himself for noblest deed
Than stones for weight, or open seas for tide.

D. A. WASSON.

BIRTHDAYS.

OH, how do passing years impersonate
   Experience !   Our birthdays come and go
Like hurrying phantoms opening wide the gate
   For Time to pass.   How fast the onward flow
Of each day's dreams and doings!   How august
   The course of ages!   How the hastening hosts
Of opportunity forewarn us that we must
   Be true to life!   And how these fleeting ghosts
Beckon us onward!   I have sometimes thought
   That in the future, when our spirits pass
From out these bodies, which are then as nought,
   Our past life will appear as in a glass,
And each year, ranged in line on either side
   The untrod pathway of Eternity,
Will meet us all aghast : Some gross with pride,
   Some lean for want of that fraternity
Of food they craved ; some, alas! bent down
   By weight of cares, and some with sickness pale ;
Some with a smile, and others with a frown ;
   Some naked, without purpose ; while the mail
As of a golden armor — earnest work
   For others' good — shines on the breast of some.
One stabs us with a look, as with a dirk,
   For time we wasted.   From another come
With earnest acclamations, when we meet,
   The gladsome benedictions for good deed,
Clapping of hands! remembering, as they greet,
   The poor we aided, or the slave we freed.
But all with more or less of sober mein,
   Clad half in sackcloth for our past neglects ;

Bent o'er with sorrow, as those wrongs are seen ;
   Each with a mirror, which those sins reflects.
Oh, what a gauntlet this through which to trace
   Our pathway in the future, as on wings
Of retribution, while the earnest face
   Of each past year stares at us, and outrings
Its special verdict! Happy, sure, are they
   Who, passing such a troop, see them as *one*,
Clad in one uniform! The whole array
   Glistening as crystals in the midday sun :
Plumed with approvals, belted with applause,
   Capped with high virtues ; and with bayonets
Such as the Love of God, the Almighty's laws,
   Illumine by a light which never sets!

JOHN T. SARGENT.

THE POETICAL PICNIC.

I 'VE been racking my brains, with no end of persuasion,
For something in verse that might suit this occasion.
I was told 't was a Picnic, though not dietetic,
But where each brought his basket of tid-bits poetic.
No dull *fête champêtre*, with flirtation and flummery ;
No summery feast, though our summons was summary ;
No lunch in the woods by some tree-shaded river, —
Just now the mere thought of the thing makes me shiver.
But a meeting where souls — I don't mean those of leather,
But the sort that can never be damped by the weather—
On the best of good footings might gather together.
Where ladies and gentlemen, gifted with talents,
Must never refuse to be weighed in the balance,
But each must be ready in *her* turn or *his* turn
To pump at the pure intellectual cistern,
That the flow of their wit and the feast of their reason
Might gladden the raw Hyperborean season.
In this March (of the mind) we are all of us trainers,
And drilled into line as recruits or campaigners.
For here are our orderly Sargents, who muster
Their companies, noted for worth and for lustre.
And surely, with two such encouraging leaders,
We should all do our neatest as speakers or readers.

Well, here we have gathered, each one with his budget, —
No strict dietitians among us to judge it ;
No grim, knotty tangles of life to unravel,
No roads up the steep mount of knowledge to travel,
No problems too weighty for mortals to settle,
And put conversation upon its best mettle :
But themes where philosophers proudly surpass us
While picnicking here on the slopes of Parnassus.

Then success to these parlors, whose large hospitality
Gives welcome so warm to the Muses' sodality!
Good luck to our hostess and host, who have ever
Made mental attractions their earnest endeavor ;
Whose circles, not Fashion, but Talent has moulded,
Like fruits in the beauty of blossoms enfolded.
Let each drink their health, though in quaffing it off, he
Should find nothing stronger than tea or than coffee.
. And let every guest at these parties remember
How summer has smiled here in bitter December ;
How the roses have bloomed in the cheeks of the youthful ;
How the sunshine of thought lit the eyes of the truthful ;
How the large open fireplace, ruddy and golden,
Linked times of new thought with our dreams of the olden ;
And the picturesque harp — needing much a repairer —
Made us think of Tom Moore and the song about Tara,
And the odors of Souchong commingled with Mocha,
Suggested those friends in the Vale of Avoca, —
A picnic poetic, no doubt, just as this is,
But somewhat *passé* for our youths and our misses.

Nor let us forget in these rooms the great-gun days
That summoned the doughty come-outers on Mondays :
How some things were upset and others were set up ;
And, spite of the "Tribune" and all it could get up
To prove that the Club was no longer a gay set,
But laid on its bier, with a mournful *Hic jacet*,
How Thor-hammer Radicals still brought their best nut
To crack at 13 in the street labelled "Chestnut ;"
Or how in the talking that followed the theses,
The ladies and gentlemen picked at the pieces ;
How ladders were scaled and how ramparts were battered,
How notions were started, how idols were shattered ;

How Weiss or how Wasson or Abbot began it,
How Emerson dreamed it, how Alcott would plan it,
How Higginson, Longfellow, Bartol, or Gannett
Would kindle a flame, and the others would fan it ;
What flashes of thought like auroras would lighten,
How old eyes would ponder and young eyes would brighten,
And how, as we homeward directed our faces,
The Universe still rested firm on its basis.

But the fluid and solid in equal division
Bear rule in the world, nor extort our decision.
Give the Muses their due, and all powers befriend us
In using the best of the gifts that they lend us !
Grace, beauty, and wit have a patent to rule us
No less than the science and morals that school us.
This sentiment closes my rhymes and my reasons,
So I beg here to stop and to make my obeisance.

C. P. CRANCH.

THE WEE BIT BIELD UPO' CARDNO BEACH.

THERE's a wee bit bield upo' Cardno Beach,
  Atween the rocks an' the ragin' water,
An' there for mony a weary year
  There lived alane an earl's daughter.

She biggit the wa's wi' her ain white han',
  An' she theekit it ower wi' broom and heather ;
O' the saut sea-kelp she made the bed
  Whaur grief an' she lay doon thegither.

Against her father and mither's will
  She had married a foreign lord, a stranger.
Wi' his souple tongue he wan her heart,
  An' she never thocht he wad be a ranger.

But when twa years war come an' gane,
  An' her gangrel Mary was prattlin' bonnie,
He sta' the bairn ae winter nicht,
  An' left the house, unkent tae ony.

There was dule the neist day at Dainrie Towers,
   When the nurse woke up frae her cruel sleepin'.
She fan' the bairn's cradle cauld,
   An' ran tae her lady's chamber, weepin'.

"The bairn ! the bairn's awa !" she cried,
   "The bairn's awa, an' I ken na whither."
"I fear me sair she's nae gane her lane,"
   As she wrang her han's, said the waesome mither.

She socht her bairn frae bower tae ha',
   Frae ha' tae stable on she socht her ;
But when she saw the black barb gane,
   Weel kent she wha the ill had wrocht her.

Oh, pale an' wan was her bonnie face,
   As she turnt her roun' ; but her cheek was tearless.
"I 'll seek her," she said, "till the day I dee."
   Her lip was proud an' her e'e was fearless.

"Gae, bring me the lock o' the gowden hair
   An' the gowd that lies aneath my pillow,
An' saddle for me my milk-white steed,
   An' tie him tae yon weepin' willow."

She hied her doon tae Mary's shrine,
   An' tauld her tale o' dule and sorrow ;
Then awa she rade o'er the prentit sna',
   Tae seek her bairn an' her faithless marrow.

She rade by day an' she rade by nicht,
   She rade by mountain, glen, an' river ;
But aye the sky an' the weary sna',
   An' the footprents on an' on forever !

When three lang days war come an' gane,
   She saw the steel-blue sea afore her,
An' a bonnie barque i' the drivin' win',
   That ower the waters swiftly bore her.

"Oh, wha is yon that sails o' the faem !"
   She cried as she cam' tae the stormy water.
"It 's a foreign lord an' a weepin' bairn,"
   Said a sailor lad to the earl's daughter.

She loupit doon frae her milk-white steed,
  An' she gae him the reins wi' the red gowd burnin'.
"Gae, tell at Dainrie Towers," she said,
  "That here I 'll wait for my lord's returnin'."

She watcht the white sails rise an' fa'
  Awa, awa, ower the waters weary ;
But when they sank ower the rim o' heaven,
  Her e'e grew dim an' her heart grew eerie.

She neither thocht o' the frost nor the sna',
  Nor the bitter win's that gart her shiver ;
But on her knees prayed ower an' ower,
  "Frae a' ill, Lord, my bairn deliver !"

Wi' rocks aneath an' rocks aboon
  She spread the bridal-bed o' sorrow.
Lang was the nicht, but langer yet
  The nicht o' grief that brocht nae morrow.

She said : "The sea gies up its dead,
  An' sall it nae the quick surrender ?
I 'll bigg a bower, an' wait for my bairn,
  Till back tae me the Lord sall send her."

She biggit the wa's wi' her ain white han',
  An' she theekit it ower wi' broom an' heather ;
O' the saut sea-kelp she made the bed
  Whaur grief an' she lay doon thegither.

An' there she watcht for mony a year,
  Through spring an' simmer, hairst an' winter ;
An' aye she prayed the Lord tae spare
  Her bairn an' him that sae sair had shent her.

She learnt tae soom i' the surgin' tide,
  O' the breakers' faem her head tae pillow ;
To guide a boat, when the win' blew high,
  An tae shoot the sea-birds on the billow.

Her name was kent baith far an' near,
  An' mony a puir man's bairn blest her ;
Nae churl sae rough but bared his head
  An' hield his breath as he gaed past her.

An' mony a nicht her lanesome licht
　　Cheert the fisher lads when the sea was thratchin',
An' mony a sailor's heart grew great,
　　As he, passin', said, "The lady 's watchin'."

But when mony a year was come an' gane
　　There cam a nicht when the lift grew surly ;
She heard the win' rair roun' her bield,
　　An' she saw the sea grow mirk an' gurly.

She trimmed her lamp, an' she kneelt her doon　.
　　O' the cauld, bare floor o' her lanely dwallin',
An' she prayed as she never prayed afore,
　　For somethin' strange in her heart was swallin'.

The saut tears trinkled doon her cheeks,
　　Frae e'en that tears had lang forsaken.
"Oh ! there 's something sair o' the sea the nicht ;
　　I 'll watch," she said, "till the mornin' waken."

She steppit oot, she steppit in,
　　As mirker grew the nicht an' drearer ;
But eerie grew she when she saw
　　The ghastly tide come near an' nearer.

She watcht it rise, she watcht it fa',
　　She prayed the Lord tae sen' the morrow ;
For aye across the waves she thocht
　　She heard the voice o' dule an' sorrow.

She clamb the rocks aboon her bield,
　　An' gazed until the east grew paler.
"O God, I thank Thee ! " — Hark ! A shriek ! —
　　She thocht her very heart wad fail her.

" I 'm here ! " she cried, " I 'm here !　O God,
　　Sen' help, sen' help, an' dinna tarry ! "
She leukit across the sea, an' saw
　　The white waves lash the Sunken Skerry.

An' in atween twa rocks she spied
　　A barque wi' sails a' rent asunder,
An' han's outstretcht tae heaven an' shore,
　　An' ower it passed the waves an' under.

Nae mair she heard, nae mair she saw ;
   But she flew like a bird tae the stormy water:
A loup, a plunge, an' a mither braves
   The rage o' the sea tae redeem her daughter.

She shot like a shaft through the buffetin' waves,
   Tae the faem flung white frae the Sunken Skerry.
Syne she raised her head frae the beaten froth,
   Hield oot her arms, and cried, "Mary ! Mary !"

"O mither ! mither !" She heard nae mair,
   But she saw twa arms outstretcht aboon her.
"Loup doon !" she cried, "loup doon !" — A splash, —
   Her bairn, — an' baith her arms are roun' her.

She kist her i' the saut sea brine ;
   She ca'd her "Mary, bonnie Mary !"
She reckit na that the sea ran high,
   As she swam tae the lan' frae the Sunken Skerry.

Licht, licht was her heart as she set her doon,
   Ayont the reach o' win' an' weather.
But the first word that her Mary spak
   Was, "Yonder, yonder, sinks my father !"

She turnt her roun' ; she leuk't at the flood,
   An' she leukit ance mair at her bonnie Mary ;
Syne she ban' a rope roun' her middle sma'
   An' plunged again for the Sunken Skerry.

Oh, mony a jaw gied ower her head ;
   I' their foamy arms they strieve tae clasp it ;
But when she cried, "A rope ! a rope !"
   A hundred han's war stretcht tae grasp it.

An' "Throw 't !" they shriekt. She threw 't against
   The breast that ance had been her pillow ;
Syne, "Pull !" she said. They heard nae mair,
   For ower her broke a thundrin' billow.

They fastened the rope aboot the prow,
   They drew it strait frae shore tae skerry ;
Syne ane by ane they faced the flood,
   They left the barque an' didna tarry.

Oh, merry and weet war they ane an' a',
　　As back they leuk't ower the stormy water. —
"But whaur is she that I wrangt sae sair?"
　　Said the foreign lord tae his weepin' daughter.

They socht her near, they socht her far,
　　They droont the waves wi' fruitless callin';
For, when the tide gaed doon, she lay
　　I' the sun, o' the san', anent her dwallin'.

The mornin' brocht nae morn tae her,
　　She wadna wake for a' their weepin' :
Her day was gane, — her weary day ;
　　Her nicht was come, an' she was sleepin'.

They carried her back tae her father's ha',
　　An' in her bridal-robes they claed her ;
An' mony a prayer was said an' sung,
　　As in her father's grave they laid her.

But lang will they mourn at Dainrie Towers, —
　　The foreign lord an' his waesome daughter :
An' this is the tale o' the wee bit bield
　　Upo' Cardno Beach, by the ragin' water.

THOMAS DAVIDSON.

INDEX.

to, in 1873, 293; poem by "H. H." addressed to, *ibid.;* poem by, on "Boston," 294; an incident of Prof. Tyndall's visit to Boston relating to, 299, 300; poem by, contributed to one of the "Poetical Picnics," 398.

Everett, Prof. C. C., 40; remarks by, 44; essay by, on "The Relation of Jesus to the Present Age," 47, 48; remarks by, 65; essay by, on "Tragedy," 212, 213; essay by, on "Imagination," 240–242; essay by, on "Don Quixote," 343–345; essay by, on "The Comic," 350–352.

Extracts from newspapers regarding the Club, 383–386.

FISKE, JOHN, 132; essay by, on "Language," 346–349.

Foster, Mrs. Abby Kelley, remarks by, on Mr. Wasson's essay on "Thou Shalt," 103; on Dr. Bartol's essay on "The Prayer Gauge," 153; on Mr. Powell's essay on "Quakerism," 181, 182.

Frothingham, Octavius B., essay by, on "Borromeo," 57–65; remarks by, on Dr. Hedge's essay on "Pantheism," 159; on Mr. Weiss's essay on "Fatality," 237; on Prof. Shaler's essay on "Darwinism," 264; letter from, 388; poem by, contributed to one of the "Poetical Picnics," 397.

Frothingham, Richard, 302.

GANNETT, W. C., remarks by, 55, 66; essay by, on "The Unseen," 67–71; remarks by, 195, 228, 233.

Garrison, Wm. Lloyd, remarks by, on Dr. Bartol's essay on "The Prayer-Gauge," 151.

Goddard, D. A., at tea with Prof. Tyndall and others, 298, 300.

Goodwin, Prof. W. W., 44; remarks by, 115.

Grew, Miss Mary, essay by, on "Essential Christianity," 117–122; Whittier's poem on, 128; remarks by, 238.

HALLOWELL, RICHARD P., remarks by, 17, 18, 125, 127, 181.

Hedge, Rev. Dr. F. H., 293; remarks by, on Prof. Everett's essay on "The Relation of Jesus to the Present Age," 49, 50; on M. Coquerel's essay on "Religion and Art," 137; on Mr. Weiss's essay on "Heart in Religion," 145; essay by, on "Pantheism," 154–157; remarks by, 158, 161; on Prof. Shaler's essay on "Darwinism," 264.

Higginson, Thomas Wentworth, remarks by, on Mr. Emerson's essay on "Religion," 7, 13, 16, 17; on Mrs. Howe's essay on "Limitations," 33, 34, 35, 36; on Prof. Everett's essay on "The Relation of Jesus to the Present Age," 50, 51; on Mr. Frothingham's essay on "Borromeo," 65, 66; on Mr. Channing's essay on "The Christian Name," 77–79; on Mr. Weiss's essay on "Music," 106, 107; essay by, on "Sappho," 109–114; remarks by, 115; on Miss Grew's essay on "Essential Christianity," 123, 124, 126; remarks by, 137; on Prof. Everett's essay on "Tragedy," 213, 214, 216; on Mr. Weiss's essay on "Fatality," 237, 238; on Mr. Potter's essay on "Buckle and Carlyle," 256; on Mr. Abbot's essay on "Darwinism," 268; in tribute to Rev. John T. Sargent, 312; remarks by, 332; on Mr. Davidson's essay on "Individualism," 337; poem by, contributed to one of the "Poetical Picnics," 400.

Holmes, Oliver Wendell, remarks by, on Mr. James's essay on "Nature and Person," 40; letter from, 362; essay by, on "Jonathan Edwards," 363–369; remarks by, on Prof. Peirce's essay on "The Impossible in Mathematics," 377, 378.

Howe, Mrs. Julia Ward, remarks by, 6, 17, 23; on Mr. Wasson's essay on "Democracy," 29; essay by,